Reluctant Allies & Competitive Partners

U.S.-French Relations at the Breaking Point?

Jacquelyn K. Davis

A Publication of The Institute for Foreign Policy Analysis

In Association with the Fletcher School of Law and Diplomacy, Tufts University

Brassey's, Inc.

Brassey's, Inc.

(Editorial)   22883 Quicksilver Dr., Dulles, VA 20166 USA
(Orders)   Brassey's Book Orders, P.O. Box 960, Herndon, VA 22070 USA

Library of Congress Cataloging-in-Publication Data

Reluctant Allies and Competitive Partners: U.S.-French Relations at the Breaking Point?
ISBN: 1-57488-671-1; $20.00
CIP information not ready at time of publication

Designed by Marci Ball
Printed in the United States of America by Svec Conway Printing, Inc.
10 9 8 7 6 5 4 3 2 1

"We must build strong and great power relations when times are good; to help manage crises when times are bad. America needs partners to preserve the peace, and we will work with every nation that shares this noble goal ... America has no empire to extend or utopia to establish. We wish for others only what we wish for ourselves—safety from violence, the rewards of liberty, and the hope for a better life ... We cannot defend America and our friends by hoping for the best. We cannot put our faith in the word of tyrants, who solemnly sign non-proliferation treaties, and then systematically break them. If we wait for threats fully to materialize, we will have waited too long."

U.S. President George W. Bush, June 1, 2002

"In life, you know, one must not confuse friends with sycophants. It's better to have only a few friends than to have a lot of sycophants. And, I'm telling you that France considers itself one of the friends of the Americans, not necessarily one of its sycophants. And, when we have something to say, we say it."

French President Jacques Chirac, September 8, 2002

Table of Contents

Forward   v

1. Introduction and Historical Overview   1
   September 11 as a Catalyst   6
   The Past as Prologue to the Future   11
   A "Certain Idea of France"   20
   The Mitterrand Years   26
   Chirac's Gaullism   29

2. The State of U.S.-French Relations Today   35
   American Power Confounds Gallic Logic   36
   Diverging U.S. and French World Views   44

3. The Genesis of a New Transatlantic Divide   59
   Using ESDP to Leverage or Constrain American Power   62
   Saint Malo: A Turning Point?   71
   Without *Tomahawks* You Have No Power   76
   Combined Joint Task Forces and NATO/EU Coalitions   82

4. Balkan Futures and Peace-Support Operations   91
   Mandate Issues and Rules of Engagement   94
   "Foot Soldiers for American Knights"   100
   Peacekeeping or Policing?   106

5. Strategic Stability and the Bush Doctrine   111
   French Nuclear Weapons and the "Non-use" Strategy   117
   Deterring Proliferation and WMD Threats   126
   Missile Defenses and Crisis Stability   133
   Arms Control and a "Paradise Lost"   140

6. The War against Terror and the "Axis of Evil"   151

New Threats and Old Nemeses   154

Iraq and the Use of Force to Compel Compliance   164

Lessons from *Enduring Freedom* for
French Military Interventions   178

Iran: Engagement or Rollback?   185

North Korea   189

7. A Final Word and a Roadmap for the Future   193

Sources Cited   A1

Charts, Maps, and Graphs

1. International Criminal Court   13

2. Composition of the 2002 French National Assembly   31

3. Major Frictions in the U.S.-French Relationship   37

4. EU Enlargement   63

5. The 1994 *Defense White Paper*   72

6. Helsinki Headline Goals   74

7. Petersberg Tasks   76

8. French Capability Shortfalls   80-81

9. Preferred French Command Structure for NATO   83

10. Bush Doctrine: A New Paradigm for Force Planning   111

11. Evolution of French Nuclear Forces (1990-2010)   117

12. Major Arms Control Frameworks   141

13. Chronology of UN Resolutions on Iraq   165

14. The French Contribution to *Enduring Freedom*   180

15. Security Planning After September 11   200

Foreword

As this book goes to press in March of 2003, France has led fellow NATO members Germany and Belgium in vetoing a U.S.-backed plan for the defense of Turkey, a NATO ally, against a prospective threat from Iraq. At no time in the history of NATO have trends in transatlantic relations seemed so ominous, in sharp contrast to the bright future envisioned at the 1999 Washington Summit when the decision was taken to enlarge and transform the Alliance. France, which long ago determined that it would choose à la carte from the Alliance menu, has sought to have it both ways; while withdrawing French forces from NATO's integrated military command structure, asserting a need to retain autonomy over French military forces, successive French governments have continued to participate in the North Atlantic Council (NAC), the Alliance's key decision-making organ, in an effort to influence and shape transatlantic political and strategic consultations. Using the NAC platform, France has been a principal instigator of dissent within the Alliance, some say because of a desire to destroy NATO—but not the Atlantic Alliance—and to promote key French objectives, from the creation of an independent European security identity to discrediting and restraining U.S. policy initiatives or positions when they are perceived to clash with French interests. The Franco-American relationship has never been easy, but in 2003 the acrimony on both sides of the Atlantic has grown harsh, so much so that it could undermine transatlantic security cooperation, although it is in neither French nor U.S. interests to allow the "new NATO" to suffer because of France's maverick behavior.

Still, on both sides of the Atlantic debate over NATO's relevance has been opened, albeit from different motivations. France is clearly experiencing an identity crisis. Like Britain, France has retreated from empire, but unlike Britain, it has been unable to accept the new global realities and has asserted its positions even when they have been at odds with those of friends and allies. The United States, too, has its NATO skeptics, although Alliance supporters urge caution when it comes to radical proposals for U.S. troop withdrawals from Europe—indeed, America's European bases can and are used for out-of-area contingency planning—or to efforts to disengage completely from European security debates. NATO's role, and that of the Atlantic Alliance more generally, in crisis management and conflict prevention continues to attract support in Congress, though there is greater interest in the "new NATO," composed of the so-called Vilnius 10 (Bulgaria, the Czech Republic, Estonia, Hungary, Latvia, Lithuania, Poland, Romania, Slovakia, and Slovenia), plus selected "old" allies who appear to appreciate the sacrifices that Americans have made in the name of European security.

If Kosovo marked a watershed for the Alliance, when for the first time it oversaw the use of NATO forces in an offensive role, then the war on terror, ignited by the events of September 11, 2001, was the moment of reckoning, as NATO, for the first time in Alliance history, invoked its Article 5 obligation to defend a NATO ally. Only this time, it was the United States that had been attacked, and its enemy was unlike any that Alliance members had previously contemplated in NATO operational circles. Differing perceptions of the Al Qaeda threat, compounded by vastly contending Alliance priorities with respect to defense spending, the war on terror, and the need to face up to real and potent proliferation threats opened a divide in NATO that persists today, as NATO debates its responsibilities to Turkey under Articles 4 and 5. Just how permanent this divide will be remains to be seen, but without question on Iraq and even with respect to next steps in the war on terror, transatlantic differences on the use of force, NATO's mission, and the role of the United Nations have occasioned new thinking on both sides of the Atlantic about the future of the Atlantic Alliance.

Of all the allies, France has been the most outspoken in the need to transform the Alliance by reining in the power of the United States. In the recent past, France sought to do this by wresting control of Allied Command Southern Europe (AFSOUTH). Having failed there, successive French governments have decided to use the European Union (EU) and its seat on the United Nations Security Council (UNSC) as a platform to restrain, challenge, and, at times, undermine American policy initiatives. Like French intervention in Ivory Coast, where French forces are becoming bogged down in a fratricidal war that may require U.S. intervention to extract them, French actions in the United Nations, including its February 2003 initiative with the Germans to fortify the UN weapons inspection regime in Iraq, may have been taken to placate various French domestic and political constituencies, as the government claims; or they may have been intended to demonstrate France's centrality to European, African, and Middle East security, the three areas where French post-colonial and national interests converge.

The inevitability of disagreement among allies, based on differing calculations of national interest or the need to support a legitimate political, legal, or moral principle, is understood and even applauded by the United States. There is a growing sentiment in America, however, that France's disagreements with Washington are less about grand principles and more malicious in intent, with the destruction of NATO—the military, operational arm of the Atlantic Alliance—from which it withdrew its forces in 1966, at the top of the list. Paris's behavior in this regard serves neither its own interests nor those of the European Union, in whose name it claims to take action. And, while successive French governments have claimed that their central motivation is to strengthen the relevance of the United Nations, France's actions undermine that very objective and weaken the united front against Iraq that was presented in the passage of UNSC 1441.

Over the coming months, the U.S. commitment to NATO will likely be sorely tested, although American hopes are that the new Alliance members will join the United States in developing a transatlantic consensus on NATO transformation and, from that, agreement on the Alliance's roll in the war on terror. France can choose whether it participates or not, according to its own interests, but French leaders should be aware that their behavior is alienating more and more of their allies, leading them to seek ways to work around the French when faced with their intransigence. The Franco-American relationship has always been challenging, but now it appears to be becoming downright disruptive to both nations. The year 2003 marks a crossroads in the relationship, and it remains unclear which path will be taken.

Introduction and Historical Overview

The Franco-American relationship has never been easy. Despite being America's oldest ally, France of late appears to be its harshest critic and among its most difficult interlocutors on issues ranging from trade to security, and even with respect to less weighty concerns such as the transmission of U.S. television programs by French media outlets. Though French-American relations have traditionally waxed and waned, the two nations have always managed to maintain an affinity for each other—at least until now, it seems. In September 2002, a Sofres public opinion poll revealed a growing animosity among the French toward the United States, manifested primarily in their opposition to American foreign policy, but reflected as well in a general distaste for and disagreement with American cultural values, perceived priorities, and even personal attributes (Courtois 2002 and FBIS 2002). At the same time, on the American side of the Atlantic, on September 12, 2002, one day after the one-year anniversary of the attacks on America, at least two prominent East Coast newspapers ran editorials that questioned the future of the U.S.-European relationship, both singling out France for particular criticism and comment (May 2002 and Rosett 2002).

Thus, today the United States and France appear to be entering a new phase in their relationship—one in which fundamental, shared interests are less apparent, a cultural gap is evident, and disputes over trade, import quotas, and industrial espionage have spilled over to affect broader global security concerns. Globalization may have created new interdependencies among nations,[1] but for the U.S.-French relationship this has been a

---

[1] For a fuller treatment of globalization and other trends affecting future U.S. security planning, see Davis and Sweeney (1999).

less than positive influence, generating fierce competition in the economic sector, while undermining the sense of fraternity that emerged from the ashes of the Second World War. The consequences for transatlantic solidarity and for the concept of collective security, which stands as the keystone of the NATO alliance, cannot be overstated. In the absence of a readily perceived and shared threat to Europe's stability and hence to its security, the habit of transatlantic cooperation that was fostered over the last half of the twentieth century is slowly but surely eroding, giving way to an intensely competitive Euro-American relationship, more often than not led, aided, and abetted by the French.

At the time of this writing, in the winter of 2003, there is a deep reservoir of anti-Americanism in France, and that sentiment has begun to be mirrored in the United States, at a time when America feels itself to be more vulnerable to security threats emanating from all sides. The roots of French anti-Americanism are frequently identified as arising from the remnants of the political left in France, but in truth, even to a casual observer, they appear to be more pervasive among French society. No less a personage than the current French president, Jacques Chirac, has been perceived in the United States as alternating between harsh and very public criticisms of the United States and expressions of sympathy, solidarity, and support for what America has endured over the last year and a half. Chirac, who attended university in the United States, and—as he is fond of relating—worked at a Howard Johnson's in Harvard Square, nevertheless has been vociferous in his efforts to moderate, leverage, or even to undercut American initiatives on the world's stage.

Viewed from Paris, America's penchant for acting alone, or for resorting to unbridled use of its military power when confronted with international challenges, lends credence to European arguments that the United States has become the new "imperial Rome." As reflected in the Sofres poll cited above, a clear majority of the French do not trust the United States "to contribute to peace and stability in the world (67 percent), to respect its diversity of cultures (67 percent), or to promote the economic prosperity of the world (72 percent)" (FBIS 2002). From this distrust, a groundswell of French resentment has built up, not least because the French fear they may be forced to accept a fait accompli on Iraq. Stated differently, the goodwill that was generated toward the United States after September 11 has effectively evaporated, replaced by what one French analyst termed "irrational anti-Americanism," which conveniently forgets "that America spared neither its men nor its resources in order to destroy the two scourges of fascism and communism" (Imbert 2002).

In a recent book about anti-American attitudes in France, noted French analyst Jean-François Revel contends that much of the impetus for French anti-Americanism stems from the fact that the Continent lost in the twentieth century the position it had held since the fifteenth century at the center of global initiative and conquest, and thus had to relinquish its role as the master of political and strategic organization and economic activity (Revel 2002). Ever since the Vietnam war, which was the direct result of European colonial expansion, Europeans alternatively have damned the United States for intervening in the world's affairs and criticized it when it remains aloof. As Revel explains, the pattern of U.S.-European relations over the last century has been marked by America's rescuing Europe from a danger that the Europeans themselves had created. If an American intervention succeeds, the United States receives no recognition, but if it goes poorly, the Americans become the instigators of the whole affair, and the disgrace is theirs and theirs alone. That this has become an "obsession" for Europeans, and the French in particular, can be seen in the now-familiar European inclination to chide the United States for inaction and reproach it for intervening. A good example is, of course, the criticism leveled at the United States for refusing to negotiate with the North Koreans to defuse the nuclear crisis, while at the same time condemning what the French still regard as precipitious action against Iraq.

Over the last several years, various French criticisms of American action or inaction on the global stage have been reduced to oversimplified rhetoric, ranging from the pejorative identification of the United States as a "hyper-power" to attacks where Washington is rebuked for taking refuge in "neo-isolationism." After the September 11 attacks, the French and others took their cynicism one step further, or so Revel has argued, by attempting to place the blame for these attacks at the feet of the Americans, as a "just response to the evil that the United States had created in the world." This strand of anti-Americanism is, according to Revel, a "way of excusing others' mistakes," while it also provides a means to divert attention from the societal failings of America's critics. As Revel sees it, American power is unlike anything ever witnessed before on the world stage, and it is as much for this reason, as for Europe's own mistakes and its inability to garner power itself, that it has become the scapegoat for European inaction. France, under the Chirac presidency, is trying to redress this trend by investing the European Union (EU) with greater power and global credibility, and by seeking to constrain America's ability to act on its own. This is bound to generate new tensions in the transatlantic relationship. But more than this, it has the potential to alienate the American public from its traditional allies, placing the future of NATO in jeopardy and forcing the United States to address the fundamental question of the role of alliances in future U.S. security planning.[2]

For their part, many Americans perceive the Europeans, and the French in particular, as "virtual" allies who more often than not endeavor to score points at the United States' expense. The Franco-American relationship, in many respects, has deteriorated into what international relations theory would refer to as a zero-sum game, where one party seeks to gain objectives at the expense of the other. Given these two countries' discordant perspectives, it is no wonder that France has become a source of concern to the United States, particularly as America contemplates its next moves in the war against terror. Neither is it surprising that a proud nation like France is struggling to find a way to hold onto its waning international power to control better its destiny and to have some say in the outcome of events that are shaping the post-September 11 world.

As considered by French elites, the best way to promote French interests and to achieve French policy objectives is to act multilaterally, through the European Union or the United Nations, using international law both to constrain or leverage American power and to ensure that U.S. actions do not in any way undermine or adversely affect French or broader European interests. Very clearly, for the French, construction of the EU and retention of France's seat on the United Nations Security Council

---

2 Revel also contends that in perpetuating this anti-American obsession, the French (and other Europeans) also risk aggravating the very "evil" that Europeans wish to avoid: discouraging the Americans from listening to valid critiques of their policies, and encouraging the very "unilateralism" that the French hope the United States will reject (2002).

(UNSC) have emerged as the sine qua non of French policy and the principal means of influencing events on the world's stage. Seen from an American viewpoint, however, the United Nations is ineffective when it comes to tackling difficult security problems, and the European Union's efforts to forge an independent European Security and Defense Policy (ESDP) are floundering in the face of disparate national priorities and policy decisions. On most issues, the United States sees its traditional European partners, notably France and Germany, as increasingly unhelpful and, on the whole, as militarily weak and ineffective allies, whose first impulse is to forestall the use of military power by any and all means.

Without question, as former State Department official Robert Kagan, writing in *Policy Review*, observed, "The United States and Europe are fundamentally different today," and "[i]t is time to stop pretending that Europeans and Americans share a common view of the world, or even that they occupy the same world" (2002a). Certainly it is true, as reflected in a recent opinion editorial by eight European leaders, not all Europeans share French world views and many reject this characterization as oversimplified. And yet, Kagan's analysis rings true for many Americans, especially when it comes to perceptions of the French.[3] This is a remarkable change in attitudes when one considers that without each other, neither nation would be where it is today. French assistance was crucial to winning America's war for independence, and French influences in America's cultural life, its economic well-being, and even in its architecture—the U.S. capital being a case in point—are readily apparent to the naked eye. Both nations share claims to the influences of the Enlightenment, and each in its own way adopted democratic principles as the building blocks of its respective governmental structures and societal mores. So, the question is: how did we get to a place where even ordinary Americans and Frenchmen are questioning the value of their relationship? What, if anything, can be done to ameliorate U.S. and French differences and establish a new basis for collaboration, even if it only involves pragmatic cooperation on a limited number of issues? And, what will this mean for NATO,

---

3 In "Europe and America Must Stand United," *The Wall Street Journal*, January 30, 2003, eight European leaders, including Prime Ministers Tony Blair (UK), Silvio Berlusconi (Italy), José Mariá Aznar (Spain), and (then) President Václav Havel of the Czech Republic, signaled their suport of the U.S. position on Iraq, while making clear that the leaders of France and Germany did not speak for their countries, dealing the ESDP a glancing blow.

not to mention the broader concept of U.S. alliance relationships, as the West confronts new security threats and challenges to its democratic principles and way of life?

September 11 as a Catalyst

There is no doubt that the events of September 11, 2001, transformed the way Americans look at the world. It is also important to recognize the profound impact of these events on U.S. alliance relationships and their role in providing for the security of the United States. For most of the latter half of the twentieth century, the United States pursued a policy of containment, directed against readily perceived U.S. enemies and based largely on the establishment of a network of alliance relationships, of which the Atlantic Alliance was arguably the most important.[4] Throughout the years, Alliance cohesion was sorely tested, not the least by French-inspired efforts to diminish America's role in NATO and to create a distinct European defense identity, independent of NATO and hence from the United States. Even as U.S. policy sought, consistently since the end of World War II, to promote the development of greater unity among the Europeans, including in the security field, over the years, French initiatives in this area have been explicitly designed to face down U.S. power, leading to considerable resentment in the United States and Congressional calls for a reassessment of the American commitment to European security. The unsatisfactory operational experiences of the United States first in Bosnia, and later in Kosovo, simply added fuel to this fire, so much so that an unlikely coalition—neo-isolationists, libertarians, and proponents of an "Asia first" U.S. policy—began to forecast NATO's demise.

Above all else, the events of September 11, 2001, called into question many of the fundamental assumptions underlying U.S. security planning. The terror attacks created a new sense of American vulnerability at the hands of a terrorist network that heretofore had attracted scant public attention, but whose previous actions, including the 1993 World Trade Center attack and

---

4   The Atlantic Alliance was created by the Washington Treaty in 1949, and was designed to provide a "collective defense," as defined in Article 51 of the United Nations Charter, for its member states. Originally established to counter the growing Soviet threat on the Continent and to help reintegrate the Federal Republic of Germany back into the community of Western nations, the North Atlantic Treaty Organization, or NATO, provided for the establishment of an integrated military command structure and a membership accession procedure by which new members can be added when they have shown that they will comply with the principles and values held dear by democratic nations.

the October 2000 bombing of the USS *Cole*, had raised alarms in the expert community over a new type of warfare being waged on behalf of the radical Islamists' cause. Even as America's response to these attacks was slow in coming, in part because of a profound intelligence failure tracing these seemingly discrete events to a systematic campaign designed to expel U.S. forces from Saudi Arabia, the United States eventually did respond with military force, first, during the Clinton administration, with cruise missile attacks against targets in Sudan and Afghanistan, and subsequently, after September 11, with an all-out war against Al Qaeda and the Taliban. But America's prosecution of the war against terrorism has exposed new and deep-seated rifts between the United States and its European allies on a range of issues, including, as Kagan observed, profound differences in their views of the role of force in contemporary international relations. As Kagan sees it:

> On the all-important question of power—the efficacy of power, the morality of power, the desirability of power—American and European perspectives are diverging. Europe is turning away from power, or to put it a little differently, it is moving beyond power into a self-contained world of laws and rules and transnational negotiation and cooperation. It is entering a post-historical paradise of peace and relative prosperity, the realization of Kant's 'Perpetual Peace.' The United States, meanwhile, remains mired in history, exercising power in the anarchic Hobbesian world where international laws and rules are unreliable and where true security and the defense and promotion of a liberal order still depend on the possession and use of military might (2002a, 1).

This, Kagan goes on to argue, has profound implications for transatlantic relations and for cooperation between the United States and its allies on contemporary security threats.

Kagan's article has sparked considerable debate in Europe, not the least so in France, where the center-right government of Jacques Chirac and his foreign minister, Dominique de Villepin, have been struggling to put into place a new, tactical approach to U.S.-French relations in order to position France better to influence U.S. policy choices. But, while the harsh rhetoric of the previous Socialist government may have given way to a slightly less acerbic tone, fundamental differences remain, including the way in which the French and the Americans view post-

September 11 security challenges and the appropriate means for meeting future threats to Western security interests. Like Chirac his mentor, Villepin knows the United States very well, having worked in the French embassy in Washington, D.C., for a number of years. In *Le Cri de la Gargouille*, published in the summer of 2002, Villepin rejects the American model as the path for France's future, while embracing a concept of what he terms "collective adventurism," by which France must redefine itself, its relationships to its former colonies, and to Europe (2002a, 245). Europe must have a heart and soul, Villepin claims. So, too, it must surpass "the traditional tools of power," to be capable of acting on issues that transcend borders and affect all of humanity (Villepin 2002a, esp. 61-97).

Thus, there is in France a growing tendency to refute the value of military power as an instrument of diplomacy, although the French, unlike other Europeans who hold this same view, would probably like to have it both ways, but their reluctance to invest in military spending over the last decade has limited their options in this regard. Still, the new French government has produced a five-year defense spending plan that is designed to rectify the glaring deficiencies in France's military posture, presumably so that it can have greater flexibility to play a more important role in future crises and conflict management.[5] Dominique Moisi, an influential French analyst, has written that just as the United States overestimates the value and influence of military power to answer and meet emerging security challenges, the Europeans "fall prey to the equally dangerous illusion of underestimating it" (Moisi 2002c). Moisi's statement was intended as a warning to both the Europeans and the Americans, but, in reality, it reflects a larger truth: that seismic changes in the global security landscape have progressively altered the transatlantic relationship, and, as a result, U.S. geostrategic perspectives no longer mirror those of many European elites, most especially those of the French.

Nowhere is this more apparent than in French and European criticisms of the Bush Doctrine. Indeed, the military concept of preemption, which is at the heart of the Bush Doctrine, has provoked an onslaught of European criticism,

---

5 See, for example, Jacques Isnard (2002d).

particularly from the French, who appear to be obsessed with the need to develop "rules" for the international system, by which they mean "binding international agreements, focused first and foremost on the United Nations Charter and its Security Council resolutions" (Gordon and Meunier 2001, 112). French—and, for that matter, broader European—preoccupation with multilateralism and collective action flies in the face of a perceived American impulse for unilateral action. However, the reality is a bit different, since at every turn in the war against terrorism, the United States has tried to fashion a coalition response, and has relied on its multilateral and bilateral relationships to confront Al Qaeda on the battlefield in Afghanistan, in the global financial community, and across the world where terrorist cells have been operating. More telling still, on September 12, 2002, President George W. Bush stood in front of the United Nations General Assembly and laid out the case for preventive action against Saddam Hussein. Far from flouting the multilateral rules and institutions that the French hold so dear, the United States has gone out of its way to give the United Nations the opportunity to enforce all of the mandates that it has passed in relation to Iraq's post-*Desert Storm* behavior. Should the United Nations fail to step up to its responsibilities in this regard, the United States does reserve its option to act; and act it will with at least some Allied support, probably even that of the French, who may do so reluctantly, but likely will participate if only to influence any post-Saddam settlement.

In the face of the challenge that is posed by Saddam Hussein's defiance of international law and his ongoing development of weapons of mass destruction (WMD), Allied solidarity with the United States would provide a lasting impression for most Americans, just as would the failure of others to stand with them. Differences over policy matters are one thing, but in a life-and-death struggle for Western values and the Western way of life, the imperative for Allied unity is perceived by many Americans as their due, given American sacrifices on Europe's behalf over the last century. And yet, very few Europeans see the current situation in quite this way, with most even refusing to dignify America's struggle as a war at all.

To most Americans, Philip Bobbitt's characterization of Al Qaeda as a "virtual state" is instructive. With a standing army, a treasury and consistent source of revenue, a civil service, an intelligence corps, and even a welfare program for its soldiers, Al Qaeda possesses all the attributes of a state, except for a territorial homeland (Bobbitt 2002), though, that, too, could change were Pakistan to veer toward a radical Islamist rule—one of two nightmare scenarios that occupy the thoughts of French analysts. But even without a territorial homeland, Al Qaeda is proving to be a formidable foe and a determined adversary, having declared war on America in 1996 and followed through on its intention to destroy American civilians, military targets, and critical infrastructure. Consequently, a majority of Americans have likewise come to accept Bobbitt's view, in sharp contrast to many Europeans, who still deny, even after Osama bin Laden's November 2002 threats, that they are joined with the United States in a life-and-death struggle to protect and sustain Western values, cultures, and lifestyles. In contrast to the Americans, many European elites tend to view Al Qaeda as a terrorist group, not dissimilar to others—including the Irish Republican Army, Basque separatists, and the Algerian Liberation Front—that have long been active in Europe. As one French analyst put it, "One year after September 11, none of America's major allies feels that the fight against terrorism is a determining factor for its vital interests" (Barochez 2002c). Another has written that "the world prior to September 11 was characterized by the dominant position of the United States in the world, increasingly greater American unilateralism, the deterioration in the Middle East, the slow convergence of Europe, an Arab world in crisis, an Africa that has failed to take off. What has changed since then? Nothing, or not much has changed" (Boniface 2002).

Thus, for many Europeans, there is a tendency to downplay American concerns about a global Islamist jihad that aims to destroy the fabric of Western society and with it the unity of the West.[6] In some French expert circles, there is even a tendency to blame the United States for this phenomenon, attributing America's "crusade" against Al Qaeda as the source

---

6 Samuel Brittan, writing in the *Financial Times* of London, notes, "Islamist militancy is a self-confessed threat to the values not merely of the United States but of the European Enlightenment: to the preference for life over death, to peace, rationality, science, and the humane treatment of our fellow man, not to mention fellow women. It is a reassertion of blind, cruel faith over reason" (2002).

of Western dissension. Dominique Moisi, for example, asked, "Could Al Qaeda terrorists achieve what the demise of the Soviet Union did not—the erosion of the Western camp?" (2002c).[7] Though this may be a somewhat extreme position, Moisi and other prominent French analysts tend to agree that the American approach to facing down the terrorist threat is having a debilitating effect upon transatlantic unity.

While divorce may not be the desirable outcome for either side, it is useful to consider that American patience has its limits. Indeed, U.S. support for its allies should not be taken for granted and can be withdrawn, as it was when the administration of President George H. Bush uprooted American military deployments in the Philippines after continued complaints over U.S. access to Clark and Subic bases. After all, U.S. alliance relationships were not created to constrain America's ability to protect or to pursue its interests. Neither have they been upheld to undercut American initiatives on the global stage.

The Past as Prologue to the Future

Even from its inception, the United States has been careful about exposing itself to the vagaries of alliance relationships. George Washington's now-famous dictum warning the young democracy against "entangling alliances" formed the essence of much of U.S. foreign policy throughout the nation's history. When Europe found itself embroiled in two world wars in the twentieth century, the leadership of the United States had a tough time in persuading Congress of the need to intervene. Indeed, some have argued that had the United States not been attacked by the Japanese, and had Hitler not declared war first, President Roosevelt may not have received Congressional approval for a declaration of war against the Axis powers in World War II. And, while isolationism really never has been a viable option for the United States, especially once its relative power became apparent, President Washington's caution in his farewell address has been firmly embedded in American statecraft, and even today, U.S. hesitation with respect to foreign interventions can be traced to Washington's legacy.[8]

7 Moisi also wrote that the U.S. efforts after September 11 were designed to make the world less dangerous for Americans. "This combination of nationalism with pure balance-of-force reasoning is weakening the concept of the West" (2002c).
8 See Walter Russell Mead (2001, esp. 57-63).

American caution regarding global interventions and its penchant to go it alone was singled out by the French very early on as an enduring attribute of America's unique geostrategic situation. When, in 1831, French aristocrat Alexis de Tocqueville traveled to America to study the young democracy and its people, he noted:

> Placed by its situation as much as by its will outside the passions of the Old World, [the Union] has neither to guarantee itself against [external interests] nor to espouse them (2000, 218).

And, indeed, for the nineteenth century and much of the twentieth, Tocqueville's observation appeared to be prescient, that is until two world wars compelled the United States to take a more activist international role, including one that demanded the establishment of "entangling" alliance relationships to support its policy of containment directed against the spread of communism and the growth of the Soviet empire.

However, the French see America's alliance relationships as a manifestation of U.S. efforts to dominate the international system. Just as the history of the twentieth century can objectively be identified with America's emergence as first a great power, then as a superpower, and finally as the pre-eminent power, it is also true that the emergence of the United States as an unrivaled superpower is a reality that many French elites find difficult to accept, and in truth, is the basis for much of the distance that is apparent in U.S.-French relations today. France's previous foreign minister, the Socialist Hubert Vedrine, once described the United States as a "hyper-power" (2001, 2-3), ready to act on its own and without the benefit of Alliance advice or consensus. And, although the new French government has distanced itself from Vedrine's sharp rhetoric, most French policy elites continue to subscribe to that view.

At the same time, however, French elites contend that as an imperial power, the United States must put itself above reproach; it has a global responsibility to set forth its vision for global stability, based upon the rule of law and an international consensus about ends and means. The view from Paris is that the United States has not yet done this, and worse, it is also considered to lack the will to impose its vision of international law on an international system that demands a new universal order (Delpech 2002). Perhaps best illustrated in the U.S. decision to opt out of the International Criminal Court (ICC),[9] or by its contemplation of the use of force to preempt emerging WMD threats, America's refusal to subject itself to international political constraints irritates the French, who

are struggling not to be marginalized on the global stage.

In stark contrast to America's unprecedented rise in power, France has been in decline—at least in the context of great-power politics. Indeed, during the last half of the twentieth century, France lost its empire after having suffered the humiliation of defeat in 1940 and subsequent occupation of much of French territory by Nazi Germany. Making matters worse, France's loss of empire coincided with the emergence of nationalism after the Second World War, a global trend that would have profound geopolitical ramifications for French foreign and security policies. Thus, as the colonial era moved to a close, France waged a last desperate struggle for empire, first in Indochina and later in Africa, with the crisis over Algeria and its subsequent independence. These were defining events for twentieth-century France, and for the way in which the French people anticipated their future.[10] For out of the ashes of the Fourth Republic and General Charles de Gaulle's return to power in 1958, modern-day France emerged, and de Gaulle's "certain idea of France" captured

9 The International Criminal Court was inspired by the United Nations and established by the Rome Treaty that has been ratified by eighty-nine nations so far, but not including the United States. The Bush administration, rightfully so, is concerned that U.S. soldiers and diplomats could become objects of political prosecutions just because nations or UN authorities objected to U.S. policy decisions. Interestingly, other nations have also not signed or ratified the ICC Treaty, including Russia, China, and India. France and the United Kingdom have negotiated exemptions for their armed forces, contrary to the picture that has been painted in the popular press portraying the Americans almost as the lone dissenters to the ICC. Of course, American concerns go beyond those of the British and the French, since the United States, in a unipolar world, is more likely to be the target of those who oppose America's omnipotence, and the West's culture, values, even its way of life, making U.S. troops and diplomats much more vulnerable as representatives of American society.

10 See, for example, Michael Kettle's *De Gaulle and Algeria* 1940-1960 (1993, 666).

public imagination, becoming the predominant French political ideology, which even today is apparent in French conceptions of the European Union.[11]

Indeed, throughout much of the twentieth century, the Gaullist philosophy united left and right in France, and pointed the way to a consensus on France's role in world affairs. Only today, in the early years of the twenty-first century, are de Gaulle's ideas being challenged by a new generation that sees itself more as European than as explicitly French, although French nationalism remains a very potent force in French political life. Still, with the advent of globalization and the trend toward greater cohesion among the European nations at least in the economic sphere, France as a nation is confronting an identity crisis—one whose resolution may not be revealed for many years to come and that may be dependent on forces over which the French themselves have very little influence.

From the beginning, France and the United States have shared a fickle and oftentimes tempestuous relationship, with each nation seeking to extract specific objectives from their association. As America's first ally, France supported the Union's declaration of independence and provided troops to help fight the British, but only after the battle of Saratoga had changed the complexion of the colonists' struggle and the benefits for France loomed larger than the disadvantages of becoming embroiled in a colonial war. With the help of Benjamin Franklin's formidable diplomatic skills, French officials perceived that by supporting the colonists, France would at last be able to exact revenge on the British, who years earlier had soundly defeated France in the Seven Years' War (1756-1763). Thus, on February 6, 1778, the French-American alliance was formalized, marking Europe's first official recognition of the United States as a national entity. French liberals, including the philosopher Jean-Jacques Rousseau and the writer Voltaire, enthusiastically supported the colonists' struggle because of what it might mean for their own pursuit of democracy in the face of autocratic regimes. The objectives of the French policy elites, however, were less

---

11 See Charles Williams, *The Last Great Frenchman* (1993), for an outline of the philosophy of what has come to be called Gaullism (335-44). De Gaulle himself first used the phrase "a certain idea of France" in his memoirs, writing, "All my life, I have felt a particular notion of what France is" (1956, 1).

altruistic and more self-serving; they supported the American Revolution out of their own self-interests, perceiving in their support a means to wrest American trade from the British and a way to ensure their sugar trade with the West Indies.

Nor did all Americans embrace the alliance with France. In the country's formative years, many, including Alexander Hamilton and his Federalists, urged caution in allying with the French, recalling the years immediately before the war when France had allied with the Indians and visited death and destruction on the American colonists. Moreover, France's "double game" with the Spanish gave impetus to American efforts to sign a separate peace treaty with the British, although in the end, in 1783, a peace treaty was signed with the full knowledge and support of the French.

In the years immediately following the Revolution, the French preferred a weak "confederation of states" and continued American dependence on Paris in disputes with the British. This approach to French-American relations worked only for a while, until the Americans jettisoned their Articles of Confederation and put into place a new constitution and the French themselves became embroiled in their own civil war. By this time, however, both the French and the Americans had tested the limits of their alliance, and when the French Revolution turned bloody, Hamilton's Federalists urged the creation of a "special relationship" with the British, to the dismay of Thomas Jefferson's Republicans.

From its very beginning, then, the French-American alliance served very specific purposes for each party in relation to the growing power of the British Empire. Throughout history, the story of America's alliance relationships in relation to Europe has centered on the tripartite dynamics of U.S.-French-British relations, and despite the closeness of Anglo-American relations today, in the country's formative years, "Great Britain, as the only global power of the day, was the country with which the United States most often came closest to war" (Mead 2001, 18). There was also a close psychological affinity between France and the young United States—an affinity that went beyond the mutual support lent to each other's revolutionary movements. America's founding fathers in many cases were steeped in the political philosophy of eighteenth-century France. The influence of

Montesquieu, in particular, on the American Constitution is apparent.[12] In turn, the demonstrated ability of the new nation to establish republican institutions profoundly affected intellectual thinking in France and, consequently, stimulated action leading to the French Revolution.

As suggested above, the story of the Franco-American relationship is also a history of the U.S.-UK special relationship, and in many respects this, too, continues to weigh on the French, particularly as they push the notion of a Franco-German "motor" as the impetus for creating a European Security and Defense Policy. France's great post-World War II leader, Charles de Gaulle, from the first regarded the Anglo-American relationship as counterproductive to French interests, and during his lifetime he treated the British as if they were little more than America's "Trojan Horse" in Europe. Certainly in the contemporary security setting, the U.S. relationship with the United Kingdom has served American interests well, far better, some would assert, than have its ties with France. Indeed, for much of the twentieth century, the close Anglo-American relationship has shaped global destinies and influenced power relationships. But in the early, formative years of the United States, the choice was not so clear. Thus, when France declared war on England in 1783, the United States faced a dilemma over whether to honor its treaty commitment to France. Fortunately, the French never demanded America's active involvement on its behalf, and the United States, for its part, enunciated a policy of neutrality that was to serve as the framework for American foreign policy up to and including the Napoleonic years, which ultimately witnessed the dissolution of the French-American alliance and the sale of all French possessions across the Mississippi to the United States.

The Louisiana Purchase opened the door to America's expansion to the west and in this regard, too, France played an indispensable if largely unintended role in the consolidation of

---

12 The Baron de la Brède et de Montesquieu, born Charles Louis de Secondat, outlined his political philosophy in *The Spirit of Laws*, published in 1748. Offering what was among the first cogent articulation in political theory of the checks and balances of the division of government power, Montesquieu borrowed from his idealized view of the English constitution, and wrote that the ideal form of government was a republic ruled by an elected leader, whose power was divided among the king (who enforced the laws), the parliament (which made the laws), and the courts (which interpreted the laws). In Montesquieu's view, law making and law enforcement powers must be distributed, otherwise there can be no liberty—a philosophy that profoundly influenced the American Founding Fathers, and which was incorporated into the U.S. Constitution, drafted some thirty-nine years later.

American power. America's declaration of war in 1812 against England illustrated, once again, the country's divisions over relationships with both France and England—an ambivalence that was reflected in American efforts to sue for peace almost as soon as the war had been declared. Coinciding with the end of the Napoleonic wars in Europe, but before their final culmination at Waterloo, the 1814 Treaty of Ghent ended the war with the Americans and bought the British time and relief from the war's drain on their resources. The Monroe Doctrine, enunciated in 1823, asserted America's sphere of influence in the New World, and reopened old wounds with the Europeans, including with the French, but it was western expansion that occupied American interests. So, while the wars in Europe continued to preoccupy the major powers, the United States was able to consolidate its gains, and did so until the Confederacy tried to secede from the Union.

French-American relations suffered during the Civil War. Napoleon III had a vested interest in supporting the Confederacy over the North, beginning with French commercial interests that were increasingly dependent on American cotton and ending with a scheme to regain possession of areas ceded to the United States in 1848. In the period immediately following the American Civil War, Napoleon III's abandonment of Mexico's Emperor Maximilian and the rise of Prussian power in Europe averted what could have been a Franco-American confrontation. Yet, as suggested by Thomas Bailey, "The Maximilian affair produced a definite rift in the somewhat illusory traditional Franco-American relationship—illusory because from 1798 to 1867 the Paris government was probably as unfriendly to the United States as that of any other power" (1946, 390).[13]

The end of the Franco-Prussian War brought about the ouster of Napoleon III, and with that, the establishment of a French republic. A republican France was a much more sympathetic nation, from the American perspective, and with

---

13 Bailey goes on to note, "When the Franco-Prussian War broke out in 1870, Napoleon had relatively few well-wishers in America, especially in the North. The Germans were fighting for national unity, just as the United States had been. Nor could the Northerners forget that while the French had been lending money to the Confederates and intervening in Mexico, the Germans had bought large numbers of American bonds. Moreover, tens of thousands of German-born soldiers, mostly volunteers, had served in the armies of the North" (1946, 390).

America's status as a world power confirmed by the opening decade of the twentieth century, President Theodore Roosevelt intervened on behalf of France in the 1906 Algeciras Conference, against Germany's claim to Morocco. When the Europeans were finally dragged into World War I, had France not been among the allies, it is doubtful, or so claimed one historian, that the United States would have actively intervened, despite the fact that German-American relations had not been particularly friendly since the 1890s (Bailey 1946, 612).[14]

Immediately after the cessation of hostilities, and the negotiation of the Versailles Peace Treaty, U.S.-French irritations resurfaced. Georges Clemenceau, the president of the Council of France, was openly derisive of President Woodrow Wilson's idealism, and French insistence on open-ended war reparations from Germany and a buffer zone to the east of Paris helped to sow the seeds for World War II. At the Naval Disarmament Conference of 1921-22, French demands for an increased ratio, disproportionate to the actual strength of the French navy at the time, further raised the ante in this regard; they also served to illustrate the lengths to which the French were prepared to go to sustain the impression of France's great-power status—a trait that perhaps belies a massive inferiority complex and that continues to characterize French involvement in Europe and with the United States today.[15]

Throughout the interwar period, World War II, and the Cold War, what the United States perceived as France's inferiority complex impeded the smooth flow of relations, and in many instances, was identified by the Americans as actively undermining the pursuit of U.S. interests. As the Americans saw it, the French were their own worst enemy. For their part, French officials perceived America to be indifferent to Europe, and they were not altogether incorrect in observing that had the Japanese not attacked Pearl Harbor, and if Germany had not declared war on America, the United States might

---

14 In truth, however, Germany's unrestricted submarine warfare, together with the fallout from the so-called Zimmermann telegram, ensured U.S. entry into World War I.

15 Robert Kagan makes this point in a November 3, 2002, *Washington Post* article, "France's Dream World." He writes, with respect to the UN debate over Iraq, "If you're France, you want these negotiations to go on forever, and then you want inspections to go on forever. When negotiations and inspections stop and fighting begins, the American global superpower goes back to being a global superpower, and France goes back to being France" (2002c).

never have intervened in Europe (Bailey 1946, 765).[16] During World War II, U.S. relations with the French government-in-exile, and with de Gaulle in particular, were vexed by the need to deal with the Vichy government before the assault on North Africa. Relations were further strained by President Franklin Roosevelt's later preference for dealing with Henri Giraud, a general officer who had attained notoriety for his exploits as a prisoner of war, and who de Gaulle thus perceived as a rival for power in post-war France. Ironically, it was not Giraud, but one of his young subordinates, François Mitterrand, who would emerge as de Gaulle's archrival in French politics for more than forty years.[17] Throughout this period, however, de Gaulle was in the ascendancy, and Roosevelt's snubs were to have a lasting effect upon the way in which de Gaulle viewed and dealt with the United States. In fact, some would say that only upon meeting Mrs. Kennedy did de Gaulle relent somewhat in his very biased criticisms of the United States.

Roosevelt's decision not to back de Gaulle explicitly to be France's post-war leader and instead to hold to the Atlantic Charter's principle of self-determination for France, became in de Gaulle's mind a personal snub, which in fact it was.[18] As a result, de Gaulle's wartime experiences with the Americans

---

16 In June of 1940, after Italy's Mussolini joined Germany in attacking France, French Prime Minister Reynaud appealed to President Roosevelt for material aid. On June 14, 1940, the American president expressed his sympathy for the plight of France, but made clear that "these statements carry with them no implication of military commitments." France was forced to surrender on June 22, 1940, despite two pleas by the prime minister for American intervention. It would not be until much later, after Pearl Harbor and Germany's subsequent declaration of war, that the United States entered the war.

17 See Tiersky's *François Mitterrand: The Last French President* (2000). Strictly speaking, as Tiersky points out, Mitterrand was not a Giraud man. He began his career as a Pétainist, and then moved to form a POW resistance network within Vichy France, as opposed to Giraud's and de Gaulle's external resistance movements. In 1943, he demonstrated his preference for Giraud's organization, but by the time that he reached Algiers, the headquarters of the Free French, de Gaulle had assumed leadership of the two external resistance movements, and the three internal resistance networks (Combat, Libération, and Franc-Tireur) soon after joined the fold, coming together in what was then called the Mouvements Unis de la Résistance (MUR). By all accounts, the first meeting between de Gaulle and Mitterrand went badly, with both men displaying their egos and their leadership aspirations. As Tiersky observes, "The meeting in Algiers was thus, on Mitterrand's part, the beginning of a long and stubborn resentment, a resistance to de Gaulle's charismatic authority, personal prestige, and assumed authority," and would have "long consequences, both in Fourth Republic parliamentary animosities toward Gaullist groups and in Mitterrand's battle with de Gaulle in the Fifth Republic" (2000, 65).

18 By all accounts, Roosevelt and de Gaulle disliked each other, and this hampered operational planning, including for *Overlord*, of which de Gaulle was not informed until days before the June 6 D-Day landings in Normandy. During de Gaulle's first visit to the United States, just after *Overlord* had been launched, Roosevelt described him as "a narrow-minded French zealot with too much ambition for his own good and some rather dubious views on democracy" (Stimson 1971, 456).

influenced his later relations with the United States. His biographers, including Jean Lacouture (1993, 332-35, 537-47), point out that de Gaulle's world view, which was to become the tenet for Gaullism, or that body of French thought designed to guide French international relations during the last half of the twentieth century and into the twenty-first century, differed profoundly from that of the more pragmatic and less theological Americans. Those differences, which are apparent today, served to create additional tensions and fissures in what should have been a close French-American relationship. But in the years following World War II, the political imperatives of Gaullist thought began to manifest themselves in practical policy choices that always put the interests of France first, even in some instances sacrificing broader principles, such as the quest for stability on the Continent when the decision was taken to evict the headquarters of the Atlantic Alliance from Paris in 1967 and to withdraw from NATO's integrated command structure, or for "the rebirth of Europe," when in 1963 de Gaulle vetoed Britain's entry into the Common Market.

A "Certain Idea of France"

De Gaulle's "certain idea of France" identifying French national interests with those of the broader European community of states was to be a constant feature of French foreign policy during the last half of the twentieth century and into the twenty-first. De Gaulle's first attempt to redress the balance of power in NATO manifested itself in his proposal for a tripartite directorate, to include France, Great Britain, and the United States. This proposal, which was received coolly by the Eisenhower administration in Washington, was doomed to fail since it marginalized the Federal Republic of Germany. There was nothing new in this, for France had spent much of its recent history trying to compete with, and to tie down, its traditionally stronger German neighbor. Still, de Gaulle, being the savvy politician that he was, recognized the need to deal with post-war West Germany if he wanted to realize his "Grand Design" for Europe, and, accordingly, extended an olive branch to the Germans by signing the Franco-German Treaty of Peace and Reconciliation in January 1963. Not only did this serve to cement de Gaulle's personal relationship with German Chancellor Konrad Adenauer, but it ensured the course toward European unity, manifested initially in the creation of the Common Market and later, during the Mitterrand presidency, in the Maastricht Treaty, which was the genesis of today's European Union. Reinforcing the development of a solid Franco-German relationship at the heart of Europe, was de Gaulle's March 17, 1959, instruction to his Council of Ministers directing French development of a nuclear weapons capability. As conceived by de Gaulle, French nuclear weapons would, in his words, ensure that all would perceive that "France is a great power; all great powers have nuclear weapons; therefore France must have them" (Messmer 1993). Moreover, implicit in de Gaulle's thinking was the idea that French nuclear weapons could one day serve a broader European constituency, although he never went so far as his successors in formally enunciating an "extended deterrent guarantee" for Germany or France's other European neighbors. He did, however, maintain that a close link existed between French security and that of West Germany, and, for his part, observed, "There is an interdependence between Germany and France. On that interdependence depends the immediate security of the two peoples. One has only to look at the map to see this. On that interdependence depends any hope of uniting Europe in the political field as also in the defense or economic fields. On that interdependence depends, consequently, the destiny of Europe as a whole" (Lacouture 1992, 340).

De Gaulle's enthusiastic campaign to win the hearts and minds of the West Germans was interpreted in some quarters as a slap in the face to the Americans, who had just floated their idea for a NATO "multilateral force" (MLF), in an effort to dilute the French push for greater European defense unity. The MLF notion caught fire in West Germany, particularly with respect to its implicit promise of providing a major role for Germany in Alliance decision-making, including with respect to nuclear weapons. This, together with French behavior in the Common Market, including the imposition of agricultural tariffs and a staged walkout over European Community voting procedures, generated new strains in the Franco-German relationship—strains that were made larger in the face of new crises over the Cuban missiles and Berlin, both of which served to reinforce to the Germans the centrality of the transatlantic tie. The post-Adenauer period proved to be a particularly difficult one for French-German relations, and the French withdrawal from NATO's integrated military command was a final straw for the Germans, who had chosen security over independence as the predominant theme upon which rested its foreign policy orientation. At this moment in history, the transatlantic connection was viewed to be of paramount importance in Bonn, and the choice, if one had to be made, between the United States and a French-dominated European entity was clear.

For the French, events—as they inevitably played themselves out—meant that Europe would forever be dependent upon the United States, unless the nations of the "old continent" reasserted themselves. Paraphrasing de Gaulle, French leftist and former defense minister Jean-Pierre Chevènement opined, "The United States of Europe would be the Europe of the United States" (Lacouture 1992, 346). Nationalist that he was, de Gaulle was among the first to think about the creation of a "political Europe." But he never believed that Europe could completely dissociated from the United States. Writing in his *Memoires d'Espoir*, de Gaulle noted,

> "My aim was to disengage France, not from the Atlantic Alliance, which I intended to maintain by way of ultimate precaution, but from the integration realized by NATO under American command; to establish relations with each of the states of the Eastern bloc, first and foremost Russia with the object of bringing about a détente followed by understanding and cooperation; to do likewise, when the time was right, with China; and finally, to provide France with a nuclear capability such that no one could attack us without running the risk of frightful injury. But I was anxious to proceed gradually, linking each stage with overall developments and continuing to cultivate France's traditional friendships" (1970, 201-2).

Thus, French nuclear developments notwithstanding, and French criticisms of NATO's command structure understood, successive French governments from de Gaulle to Chirac today have maintained the importance of the transatlantic connection as, to use de Gaulle's own words, "the ultimate precaution" (Tournoux 1967, 364-65). Still, the predominant French world view was one of partnership with Russia, creating a "Europe from the Atlantic to the Urals." In this regard, it may plausibly be argued that de Gaulle foresaw the collapse of the Soviet Union. In his public statements he referred not to the Soviet Union, but to Russia. He looked to a Europe that was built from a family of nations in which Russia might someday play a constructive role. In de Gaulle's own Grand Design, which continues to shape the

French political outlook today, the Soviet Union and its Warsaw Pact allies were identified as artificial creations, doomed to ultimate failure as the nations that composed the Soviet empire asserted themselves and broke from their communist yoke. In this sense, de Gaulle had a vision of what was to come to pass some twenty years later, where a broader European entity, with its core in Western Europe and led by France, would emerge to act as a counterweight to the global power of the United States, and in the face of the rising power of the Chinese in Asia.

So, despite Russia's incarnation during the Cold War years as the communist Soviet Union, against which Western nations had directed their security planning, France sought to engage the leadership in Moscow, and announced that French nuclear strategy would be *tous azimuts*, or directed against all potential threats, including presumably that of the United States. While Americans took this as an affront, the French contended that it was never meant as such. Indeed, expanding upon the ideas of Generals Pierre Gallois and Charles Ailleret, French strategic analysts from Lucien Poirier to Pierre Lellouche and François Heisbourg contended that the *tous azimuts* strategy was designed to take into account the breakup of the Soviet empire at some point in time and the possibility of new threats to France, including those that might manifest themselves from unexpected quarters.[19]

Needless to say, French motivations were suspect in the United States, and France chose to operate on two levels for much of the Cold War era: as a responsible Western ally and as an independent actor who was not above playing the NATO allies off against each other to further a specific French objective. This

---

19 General Charles Ailleret was at the time the chief of the defense staff. He first articulated the *tous azimuts* concept in a 1967 article (Ailleret 1967a, 1923-32). Together with Air Force General Pierre Gallois (in his seminal book *The Balance of Terror* (1961)), and (then) Army Colonel Lucien Poirier, General Ailleret provided much of the intellectual underpinning to French deterrence theory. Subsequent refinements were made to the *tous azimuts* strategy, to include the concept of the "enlarged sanctuary," articulated during the presidency of Giscard d'Estaing, and designed to take into account French conceptions of the importance of Europe to French foreign policy and strategic interests; and the concept of "concerted deterrence," which was articulated by Prime Minister Alain Juppé, during Chirac's first presidency, and which embraced the notion of a test use of "pre-strategic" weapons. Both Pierre Lellouche, a senator and former security analyst, and François Heisbourg, a defense official in the Mitterrand government and now head of a major think tank in Paris, argue the need to anticipate wholly new defense challenges. Each, from his own perspective, defends the integrity of the French strategic deterrent, so long as nuclear weapons are a factor in power politics, although both also suggest that their role in French security planning has declined in the face of new and emerging transnational and non-state threats to French security interests.

being the case, it was predictable that U.S. and French interests would clash, and clash they did on policies toward the Soviet Union, America's involvement in Vietnam, and U.S. support for Israel during and after the 1967 war. To a considerable extent, Franco-American policy differences were exacerbated by the personalities in power at the time. More fundamentally, however, they reflected contending world views, which themselves were reflections of profoundly different prescriptions for international stability. The French were never comfortable with the bipolar order of the Cold War international system, and most of their international initiatives were derived from an impulse to create an additional pole in the international system, and/or to level the playing field by diluting American influence in the world.

It should not come as any surprise, therefore, that even with de Gaulle's departure from office in 1969, the broad framework of his policies remained in place, having been defined in the context of French national interests and retaining a *mondialiste*—or worldwide presence—approach and continuing its pursuit of *francophonie*, or the cultural cohesion of all French-speaking peoples. Georges Pompidou's short tenure as president, followed by Valéry Giscard d'Estaing and his departure from the Gaullist line in his preference for a more ambitious vision of European convergence,[20] nonetheless served to sustain de Gaulle's overall conception for French foreign and security policies. In major respects, including the affirmation of France's world role and the maintenance of the French *force de frappe* (nuclear strike force), Giscard toed the Gaullist line, departing really only on Europe and then not very far. Like de Gaulle, Giscard, who was more a technocrat than a deep thinker, saw in the European Economic Community (EEC) a framework for advancing French interests, while challenging what was generally viewed as American economic imperialism.

In four particular areas—relations with the former Soviet Union, energy policy, Middle East diplomacy, and arms control—the government of Giscard d'Estaing proved to be a major obstacle to U.S. policy interests and initiatives. Giscard's

---

20 Giscard d'Estaing favored the (Jean) Monnet school of integration, and actively pushed for a confederal structure based on economic and monetary union and the "co-ordinated evolution of European currencies" (Frears 1981, 14). Nothing in Giscard's writings suggests, however, the need to abolish the nation-state, although on that issue Giscard was never so doctrinaire as were the fervent Gaullists. Still, in his own words, France is described as a *rayonnement*, a beacon of culture and enlightenment, and an example to the rest of the world.

presidency coincided with Dr. Henry Kissinger's "Year of Europe" initiative and the Arab oil embargo of 1973-74. Despite the Nixon administration's greater affinity for the French (as compared to the Johnson administration's), successive French leaders, from de Gaulle in his last years in office to Giscard's assumption of office in France in 1974, evidently concluded that the greater their independence from American policy lines the better chance they would have of sustaining the now apparent French consensus on national security policy.

Thus, for many reasons, the period between 1973 and 1980 turned out to be one of the most contentious in U.S.-French relations. Not only did the French widely deride the Kissinger "Year of Europe" and his International Energy Agency (IEA) initiatives—because of their overwhelming dependence on imported Persian Gulf oil—they aggressively undertook a campaign in support of the Palestinian Liberation Organization (PLO), and played upon so-called Third World sensitivities to a perceived North-South divide in international politics. As a result, France's relations with the Arab world progressively took on a less objective flavor. Accordingly, France was critical of U.S. Middle East policy and undertook an aggressive campaign for international recognition of the Palestinian cause, even calling for Israel's withdrawal from territories captured during the 1967 Arab-Israeli war.

During this same period, U.S. relations with France also suffered from differences over relations with the Soviet Union, including with respect to American approaches to arms control in Europe, which were then based on talks designed to achieve mutual and balanced force reductions (MBRF) between NATO and the Warsaw Pact. The French approach was to bypass NATO and call for a conference on disarmament (CDE) under United Nations auspices—another emerging and consistent theme of French diplomacy into the twenty-first century. Despite the appearance of closer cooperation with the Western allies in his "enlarged sanctuary" concept, Giscard preferred to consider a more maverick approach to security in Europe, first by establishing a broader détente with the Soviet leadership and later, in 1979, by preserving relations with Moscow and standing apart from the rest of the Western allies in their vociferous condemnation of the Soviet invasion of Afghanistan, dissociating France from any of the American reprisals, including economic sanctions and the 1980 boycott of the Olympics. Coming on the heels of France's perceived indifference to the American hostage crisis in Tehran, the lack of support by the Giscard government on sanctions against Moscow only served to reinforce a growing American frustration with a reluctant French ally.[21]

The Mitterrand Years

The results of the historic election of the first avowedly non-Gaullist and political arch-rival of the General, François Mitterrand, in 1981, turned out to be deceptive in terms of foreign and defense policies. In many ways, Mitterrand was more Gaullist than de Gaulle in his pursuit of French *grandeur* and *mondialisme*. This was perhaps no better illustrated than in French efforts to resolve the crisis that eventually led to the 1991 war in the Persian Gulf. Never convinced that war was inevitable, and convinced that if it did come, French oil interests in Iraq would be adversely affected, Mitterrand and his government put the prestige of France on the line with persistent efforts to frame a diplomatic solution to the crisis. Thus, even as late as January 1991, French diplomats were still working feverishly to avoid the impending "desert storm." When war did come, the French joined the coalition operations, despite the fact that the French government had great difficulty in attracting sufficient numbers of volunteers, a reflection, no doubt, of the widespread French opposition to Mitterrand's last-minute decision to participate in *Desert Storm*.[22] Certainly, no one in France wanted to be

---

21 For an in-depth treatment of French policies during the Giscard presidency, see Frears (1981). Frears observes, "Resentment of American power and fear of American domination are components of nationalism in France..." (99). And, "[b]y pursuing an independent and *mondialiste* foreign policy, taking no risk to its security, France may infuriate its allies but obtains some prestige and, in a world where trade is awarded by dictatorships from political considerations, some tangible economic benefits. Furthermore a grandiloquent foreign policy is undoubtedly part of the expectation that the French public has come to have, and constitutes an adhesive for French national unity and the legitimacy of the presidency" (103).

22 Because of the peculiarities of the French constitution and the power that is conferred on the president in matters of foreign affairs and national security, Americans may tend to overlook the importance of domestic politics in shaping French foreign policy. Apart from the obvious, that is, the direct election of the president, the need to appeal to disparate constituencies, including a very strong "workers' sector" has underpinned French policies toward Europe, Russia, Africa, and the Middle East. Moreover, since France is home to between five million and six million Muslims and a large immigrant population from its former African colonies, French policy has a need to be sensitive to "the Arab street." As with all nations, economic policy is domestic politics, and domestic politics form the basis of French foreign policy, though Mitterrand, like de Gaulle before him, was an expert in manipulating public opinion to suit broader French national interests. In the case of *Desert Storm*, this included, from Mitterrand's perspective, the need to have a say in the post-conflict resolution and recovery of Iraq, since France maintains considerable oil and other commercial interests In Iraq.

dragged into a war that went beyond the UN objective of liberating Kuwait, to topple the regime in Baghdad, as they thought the Americans intended to do. Thus, throughout the military operation, French officials repeatedly tried to influence the U.S.-led offensive, and they were adamant at the war's end about holding to a cease-fire that provided for regime survival.

Without question, the Mitterrand years, with few exceptions, were difficult for U.S.-French relations. The one shining exception was when France demonstrated its solidarity with the West during the so-called Euro-missile crisis of 1979-81. This crisis erupted when the Soviet Union installed SS-20 intermediate-range ballistic missiles (IRBMs) on East German and Czechoslovakian territories at the end of the 1970s. NATO, in response, opted to deploy its own intermediate-range nuclear systems (128 *Pershing* IIs) in West Germany and 464 cruise missiles elsewhere in NATO countries, after Moscow rejected Western disarmament initiatives (the so-called double-track decision). The crisis was finally resolved when the Reagan administration proposed the "zero option," by which both the SS-20s and the *Pershings* and cruise missiles were withdrawn from their deployment sites in forward areas in Europe.

As viewed in the United States, France's support during this crisis was considered all the more remarkable given its potentially profound ramifications for the French defense consensus. At the time, there was a real fear that if the German peace movement had managed to pressure the NATO allies into a unilateral withdrawal of NATO's *Pershing* II and cruise missiles from German soil, then the French government might have opened itself to domestic criticism over France's own nuclear force deployments.[23] Notwithstanding that it was very much in the French national interest, as conceived by Mitterrand, to do everything in his power to maintain the credibility of the nuclear deterrence concept, without his very public intervention in front of the German parliament, the Alliance might not have received German backing at this crucial time. Still, the very fact that Mitterrand had come to power on the basis of a "common program" with the French Communist Party (PCF) and in fact had named four Com-

---

23 For an in-depth analysis of the Euro-missile crisis, see Davis, Perry, and Pfaltzgraff (1989).

munist Party members to be a part of his first government, was worrying to the Reagan administration, and, in point of fact, colored U.S.-French relations for much of Mitterrand's tenure (Tiersky 2000, 127).[24]

If the Euro-missile crisis represented the high point in U.S.-French relations during the Mitterrand years, German reunification could be characterized as the nadir. Mitterrand's own personal experiences, from his birth in 1916, the year of the Battle of Verdun—an event that was to haunt him throughout his life—to his escape from a German prison camp during World War II, and his subsequent work in the Resistance, ensured that his vision of French security was firmly anchored in the view that German power on the Continent must always be contained. Like de Gaulle before him, Mitterrand launched new initiatives designed to contain German power by integrating it into Europe's evolving institutional frameworks and by tying it more closely to that of France, creating what was later characterized as the "motor" of Europe. When German unification emerged as a real possibility during the Gorbachev era, Mitterrand's first impulse was to attempt to slow down the momentum of reunification by demanding formal treaties to codify boundaries, especially that between Germany and Poland. When that failed, he redoubled his efforts to establish a broader basis for security collaboration among the European states.

Mitterrand's preoccupation with German unity was not unrelated to his concerns about European equilibrium as the Soviet empire began to dissolve. Hubert Vedrine, the former French foreign minister, was one of Mitterrand's "technical counselors" in the 1980s. He has characterized Mitterrand's behavior with respect to German unification as consistent with France's geopolitical interests at the time. From this perspective, failure

---

24 It is important to note, in this context, that the French Communist Party was the most pro-Stalinist in Europe at that time. As described by Tiersky, "A Socialist party alliance with a Stalinist Communist party in a major NATO country was hardly a situation Washington could put on a back burner." He goes on to quote Mitterrand on this issue: "Joining the Socialist party was in no way for me a rally to Marxism; it was the means for the left to win power, and also a means to bring communism back to its genuine level. In France, communism attained an exaggerated level of support, partly because of its heroic attitude during the war. But, politically and historically, the most important moment (in France) since the Liberation was when the Socialist party surpassed the Communist party. We got to a situation then in which, for a left-wing voter, to vote "useful" no longer meant to vote Communist. To have them inside the government takes away their originality, since they are associated with the Socialists in all decisions. They should therefore be less and less capable of getting votes beyond those of Communists [i.e., of sympathizers and protestors]."

to slow the momentum of German unification could only result in the need to speed up European integration. In this way, any German impetus for a resurgence of its great-power status in Europe could be modulated within an institutional framework that would channel it and direct it to support broader interests, in tandem with those of France and Germany's other European neighbors. As assessed by Vedrine, Mitterrand's promotion of the Maastricht Treaty's objective of monetary union and his subsequent efforts to promote a common European foreign and security policy were fundamental aspects of his policy toward Germany (Vedrine 1996, esp. 562-67).

To achieve his goal, Mitterrand saw a need to reinvigorate Franco-German relations, both as the essential "motor" to get European integration moving and to balance America's growing power, now that the Soviet Union was imploding. Early in his presidency, Mitterrand had reached out to the Germans, arguing that their collaboration was a necessary counterbalance to American power. On September 22, 1984, he and German Chancellor Helmut Kohl clasped hands at Verdun, creating new expectations that their historic enmity had been cast aside. When, several years later, at the height of negotiations for German re-unification, the old rivalries seemed to resurface, the persistence of these two leaders in moving the European agenda forward survived even the greatest of slights when France maintained its insistence on a formal treaty specifying Germany's borders.

Chirac's Gaullism

Throughout the Mitterrand years, and into the tenure of Jacques Chirac beginning in 1995, French foreign and security policy followed its predictable course, delineated by Gaullist principles, but conditioned by the emerging realities of the day. From 1986 to 1988, and again from 1997 to 2002, French foreign and security policies were enunciated by the French president, but modulated to take into account the practical politics surrounding "cohabitation."[25] As the election of 2002 ultimately demonstrated, there was little light between the candidates' positions on

---

25 Cohabitation is defined as a mixed-party government in which in the first case, France had a Socialist president and a "neo-liberal" prime minister, while in its second incarnation the politics and positions were reversed. The differences between the two political groupings are most noticeable on domestic policy questions, and less so in foreign policy, where the much vaunted French consensus appears to be real. However, as the World War II generation passes away in France and the country becomes more multicultural real questions arise about the ability of French leaders to rely on this consensual approach to foreign and security policy development.

foreign and security policies, though the Socialists did champion a greater distance in France's relationship with the United States. Indeed, the former French Socialist government of Prime Minister Lionel Jospin registered the harshest of critiques of American foreign policy, particularly after the election of George W. Bush, although it is also true that across the political spectrum in France there was and remains a profound distrust of the Bush administration's policy choices. Consequently, the coalition of center-right political parties created to support Chirac's second presidential bid, then called the Union for the Presidential Majority and subsequently changed to the Union for a Popular Movement (UMP) promoted greater solidarity with the Americans in the war against terror, but on issues related to the Middle East more generally and European security planning very specifically, Chirac's coalition made clear its differences with U.S. policies.

That said, it was neither foreign nor defense policy matters that pre-ordained the outcome of the French presidential election in 2002. Of far greater importance were issues relating to local security, that is, crime, unemployment, race relations, and illegal immigration. The import of these issues was such that the Socialist prime minister, Lionel Jospin, who had widely been considered (along with Chirac) to be one of the final two candidates in the second round of voting, was eliminated and in his place Jean-Marie Le Pen, running on an anti-immigration platform, faced Chirac in the run-off. Even as Le Pen's first-round victory over Jospin shocked a majority of French voters because of his extreme positions on immigration and law and order, Jospin's defeat reflected the French electorate's alienation from both of the apparent front-runners, contributing to widespread voter apathy that resulted in a high percentage of abstentions and a protest vote for Le Pen. Consequently, in the second round of voting, for a majority of French voters there was no choice but to elect Chirac, which they did, whereupon the president formed an interim government composed of members of his coalition, headed by centrist Jean-Pierre Raffarin. After their successful result in the French National Assembly elections in June 2002, Chirac gave Raffarin, the interim prime minister, the job of forming a permanent government. The resulting French government comprises a combination of Chirac loyalists—so-called Chiraquiens—including Foreign Minister

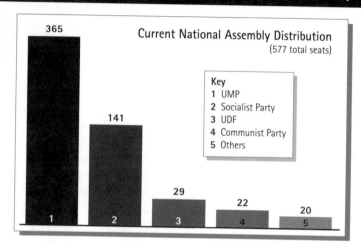

Current National Assembly Distribution
(577 total seats)

365

141

29

22

20

1   2   3   4   5

Key
1 UMP
2 Socialist Party
3 UDF
4 Communist Party
5 Others

The Majority Parties and Their Issues

Union for a Popular Movement (UMP)
Leaders: Jean-Pierre Raffarin, Prime Minister,
and Jacques Chirac, President
1. Restore the authority of the state by augmenting police forces and placing them under a central command authority. Establish new controls to deal with illegal immigrants and create detention centers for young offenders.
2. Revitalize the economy by reducing the income tax by 5%, altering work laws to allow for a work week beyond 35 hours. Create incentives for youth employment, endorse the establishment of small businesses, and revamp the pension system.
3. Increase the defense budget.

Socialist Party (PS)
Leader: François Hollande
1. Revitalize the economy by cutting taxes for low-income earners, raise the minimum wage, and reduce the jobless rate.
2. Reorganize public services by ending homelessness, stopping deregulation, and preventing further privitization of state services.
3. Reduce crime by strengthening police powers and enhancing the justice system.

Union for French Democracy (UDF)
Leader: François Bayrou
1. Reduce crime by rewriting existing laws to accentuate police power, create a Ministry of Public Safety, and toughen juvenile delinquency laws.
2. Revitalize France's economic base by involving management and labor more closely in the government (as in Germany and Spain), giving employees a greater say in the management of companies, and establishing a higher minimum wage.
3. Establish France as a stronger power in the European community by working towards majority voting in the European Union.

Communist Party (PC)
Leader: Robert Hue, President, and National Secretary
1. Redistribute economic benefits by granting poorer districts more benefits and levying higher taxes on high-income earners.
2. Reorganize businesses by doing away with redundancies in profit-making companies, ceasing privitization, and granting workers more power in company management.
3. Adopt stricter policies on crime.

Source: French National Assembly website (http://www.assemblee-nat.fr/qui/declarations-groupes.asp)

Chapter One: Introduction and Historical Overview ❖

31

Dominique de Villepin and Interior Minister Nicholas Sarkozy, and technocrats like Finance Minister Francis Mer.

Unencumbered by the politics of cohabitation, the new Chirac government has greater leeway in policy development, and while the main outlines of French foreign and defense policies are unlikely to change, the tone of the relationship with the United States has moderated, though criticisms remain. And, on some issues, notably the campaign to eliminate Al Qaeda, French officials have demonstrated greater solidarity with the United States than did their predecessors, in part no doubt because of Al Qaeda's May 8, 2002, attack against French nationals in Karachi and their apparent complicity in the October 2002 explosion that ravaged a French oil tanker off the Yemeni coast, both of which brought home to the French their own vulnerability to the non-state, transnational terrorist threat. So, too, French suspicions still linger about the source of the blast at a Toulouse chemical plant in September 2001, just after the World Trade Center and Pentagon attacks. As a result, the French government momentarily backed away from the confrontational rhetoric of the Jospin era, and in its place attempted to introduce a more conciliatory approach that, at least initially, aimed at delineating areas of potential cooperation and a commonality of interests.

Villepin's first visit to the United States in July 2002 was intended to signal very publicly this new French approach to dealing with the United States. The nuances of the previous government's disdain for Bush administration policies have been replaced by a more open atmosphere that seeks to enable a new line of communication between Paris and Washington. Even so, political styles aside, specific U.S. initiatives and Washington's general approach to international relations remain a concern for the French. In this respect, there is more than a kernel of truth in Robert Kagan's analysis in which he maintains that there is much that divides the Americans and the Europeans, starting with discrepancies in the way in which Americans and the French view the world. Nevertheless, it is necessary to ask if there are not also synergies in the ways in which the two nations perceive the challenges and opportunities of the twenty-first century world. The central issue, therefore, becomes one of how the United States can best work with its French ally on issues in which both have vested interests, and if constructive collaboration is not possible, how the two countries should move ahead with key initiatives and yet minimize the potential for irreparable damage to the U.S.-French relationship. Is this possible? And, should we even care?

Subsequent chapters of this study address the major security issues affecting Franco-American relations in an effort to address these questions. Chapter 2 provides an overview of the state of U.S.-French relations today, highlighting areas of tension and those in which collaboration may be possible and even fruitful. Other chapters examine specific issues of concern to U.S.-French relations, including NATO and the European Union; Balkans futures and peace-support operations; the Bush Doctrine and strategic stability; and new threats and old nemeses. Finally, the last chapter presents the major study conclusions and offers a roadmap for consideration by U.S. policy-makers. Coming on the heels of the 2002 French elections, and in the first years of the Bush administration, this monograph has as its goal to inform, challenge, and lend insight to the conventional wisdom about U.S.-French relations. As America's oldest "friend" and a reluctant ally, France has much to contribute to U.S. policy initiatives and diplomacy, but its views must not be allowed to derail or otherwise undermine U.S. interests.

CHAPTER 2

The State of U.S.-French Relations Today

The election of George W. Bush marked a sea change in the French-American relationship. Europeans who had become sanguine about American leadership suddenly had to sit up and take notice. The Americans had elected a new president, whose positions on foreign policy issues were straightforward, opinionated, and very much defined from an interests-based perspective. Gone were the Clinton years of multilateral diplomacy when U.S. foreign policy positions were often arrived at by consensus, invariably resulting in policy initiatives based on the lowest common denominator. Missing as well in the new Bush administration was the lip service paid to international organizations and the political correctness that allowed liberal agendas to influence national security strategy.

In place of the previous administration's approach to security planning, which included an emphasis on non-traditional agenda items, such as environmental protection and AIDS as national security issues, Bush government officials called for development of a national missile defense system and the abnegation of formal arms control agreements that were outdated by the march of technology and the changes that had taken place in the international environment. They also went on record as favoring the wholesale transformation of the American military establishment to meet new and emerging threats to American security, especially those of non-state transnational terrorist groups that were likely to employ asymmetric tactics to threaten American society where it was most vulnerable. Most significant of all, from the European perspective, the American approach to dealing with friends and allies appeared to be undergoing great changes, as unilateralism emerged as a favored option for U.S. operational planners and multilateralism came to be viewed in some instances as an impediment to timely and decisive action. [26]

Initial European reaction to the new American president was generally critical, with the exception of the Spanish and Italian conservative government leaderships. In France, elites at both ends of the political spectrum had held out hope that the U.S. election drama would play out in favor of Al Gore. When George W. Bush was officially identified as the winner, the French were unprepared and unforgiving in their criticisms of the new president's world view. In particular, the French were highly critical of the Bush administration's solid support for missile defenses, and predicted a new era of instability in U.S.-Russian relations now that the arms control frameworks of the Cold War era appeared to be in jeopardy. Many among the French elite view arms control frameworks as indispensable instruments for attaining predictability, a key element in ensuring strategic stability. When comparing the uncertainties of the contemporary security setting with the strategic stability of the Cold War era, French government official Marc Brichambaut (2002) called the earlier era a "lost paradise," a characterization that in many respects reflects a broader French desire to cling to the status quo that was conferred by earlier decades' arms control mechanisms.

American Power Confounds Gallic Logic

From a status quo perspective, the Bush Doctrine is a dangerous and destabilizing development that threatens to undermine the enduring value of arms control and multilateralism as the basis for both strategic and crisis stability. Even as specific arms control regimes may be less than perfect in monitoring transparency—French analysts frequently cite the Chemical Weapons Treaty in this regard—and their shortcomings readily apparent, most French officials still view these treaties as useful, suggesting that the lesson is not to abolish existing treaty regimes but rather to seek stronger enforcement mechanisms. For the French this means a

---

26 Many of the ideas that are shaping the Bush administration's foreign and security policies were outlined by candidate Bush in a series of speeches during his presidential campaign. Among the most notable in this regard were his Citadel speech of September 23, 1999, and his May 24, 2000, speech at the National Press Club, in which he outlined his views on nuclear deterrence and missile defenses. Now that he is president, these ideas are encapsulated in a new national security strategy document produced in September 2002, "The National Security Strategy of the United States of America" (Executive Office of the President 2002).

Major Frictions in the U.S.-French Relationship

NATO–ESDP

With the Southern Command issue behind them, France and the United States have continued to spar about NATO issues, and tensions heightened during the Bosnia and Kosovo wars. France continues to try to chip away at NATO's political legitimacy and has endeavored to strengthen the EU's defense and security policies to provide a counterweight to American domination in the Alliance.

Middle East

As seen from Paris, U.S. national interests, oil, and domestic politics combine to drive American support for Israel, to the detriment of Palestinian statehood, which is favored by a majority of French elites. American pro-Israeli positions have clashed with France's Arab policy in the past over Israeli actions, particularly their settlements policies. There are also differences with respect to Syria, which the French see as a key to regional stability, and over Lebanon, which the French continue to regard as their "colonial protectorate."

Bush Doctrine

The French vehemently protest the Bush Doctrine's emphasis on preemption and find its focus on coercion to be at odds with their interest in engagement. There continues to be significant French criticism of President Bush's "axis of evil" speech, and U.S. aspirations to roll back these three countries' WMD capabilities. France and the United States also differ over missile defenses, arms control, and the role of force, more generally, in international relations.

Iran

U.S.-French differences over Iran date to the days of the shah, but it was the American hostage crisis that really differentiated U.S. and French views, as the French attempted to develop a special relationship with the mullahs. Oil is the prize, but the French also view Tehran as central to regional power dynamics, and they believe that the reformist tendencies of the Khatami government should be nurtured through engagement and not threatened by U.S. talk of WMD rollback.

Iraq

France and Iraq have long had a special relationship, and since 1972 France has been a privileged trading partner in the oil sector. Apart form their oil interests, the French have viewed their position in Iraq as a counterweight to the U.S. and UK presence in the Gulf region. While the French ultimately went along with the *Desert Storm* operation, policy elites feel that the sanctions regime must come to an end, and there is virtually no elite support for ousting Saddam Hussein, since that could negatively affect France's trading position. On that basis, the French have not participated in the Allied NFZ activities; neither are they overly concerned about Saddam's nuclear potential, contending that the UN weapons inspections largely dealt with that issue. They do, however, support a return of the weapons inspectors, but that is a tactic intended only to stall American military action.

Missile Defenses

The French have long been opposed to U.S. development of missile defense technologies, in part because of their potential implications for French offensive nuclear forces, but more fundamentally because of their impact on the 1972 ABM Treaty. Now that the ABM Treaty is no longer in force, and the Russians have agreed to its demise, the French are struggling to find a niche for themselves and Europe both in the U.S. concept and in its technology research and development programs.

broader engagement of the United Nations, including with respect to treaty violations. This helps to explain why, among other reasons that are discussed more fully in chapter 6, the French continue to insist on the primacy of the UN Security Council in assessing Iraqi compliance with UNSC resolution 1441, adopted on November 8, 2002, calling for the re-introduction of UN weapons inspections to determine Iraq's compliance with previous United Nations resolutions directing Iraq's disarmament of its chemical, biological, nuclear, and radiological weapons (CBNR) programs.

Non-proliferation has emerged as a central issue for the French, as it has been for the United States for many years. One of the lessons learned from the wars against Serbia and Al Qaeda is that regime survival depends on dissuading the United States from military intervention, and for an increasing array of state and now non-state actors this appears to require the acquisition of weapons of mass destruction. The French also worry, in this regard, that failing states may consider nuclear weapons as an attractive means by which to retain power, or even as a means of exacting a heavy toll for actions directed against their regimes in a crisis contingency. With these considerations in mind, French experts contend that proliferation can best be dealt with through a combination of "carrot and stick" initiatives, in which the emphasis is on negative security guarantees and positive incentives or rewards for "good" behavior. Accordingly, there is a fundamental difference between the French and American approaches to North Korea, Iran, and Iraq, with the French persuaded that there is more to be gained from engaging these regimes in patient diplomacy than there would be from relying on military force to confront prospective adversaries. Thus, with respect to the emerging contours of the so-called Bush Doctrine, there is considerable French criticism of the twin notions of forward deterrence and preventive defense. More specifically, as this relates to counter-proliferation planning, the Bush Doctrine's emphasis on rollback is derided in France as a fig leaf to cover the American desire for regime change in Iraq, Iran, and North Korea, rather than a serious option for dealing with WMD proliferation.

Arms control, as noted earlier, remains central to French conceptions of non-proliferation planning. In this context, the French have a decided preference for keeping in place the Non-Proliferation Treaty (NPT), even now that certain powers (India and Pakistan, and very probably North Korea) have publicly avowed their respective nuclear weapons capabilities. As viewed from Paris, while the West may inhabit a "post-nuclear" world in which advanced and emerging non-nuclear weapons technologies have assumed greater relative importance in national and Allied security planning, other states contest this marginalization of nuclear weapons and, indeed, perceive them to be central to their security planning paradigms.[27] While hailing the NPT's efforts in the past to dissuade several countries—Brazil, Argentina, and South Africa are often cited in this regard—from proceeding with their nuclear programs, the French recognize the need to reinforce NPT proscriptions, and they have supported doing so by strengthening the powers of the International Atomic Energy Agency (IAEA) to inspect NPT compliance, and by establishing stronger enforcement mechanisms to promote transparency, verification, and complementary disarmament measures.

In addition, the French have been among the most ardent proponents of a code of conduct for supplier nations, and are in the forefront of efforts to promote a new, multilateral arms control paradigm that entails a more explicit declaratory policy to reduce the proliferation incentive. Previously, French policy elites had dismissed such a stark approach to non-proliferation planning, preferring to rely on so-called negative security guarantees, such as their pledge in 1982 not to use French nuclear weapons against countries that abstained from their own nuclear weapons development programs, and their reaffirmation in 1995 not to use nuclear weapons against non-nuclear signatories of the Non-Proliferation Treaty. Now, however, the French are said to be flirting with an approach that explicitly considers a declaratory policy about the prospective use of French nuclear weapons in certain scenarios, including those that involve terrorist actors striking at the heart of French interests. Just as the French have long recognized the importance of backing up their deterrence concept with credible capabilities—even under the non-use doctrine that they espouse, and which is discussed in detail in chapter 5—they now identify a need to make the con-

---

27 This point and the so-called North-South dichotomy in perspectives of nuclear weapons are explored in considerable length in "France and the Challenge of WMD Proliferation: A Report of the Defense Commission of the French National Assembly," issued on December 7, 2000, by Deputies Pierre Lellouche, Guy-Michel Chaveau, and Aloyse Warhouver. According to this report, three groups of states seek or have already acquired nuclear weapons outside of the NPT framework. These include the de facto nuclear states of India and Pakistan, Israel, which is considered a "threshold" state, and states suspected of having clandestine programs, including North Korea (which since has confirmed the existence of a covert program), Iraq, although among the French there is disagreement on this issue, Iran, Libya, and Syria. Brazil, more recently, has hinted that it, too, might reasses its adherence to the NPT.

cept of security guarantees more credible, in part to obviate the need to take the preemptive path, as the Bush administration appears prone to do.

In keeping with their preference for engagement rather than containment or preemption, the French are also seized with the importance of identifying the so-called root causes of proliferation. In this respect, French officials are inclined to attribute a cultural basis to their policy approaches, which in itself is not a bad idea and is one that has been considered by the United States in its own thinking about deterrence and counter-proliferation planning in the post-Cold War era. That said, the French approach is to focus on alleged complaints against the United States, especially from the Arab Middle Eastern states that contend that Israel's nuclear weapons holdings are reason enough for Arab proliferation activities. Expressing a very different view from the one held by the United States, many French policy elites trace everything from Saddam Hussein's WMD pretensions to Pakistan's nuclear development to U.S. policies, very explicitly including American support of Israel. From this emerges the French position that before the West takes on Saddam Hussein in Iraq, it first should address the Palestinian issue, which, from a broader perspective, must include Israel's possession of nuclear weapons. However, French predilections for explaining away Arab state-sponsored proliferation activities by singling out Israel as the principal motivating factor is highly suspect, considering France's own behavior in this regard and its late adherence (1992) to the Non-Proliferation Treaty. As an instrument of national independence and the sine qua non of state survival, Israelis, like the French before them, have determined that nuclear weapons remain essential to their national survival, especially in the face of a determined adversary who has much to lose by exposing his nation to the threat of nuclear reprisal.

Alternatively, however, French analysts consider Al Qaeda's pursuit of nuclear weapons to pose a different kind of challenge to non- and counter-proliferation planning. Since the transnational terrorist group has no base to protect and is willing to risk the survival of its members, neither positive nor negative security pledges are likely to hold much sway in influencing the behavior of the likes of Osama bin Laden. As the French see it, considerations of strategic stability that long have been central to deterrence among states are irrelevant factors when contemplating deterrence of what the French refer to as non-governmental criminal organizations (NCOs). From the French perspective, NCOs are essentially "undeterrable," since today's terrorists have shown themselves willing to make the ultimate sacrifice. This is why, the French agree with the Americans, it is important to go after their state sponsors and their financial networks, and in this context, the French are promoting the creation of an environment that is "terrorist averse," or an environment in which states have a vested interest in turning against terrorist clients. As part of a broader French effort to promote a code of conduct for nation-states, including with respect to technology transfers and efforts to stem the flow of fissile materials, the French government has proposed creation of an incentives-based framework for devising institutional responses to the terrorist challenge. Prevention rather than preemption is the French preference, and against the challenge of mass terrorism, the French see an opportunity to be more utopian, with the possibility of combining two French objectives: to use multilateralism as the basis for formulating responses to major security challenges, and to develop new arms control mechanisms to perpetuate Western conceptions of strategic and crisis stability. In this sense, there is considerable French support for stronger enforcement mechanisms and broader engagement of the United Nations and the group of industrial countries (the G-8) to stem the tide of technology transfers and the illegal sale of fissile materials, starting first with tighter controls over states that may be engaged in illegal arms sales or the covert transfer of WMD technologies, as some in the United States fear to be the case between Saddam's Iraq and Hamas, Al Qaeda, or other WMD-aspirant states, in this case, Libya and Syria.

Specifically in the case of Al Qaeda, the French do not accept the proposition that there is a formal tie to Iraq, as many analysts in the United States and the United Kingdom have come to believe. Like the United States, France perceives dangers in Iraq's quest for nuclear, chemical, and biological weapons, but insists that there is no verifiable evidence of a link between Iraq and Al Qaeda's pretensions to gain access to the same. This viewpoint has certainly influenced French behavior with respect to American actions to disarm Iraq, and it has stood at the basis of French views of the need to separate the situation in Iraq from next steps in the war on terror. Iraq's compliance, or lack thereof, with UN-mandated resolutions requiring the dismantlement of Saddam's WMD programs is a matter for the UN Security Council, whose structure perpetuates the illusion of great-power status for France, as one of its five permanent members. By resorting to the machinery of the United Nations, France has been able to constrain U.S. unilateral action on a number of issues, though not in 1998, when Iraq forced the withdrawal of the UN weapons inspectors and the United States, together with the United Kingdom, bombed Iraq without seeking a new Security Council resolution. Vowing never to let the United Nations be sidelined again on matters pertaining to Iraq, the French led an effort to get the UN to define proliferation as a "threat" to international peace and stability and, as noted above, promulgated an explicit declaratory policy to bolster the legitimacy of the Non-Proliferation Treaty regime.

In keeping with the dictum that there is no one so exacting as a determined convert to a cause—even if it was a relatively late conversion at that—the French have redoubled their efforts, if not their enthusiasm, to use multilateral frameworks to amplify their support of a UN-mandated effort to contain and disarm Iraq, should the international community become convinced of Saddam's complicity in developing a WMD capability for Iraq. The previous inability of the international community to compel Iraq to agree to the reintroduction of the weapons inspectors was viewed in Paris as arising, in part, from the Bush administration's intransigence on many fronts: its denunciation of formal arms control mechanisms; its defiance of international consensus on agreements such as those to constrain environmental emissions (the Kyoto Treaty) and to establish the International Criminal Court; and its renunciation of the ABM Treaty, which most French and European analysts had long considered to be the foundation of global security. In their own Gallic logic, the French contend that by flouting international law and rejecting established arms control frameworks, the United States has established an unhealthy precedent that could be seen as encouraging other nations to withdraw from arms control agreements that no longer suit their national interests. Egypt's prospective withdrawal from the Non-Proliferation Treaty in 2005, during the next NPT review conference, is frequently cited as a particular worry in this regard.

Even though the correlation between America's withdrawal from the ABM Treaty and global proliferation is tenuous at best, the French are sincere in their strong belief that such a relationship does in fact exist.[28] As they see it, the ABM Treaty was the centerpiece of superpower arms control for three decades, and its demise may well occasion the unraveling of other established arms control mechanisms, from the INF Treaty in Europe to the nuclear Non-Proliferation Treaty signed in 1968 to the so-called Suppliers Group, which aims to get a handle on the transfer of fissile materials and ballistic missile technologies. Even as many in French policy circles have expressed surprise at just how long the ABM Treaty actually remained in place, they nevertheless appear to have been astonished at the swiftness of its demise once the Bush administration came to office.

That, and Russia's relatively quiet acceptance of the American fait accompli, has forced the French into a fundamental review of their own defense posture, based, as it has been for the last forty-plus years, on nuclear deterrence and the *force de frappe*. The French have begun, with their enunciation of a new five-year defense program, to explore future security options, though hardly anyone expects this or any future French government to jettison the central role of nuclear weapons in the nation's security planning. What is open for debate is the relative importance of nuclear weapons in deterring emerging non-state threats, and the weight that a collective European security entity will bring to bear in the formulation and implementation of French defense and foreign policies, both subjects that are examined in greater depth in chapters 3 and 5.

If the Chirac-Raffarin government has come to terms with the U.S. effort to establish a new strategic relationship with Putin's Russia—a relationship based on deep cuts in both countries' offensive nuclear arsenals, a closer Russian relationship with NATO, and cooperation in the war against terrorism—it has also expressed concerns about Europe's marginalization in those areas. For that reason, Paris is re-

---

28 In May 1972, the Nixon administration signed two landmark arms control agreements with the Soviet Union. The first was an interim agreement limiting offensive ballistic missile deployments, with ceilings on launcher numbers and warheads. Tied to this was a treaty on anti-ballistic missile development and deployments.

energizing efforts to get Europe's Security and Defense Policy back on track. Of all the European allies, France has been the most vociferous in promoting ESDP, with the ulterior motive, some suspect, of undermining once and for all NATO's integrated command structure. French defense elites and government officials from both left and right deny that this is true, but they do contend that the emergence of a separate European defense entity is key to the establishment of another pole in the international system, in accordance with the French preference for a multipolar world to check the power ambitions of any single actor, in particular the United States, on the international stage.

Diverging U.S. and French World Views

Nowhere is the dichotomy between U.S. and French world views more apparent than in each country's responses to the post-September 11 world. Having declared war on Al Qaeda and the Taliban, the United States marshaled its resources to take on that mission. It quickly deployed forces to a distant theater of war, where it lacked the luxury of an established basing infrastructure, and it set out to reorganize its internal security, focusing on homeland defense and contingency planning to address terrorist threats in the United States and against U.S. interests abroad. It did all of this even as Americans continued to participate in SFOR in Bosnia and KFOR in Kosovo and while U.S. forces remained on alert in Japan, Korea, and the Persian Gulf and deployed to new locations in the Philippines to fight the global war against terrorism.

When the illusion of American invincibility was shattered by the events of September 11, the predominant American impulse was to go on the offensive and by October 2001, U.S. forces were engaged in battle in Afghanistan, the safe haven for the terrorist network. The U.S. decision to use military power was not a knee-jerk response, as some in Europe had feared it might have been; rather, it was a measured and decisive answer to a pressing security threat. While the French and the European allies expressed solidarity with the United States, there was in certain quarters a sense that America had gotten what it deserved (see Baudrillard 2001 and Revel 2002). Many in Europe, particularly in France, identified the source of the terrorists' attacks as emanating from U.S. policy choices. In so doing, they have endeavored to insulate themselves from the repercussions of American initiatives, and in some instances have done this by actively promoting policies that contested directly those of the United States. To be sure, successive European leaders, with France's Chirac being the first, hurried to Washington to express sympathy and support for the United States. But the penchant to avoid direct confrontation with state sponsors of terrorism remained strong and sharply colored their outlook with respect to operations in Afghanistan, and talk of operations in Iraq and Asia.

To support the United States, the NATO allies, for the first time in the history of the Alliance, invoked their Article 5 treaty commitment and deployed AWACS forces to help monitor the airspace over the United States. Though largely symbolic, the action, if only momentarily, silenced critics who had been complaining of NATO's irrelevance in the post-Kosovo world. But U.S. military leaders initially brushed aside offers to help U.S. forces in Afghanistan, remembering all too well their experiences in Bosnia and Kosovo and vowing not to be hampered by the constraints of coalition warfare. After several months, however, when it became apparent that certain U.S. military skill sets needed reinforcement, Allied contributions were welcomed on a selective basis, and new thought was given in Washington to the post-conflict stabilization of Afghanistan, using Allied/coalition partner forces to assume the burden of the peace-support missions.[29] Washington envisioned a division of labor between U.S. and Allied/coalition partner forces, where the United States would assume the war-fighting burden, while Allied forces would perform the bulk of the peace-support missions, as they themselves had suggested very often in Alliance forums.

However, the Europeans saw this as an unacceptable division of labor, particularly since it required the deployment of European forces outside of Europe. Most Europeans are rather parochial in their conception of security planning, and even Britain and France, which maintain residual global deployments, find the present division of labor difficult to

---

29 Notable among these were special forces for intelligence and missions in the mountainous regions, maritime assets for intercept operations, including in the Mediterranean area, and infantry forces for stabilizing missions throughout Afghanistan, especially to separate warring tribal factions.

accept. Dominique Moisi (2002a), writing in the *Financial Times*, noted that during the 2002 French national elections, defense and security issues were hardly mentioned. Instead, French concerns were focused on local issues, from unemployment and petty crime to violence in French cities, as well as the entry, illegal or otherwise, of large numbers of immigrants into France. When national security issues are considered, it is largely out of concern for their local ramifications. Thus, there is broader French interest in the Middle East than there is in Korean stability because of France's large Muslim population, and its vast network of energy and other commercial interests in the Arab world According to Moisi, "For most French voters in 2002, security ha[d] little to do with abstract and distant geopolitics" (2002a).

French elites, on the other hand, devote considerable time to foreign policy issues; for many, France's historic mission is to bring greater morality and vision into international relations, to substitute, as Kagan suggests, the Kantian global order paradigm for the chaotic, anarchical, Hobbesian international system. The clear French preference for a multipolar international system reflects this vision of France's pre-ordained role, but it also appears to be a rather transparent effort to enhance the French capacity to act on the world's stage. When, in March 2002, French President Chirac appealed in the EU for creation of a federal Europe, most observers saw this as an attempt to establish a counterbalance to unparalleled American power.[30] In the aftermath of September 11, the French have been particularly worried about American plans for the next phase in the war against terrorism, and especially its desire for regime change in Baghdad. New frictions in the U.S.-French relationship have developed over American intentions with respect to Iraq and even Iran and, more recently, North Korea, the three countries singled out by President Bush in his 2002 State of the Union Address as belonging to an "axis of evil," and housing regimes that support terrorism to gain national objectives and that repress their peoples for the sake of regime control. Without ques-

---

30 In calling for a "federation of nation states," with its own constitution, president, and parliament, President Chirac is attempting to reinvigorate the European Union and provide France, through what he calls a "pioneer group," with a major policy role in heading and delineating European policies in the defense and foreign policy arenas. See Evans-Pritchard and Helm (2002).

tion, U.S. and French positions on the so-called axis of evil, and very particularly on how to handle their proliferation-related activities, are diametrically opposed, despite agreement that the development and deployment of WMD by any one of the three would be destabilizing and profoundly dangerous to regional stability.

In discussing the state of U.S.-French relations today, one French analyst has observed that "the U.S. has less patience for us, and the French have less understanding of you" (Moisi 2002b). President Bush's 2002 State of the Union address, in which he characterized Iraq, Iran, and North Korea as an "axis of evil," illustrated the deep divide between the United States and France in their approaches to international relations. For the French, the president's remarks sharpened an image of America as operating in a high-risk fashion, as in the days of the Wild West. Bush's speech was particularly difficult for French elites to understand, since they had been engaged in painstaking efforts to persuade the UN to lift the sanctions against Iraq, a country with which successive French governments have shared a special relationship, and to engage Iran, where French leaders perceive a real opportunity to separate the moderate public from the repressive leadership of the mullahs. North Korea's inclusion in the "axis" was of less interest to most in France, although the 2003 nuclear crisis is perceived in Paris as a threat to global efforts to stem the tide of proliferation. That said, the potential for lucrative commercial deals with a South Korean government that is committed to détente on the Korean peninsula provided yet another basis for French derision of the Bush administration's policy approach. Paradoxically, however, French commercial interests may actually benefit from the Bush speech, if only with respect to Iran, but conceivably with respect to Iraq and the two Koreas as well.

Commercial interests, in particular trade and arms sales, have always played a major role in U.S.-French relations, not the least affecting collaboration on defense and security issues. Today, with the size of prospective markets shrinking, and the greater reliance of military forces on commercial technologies, from global positioning receivers to laptop computers, trade, arms sales, and technology transfer issues have emerged as a central concern for defense decision-makers. In both France and the United States, intelligence agencies have begun to concentrate on economic security issues, and in the United States, critical infrastructure protection (CIP) has emerged as a central aspect of homeland defense. The future does not look promising in this regard for U.S.-French relations, particularly given the sizeable and increasing technology gap that exists between U.S. and Allied military forces.

As is the case for the majority of U.S. allies, France made a conscious decision to cut its defense spending and to sacrifice modernization accounts while continuing to depend on the United States for strategic cover in the event of an "emergency" in Europe.[31] The widening capabilities gap that is in evidence today between the United States and its allies has affected U.S. operational planning and has reinforced a unilateral approach or a division of labor that most Europeans have found distasteful. Yet, the reality is that even in NATO, which has fostered the habit of multilateral planning and cooperation, the capabilities gap has made it very difficult to plan and execute operations, particularly in distant theaters. Furthermore, Alliance operational planning has proved to be contentious at the political level, with differences apparent over rules of engagement (ROE), over-flight rights, and even access to bases and logistical infrastructure.

Still, the United States has maintained the need for Alliance cohesion, and, at the November 2002 Prague Summit, endorsed a second round of membership expansion in NATO. While in many U.S. decision-making and analytical circles the relevance of NATO to twenty-first century security planning is not immediately obvious, the Bush administration has accepted its geopolitical importance both as a framework embracing the shared democratic values of the Euro-Atlantic community and as a means of ensuring that a power vacuum in Central Europe will never again become the object of great-power politics. The administration's challenge is to communicate that rationale to an increasingly skeptical American public that has no collective memory of the events that led to the formation of NATO and appears to be disenchanted with perceived Allied slights across

---

31 The Chirac-Raffarin government is aiming to counter this trend by increasing its defense spending and moving ahead with the modernization and transformation of its military forces, using the United Kingdom as its model for force-sizing, program priorities, and modernization. Chirac was very clear about this in his speech on the eve of Bastille Day 2002.

a range of issues. Fairly or not, the French tend to be singled out in this regard, largely because, in the words of Henry Kissinger, "France has pursued its interests by making it too painful to ignore them" (2001, 50).

The dissolution of the Soviet Union was a defining event for the Atlantic Alliance, U.S.-Allied relations, and particularly the Franco-American relationship. The fundamental transformation of the European security environment that accompanied Moscow's loss of empire gave greater urgency to French efforts to forge a constructive and cooperative relationship with the Soviet Union's successor states, particularly the Russian Federation and Ukraine. To a certain extent, French actions in the immediate post-Cold War era could be understood in the context of traditional French diplomacy that previously had sought to contain German power by entering into an alliance with Russia. However, these actions can also be explained as a concerted effort to curtail U.S. influence in Europe and elsewhere, particularly after the Persian Gulf war and the establishment of a quasi-permanent American presence in the Persian Gulf states—an area that was traditionally viewed as the domain of the European powers. Dr. Kissinger has portrayed France's relations with the United States as a zero-sum game, and from the perspective of U.S. interests, this certainly appears to be true for many issues (Kissinger 2001, 50). However, very likely, the fact that the French are unashamed to admit this irritates Americans just as much if not more than their actual policy stances. Thus, not for the first time in the history of their relationship has style contributed just as much as substance to French-American disagreements.[32]

The "age of globalization," to use Vedrine's phrase, has had a profound impact on French thinking, in particular on the way in which the French view themselves in the international system. For elites in France, globalization is equated with the

---

32 Hubert Vedrine, France's foreign minister in the 1997-2002 Jospin government, makes this point in *France in an Age of Globalization*, when he says, "In our relationship with the United States, we must perform a delicate but indispensable balancing act. French foreign policy after 1958 leaned in general toward criticism. . . Today, we should be capable of saying yes [to U.S. initiatives] when it is in our interest to do so, notwithstanding those who gauge our diplomacy according to the sole criterion of how much disagreement it creates with Washington. And I think that we should also be able to say no when that's in our interest—when our view of the world is different ..." (2001, 45).

growth of American power and influence, and from that perspective, it is a trend that is to be resisted at all costs. Just as José Bove took on the McDonald's chain in France, French elites have variously criticized America's economic policies, its cultural imperialism, and other aspects of its "soft" power that have had and will continue to have a major influence on the daily lives of people and governments around the world. In coining the word *hyper-power*, the French may have sought to demonize America's global reach, and to use it as a rallying call for all who oppose or contest U.S. interests. For their part, in this regard, the French are performing a dangerous balancing act, on the one hand sniping at America, while on the other hand depending upon its very power to be able to act so derisively toward it. When former U.S. Secretary of State Madeleine Albright referred to the United States as "the indispensable nation," the French were the first to criticize that characterization. But when the Europeans, led by the French, were unable to act in Kosovo, it was the Americans who devised a strategy and employed their leadership role in the Alliance to organize a defense of the beleaguered province.

These are the kinds of issues that weigh upon American thoughts today. The fear is that the French, with their penchant for "independent" thinking, may push the United States further and further away from its European partners, a fear that appears to have greater credence every day, with the passing of the Atlanticist generation that emerged after World War II, during the heyday of Alliance solidarity and cohesion in the face of a readily identifiable external threat to European security interests. The Chirac-Raffarin government in France is composed of a generation of technocrats whose perceptions and conceptions of their interests differ in important respects from those of their American counterparts. For the Bush administration, September 11 was a defining moment, when the sense of American invulnerability was lost and the threats to U.S. security became ever present and very dangerous. The French, who have long lived with the legacy of Algerian terrorism on French soil, may have failed to appreciate the extent to which America has changed after the terrorist attacks.

Even as there has been much apparent cooperation between the two governments on tracking and preventing future terrorist threats, they still seem to be talking past each other, especially with respect to future courses of action. For the United States, a military response to the attacks of September 11 was not only expected but widely supported among the American public and political elites. The French appeared to have understood, and indeed participated in and supported, the U.S. efforts to destroy Al Qaeda and its state sponsors in the Taliban regime. Where U.S. and French policies are now diverging is on the question of what to do next. For many in the United States, the answer is more or less apparent: continue to pursue Al Qaeda and its state sponsors through a combination of military and other means. The French would not necessarily disagree with this formulation, though it is clear that they are much more selective in designating targets and far more reluctant to resort to the use of military power. Clearly, this reinforces, once again, Kagan's thesis that Kant and not Hobbes provides the more persuasive philosophy for the Europeans.[33]

On the issue of Iraq, as noted above, there is fundamental disagreement over how to deal with the regime in Baghdad, although the French, like the Americans, would be happy were Saddam Hussein to be deposed. The French believe that a war with Iraq would be counterproductive: it would place an unfair burden on Iraq's civilian population, and it would destabilize the broader Middle East region, including North Africa, and threaten friendly Arab regimes in the Persian Gulf region. So, too, some French officials contend that a war with Iraq would divert attention from efforts to destroy Al Qaeda and may even embolden the terrorists to act anew. Always preferring the diplomatic approach as compared to what they see as the American tendency to resort to the use of military power, French policy elites are very concerned about regional stability once Saddam's Ba'athist regime is deposed from power. There is little confidence in the Iraqi National Congress (INC) in French

---

33 In his major work, *Leviathan*, Thomas Hobbes set forth his political philosophy, asserting that in the absence of a social structure, man is ultimately self-serving and that the natural condition of human beings is a perpetual state of war, unconditioned by moral strictures (1914). Immanuel Kant, on the other hand, believed that two classes of beings exist: the animal and the rational, who would act only in accord with strict moral strictures and according to the dictates of reason. Human beings, who are likely to give in to irrational impulses without the rule of law, therefore require rules of conduct and have the ability to select those principles that will guide their actions. Kant's political philosophy is elaborated in *Perpetual Peace*, which also contains guidelines for inter-state relations, the arbitration of conflicts, and the construction of a civil society that would facilitate the development of supranational laws and eventually "universal hospitality" and "world citizenship" (1939).

policy circles and there is no support for a protracted military campaign that exacts civilian casualties and requires a sizeable peacekeeping contingent after the operations are completed. French oil interests also worry about the stability of the Persian Gulf sheikdoms and the impact of any operation against Iraq on Iran, with whom the French government is investing considerable time, resources, and energy to engage. In this context, a French view has emerged that alleges, "U.S. strategic objectives in Iraq have little to do with the antiterrorist struggle." Rather, it is contended, "the installation of a pro-Western regime in Baghdad would allow the United States to control the world's second largest oil reserves, at a time when the largest, the Saudi reserves, seem gradually to be slipping away. The toppling of Iraq would make it possible to remodel the geopolitical face of the Middle East, to encircle Iran, and to facilitate a solution to the Israeli-Arab conflict in conformity with Israel's ambitions" (Barochez 2002b). A further motive, that of retaliation for the attempted assassination of the U.S. president's father, is also frequently cited in this regard.

From the American perspective, each of these motivations would, in fact, support broader U.S. strategic interests and contribute to regional stability. However, Paris sees them as potentially conflicting with French interests and points out once again the divergence between the two allies' world views now that the Cold War has ended. And yet, with respect to both Iraq and Iran, the Bush administration's priority interest in non- and counter-proliferation is remarkably consistent with that of France, but with some important differences. For example, in contrast to U.S. concerns about Iraq's nuclear proliferation potential, the French tend to dismiss that possibility as the main concern, worrying more about Saddam's biological weapons, which are also of concern to the United States, but more from a terrorist perspective. Iraq's ability to use biological weapons against the U.S. homeland, for example, or in support of an NCO terrorist operation, raises a different set of issues and challenges for U.S. security planners that are just as serious as those attendant upon nuclear weapons proliferation, but are of a completely different order in terms of operational planning and consequence management priorities.

From the French perspective, the United States tends to wrap itself in nuclear mythology and, as a result, continually emphasizes the worst-case scenario instead of concentrating on the more likely possibilities. In the case of Iraq, the French view is that the UN inspections regime that was set in place after the Gulf war oversaw the destruction of Iraq's nuclear programs, and even though weapons inspectors were expelled from Iraq in 1998, the sanctions regime that has been in place has made it virtually impossible for Saddam to gain access to nuclear-related materials. In fact, the French further argue, now that a new weapons inspection regime has been established by the United Nations, sanctions against Iraq should be modified to resemble the "smart sanctions" proposal that was put forward by the U.S. State Department's policy planning staff, if not dropped altogether because of their alleged adverse effects upon Iraq's civilian population.

The issue of Iraqi compliance with UNSC resolution 1441, and the questions raised by the report of chief UN weapons inspector Hans Blix in late January 2003, as to whether Iraq was in "material breach" of Security Council resolutions, have also generated new divisions between the United States and France, particularly in light of President Bush's reservation of the right to act unilaterally should the UN fail to take action. Notably, French and U.S. differences regarding a second and separate Security Council resolution to sanction the use of force against Iraq, followed by the unveiling of a Franco-German plan to augment the weapons inspections process, generated anew American fears that Baghdad would be emboldened to continue to defy UNSC 1441, while undermining NATO unity. French views of Iraq and U.S. policy are explored in greater depth in chapter 6 of this study. Suffice it to note here, however, that Iraq and the broader question of non-proliferation planning are destined to influence U.S.-French relations for the immediate future, and on these issues there is ample opportunity for questioning what each side stands for and what our interpretation of the answer to this question means for the future of U.S. and European security planning, including with respect to Iran, another point on the "axis of evil."

Unlike Iraq, whose Ba'athist regime Chirac has openly criticized, Iran marks a totally different case for the French, who long have sought "normal" relations with the regime of the ayatollahs, particularly since the election of Moham- med Khatami, who those in French policy circles perceive to be a moderate leader with no other agenda than to inject an element of modernity into the stalled economy and to bring a breath of liberalism into the staid political environment of the mullahs' fundamentalist preferences. The French inclina- tion toward engagement rather than containment of Iran was manifest early on during the 1979 hostage crisis when Washington perceived the government of Giscard d'Estaing as being "indifferent" to the plight of the American embassy personnel. In truth, the French were acting in their char- acteristic fashion, putting French national interests above Alliance considerations. France is almost totally dependent on imported energy, and its policies toward the Persian Gulf states, throughout the Fourth and Fifth Republics,[34] have consistently reflected the need to ensure French energy sup- plies. Even as Iraq remains the prize in this regard, the need for diversification of sources of energy supply has not been lost on the French, who were particularly hard hit by the oil shocks of the early 1970s. For that reason, Iran looms as a potentially important target of French diplomacy, more so when consideration is given to Iran's prospective emergence as another pole in the multipolar system that continues to influence profoundly French foreign policy and national se- curity decision-making. In keeping with this view, the Bush administration's inclusion of Iran on the "axis of evil" re- inforced French contentions that the United States seeks an imperial rule in which regime change in Iran would pave the way for consolidation of American influence in the energy- rich Persian Gulf region, and thereby encircle China and Rus- sia, to support U.S. global interests.

As for Washington, President Bush noted in his 2003 State of the Union address that "different threats require different strategies." Specifically with respect to Iran, he seemed to

---

34 During the Giscard years, France embarked on an ambitious program to develop alternative energy sources, in particular nuclear power generation, which was to culminate in a network of civilian nuclear power plants, a reprocessing capability in country, and an almost 80 percent dependence on nuclear-generated electricity, to reduce the country's dependence on energy imports from the Middle East. Since 1981, however, successive French governments have backed away from investments in nuclear power, and it is only now, with the Raffarin government, that discussions have begun anew of a civilian energy program aimed at developing new-generation reactor technologies.

signal the prospect of U.S. support for that country's democratic forces. While the president stopped short of embracing a new engagement strategy, noting that "in Iran we continue to see a government that represses its people, pursues weapons of mass destruction and supports terror," he nevertheless opened the door to so-called Track 2 engagement, in which non-governmental exchanges are commonly used to push official agendas. That said, there is little expectation that, even with a regime change in Tehran, a successor government would jettison Iran's nuclear weapons program. Nuclear weapons have become a great power currency, and in the broader Middle East region their possession lends political legitimacy, commanding the respect of regional neighbors. Thus, even were the United States to alter its strategy vis-à-vis Iran, it can never be sure that regime change in Iran would be accompanied by a willingness to abandon Iran's WMD programs, and this is proving to be a stumbling block in current U.S. efforts to forge any kind of dialogue at all with the Khatami government.

Certainly, as viewed from the United States, French efforts to influence state behaviors through an incentives-based policy approach have yielded little of substance, and in the instance of Iran, Iraq, and North Korea, these efforts may have had the unintended consequence of legitimizing their proliferation efforts. To defuse and even counter French and other Allied criticisms about the more confrontational nature of U.S. policies, the Americans have begun to build the case against each of the "axis" nations, though the evidence is likely to be filtered out by those who prefer to follow a less confrontational policy line. When the European Union led a delegation to Pyongyang in 2001, there was no question but that it embodied an effort to undermine the harsh stance that the new administration in Washington had adopted vis-à-vis both the North Korean regime and South Korea's so-called sunshine diplomacy. The EU mission, followed by French policy overtures to Pyongyang, has put the Europeans, and in particular the French, on a confrontational footing with the United States in Northeast Asia. Apart from mixing into an area (the Korean peninsula) that since the Korean war has, more or less, been accepted as the domain of the United States, the French have raised American ire by floating arms control initiatives targeted on the peninsula, without consulting with the United States, and by openly criticizing U.S. military deployments on the peninsula as vestiges of the Cold War.

The revelation in October 2002 that North Korea was pursuing development of a covert nuclear weapons capability is only likely to exacerbate U.S.-European differences in this regard. Now, with North Korea's withdrawal from the nuclear Non-Proliferation Treaty, and with the apparent demise of the 1994 Agreed Framework (which provided Western material and aid to alleviate North Korea's energy shortages in return for renunciation by the DPRK of its nuclear weapons programs), the United States has gone on record as refusing to enter into negotiations with the DPRK regime until Pyongyang halts all of its proliferation-related activities. And, despite agreement by all of the sponsors of the Korean Energy Development Organization (KEDO), including the European Union, that nuclear blackmail must not be rewarded, the Europeans are unwilling to back entirely away from engagement of the North, citing the need to keep a dialogue alive, particularly between North and South Korea themselves. To be sure, the French appear to be less interested in the third "axis" state, although because events on the Korean peninsula affect broader regional stability in Northeast Asia and have a direct influence on China's world view, the French have determined to keep their hand in peninsular affairs, as much to attempt to influence American presence on the peninsula as to create new markets for French goods. Thus, even here, there is the prospect for Franco-American discord, particularly as U.S.-South Korean relations experience their own ups and downs.

From this brief overview of issues bearing on the U.S.-French relationship, it is readily apparent that the two nations face serious challenges, several of which could pull them apart and wreak havoc with broader U.S. interests, including with respect to the future of the Atlantic Alliance. Taken together it is easy to conclude that U.S. and French interests may not be so symmetrical after all. If so, what this portends for transatlantic relations, particularly Alliance politics, is difficulty on the road ahead, not the least regarding the transformation of NATO, its role in U.S. and European security planning, and its relationship to the nascent European Security and Defense Policy that the French have embraced as their own to advance their own power and influence on the world stage. The next chapter explores in greater depth French views of NATO and the emerging ESDP, and how they may affect transatlantic collaboration on defense and broader security planning.

CHAPTER 3

The Genesis of a New Transatlantic Divide

NATO has long been a source of tension in the French-American relationship. Shortly after its creation, conflict arose over questions involving command relationships, the scope of Alliance responsibilities, and membership issues. For the French, NATO's initial utility was in the framework it provided for German rearmament to take place without threatening the stability of the European continent. At the same time, during the height of the Cold War, the Atlantic Alliance provided tangible evidence of America's security relationship with Western Europe, even if most French strategists readily dismissed the credibility of the American extended deterrence guarantee. The French were not convinced that Washington would sacrifice the security of New York for that of Paris, Berlin, or even London. So the only way to ensure French security was for France to develop its own deterrent capability, which was begun under de Gaulle's watchful eye in the late 1950s.[35]

France's determination to develop and deploy a national deterrent capability was motivated by many reasons, which are explored in chapter 5. Here, it suffices to note that de Gaulle's ambitions for France demanded that France should possess nuclear weapons since they were a clear manifestation of great-power status. Without nuclear weapons, France could not claim this status alongside the United States and Great Britain.[36] Viewed from this perspective, it is clear that American dominance of NATO, solidified by its nuclear weapons supremacy, was not only irritating to the French, but perceived as working against French interests, as it surely had done years before and during the 1956 Suez crisis, when the United States failed

---

35 For an examination of the origins of the French nuclear program, see Kohl (1971, 15-47) and Goldschmidt (1980, 136-70).
36 For an insightful treatise on de Gaulle's thinking during this period, see Williams (1993, 408-22).

to back the Anglo-French-Israeli initiative to counter Egypt's nationalization of the Suez Canal.[37] The Suez crisis occurred just as the national liberation movement in Algeria was gaining momentum and a mere two years after France's disastrous defeat in Indochina led to French withdrawal from Southeast Asia. Algerian independence was the issue that brought de Gaulle back into power in France, and it was a constant distraction with which the Fourth Republic had to contend. In 1959, when the Soviet Union, under Nikita Khrushchev, sought to reassert Soviet authority over Berlin, again in 1961, with the construction of the Berlin Wall, and in the 1962 crises over Berlin and Cuba, France had little choice but to adhere to the U.S. and NATO lead. In this situation, de Gaulle was unable to advance his agenda for propelling France toward a leading role in Europe and onto the global stage, though the crises in Europe and in U.S.-Soviet relations over Cuba gave him time to address and resolve the Algerian issue, after which he could move on to focus on what really interested him—establishing France as the leader of Europe.

Very early on, in the aftermath of World War II, de Gaulle's vision of Europe—his so-called Grand Design—clashed with emerging global realities. Through the creation of the Atlantic Alliance, and with it the NATO framework for organizing the defense and security of Western Europe, the United States had assumed the leading role in European security debates. Not content to be playing a minor role to the American lead in Europe, de Gaulle in 1958 proposed the creation of a NATO directorate, composed of the United States, Great Britain, and France, to oversee decision-making in the Alliance. Despite his earlier overtures to the Germans with respect to the European Economic Community (EEC), which came into being on January 1, 1959, and his personal relationship with German Chancellor Konrad Adenauer, de Gaulle was adamant that the Germans be excluded from the directorate, as well as being prohibited from developing nuclear weapons or reuniting with the German Democratic

---

37 The military action ended in disaster and has been identified as one of the motivating factors behind the French view of America as an undependable ally. For the French, the requirement to act sprang from Gamal Nasser's role in supplying the Algerian separatists and terrorists (FLN). By all accounts, the French government at the time considered that the FLN could not be defeated until Nasser was ousted from power. See Gildea (1996, esp. 5-29).

Republic, which since World War II had been under Soviet occupation and later was the linchpin of the non-Soviet Warsaw pact nations.

De Gaulle's arguments in favor of the directorate were predicated on a world view that featured a major role for France and depended on an effort to pry the British away from their longstanding "special relationship" with the United States, to allow for a "European" majority in directorate voting. It is not clear whether this was a serious proposal, although it established a pattern of demands that continue to this day in Alliance decision-making. De Gaulle biographer Charles Williams suggests that the real motive behind the directorate proposal was to gain access to U.S. aid for the French nuclear program (Williams 1993, esp. 394-407). Whatever the precise motivation, de Gaulle's efforts to attract U.S. help with French nuclear developments were, at this time, unsuccessful, leading to a renewed determination on the part of de Gaulle to create an independent deterrent force, one that could be invoked in a crisis by the French president alone (although in consultation with the French Defense Council).[38]

Over the years, however, France eventually did receive some help from the United States for its nuclear programs, specifically in the areas of warhead miniaturization and in its simulation program called PALEN.[39] Yet the myth that it did not persists.[40] That said, for all practical purposes, the French nuclear force is a national capability at the disposal of the French president to call upon in the name of the French nation if a crisis dictates its use. Armed with the power conferred on him by the French nuclear program, and after having extricated France from Algeria, de Gaulle was free to return to the issue of NATO and its American-dominated command structure. From that point onward, de Gaulle and his successors devoted considerable time to devising alternative

---

38 The first French nuclear test took place in February 13, 1960, and the first squadron of nuclear-capable *Mirage*-IV bombers became operational in 1964. The first French strategic nuclear submarine class, the *Redoutable*, was commissioned in 1967, and the first boat became operational in 1967. In 1971, eighteen nuclear-tipped land-based intermediate-range (IRBM) surface-to-surface ballistic missile launchers were deployed on the Albion Plateau in southwest France.

39 Preparation à la Limitation des Essais Nucléaire, or PALEN, involves a series of computer simulations and was designed to take the place of operational warhead testing so that France could sign the Comprehensive Test Ban Treaty.

40 Over the years, as Princeton University Professor Richard Ullman (1989) has noted, the United States, in fact, has provided help to the French nuclear program.

frameworks for European security—frameworks that were calculated to diminish American power in European decision-making and to undermine the capacity of the British to act as America's Trojan horse in the Alliance. Neither de Gaulle nor any of his successors, especially throughout the Cold War, challenged the importance of retaining a formal tie to the United States for political and military consultations on security issues. They did, however, contest the American ability to act unilaterally on issues affecting NATO as a whole.

Using ESDP to Leverage or Constrain American Power

American unilateralism has been a constant complaint levied by the French over the years. For periods during the Cold War, notably when the United States and the Soviet Union met in 1972 to sign the Strategic Arms Limitation Agreements, and later, as Germany's *Ostpolitik* took hold and German unification was about to become a reality, French complaints about American unilateralism were joined with apprehensions about a superpower "condominium," in which—or so it was alleged—European security interests were being sacrificed for those of the United States, for the first time publicly articulating charges that American and European security interests were not symmetrical after all. French concerns over the growing asymmetries between U.S. and French policy positions on a range of issues, from the Middle East to arms control with the Russians, to German reunification, provoked new thinking in France about Europe's security arrangements, culminating in efforts to create a pan-European security system that would embody all of Europe from the Atlantic to the Urals. While hardly a new concept—indeed de Gaulle had first articulated this idea shortly after he announced the decision to pull French forces out of NATO's integrated command structure in 1966[41]—the concept of a pan-European collective security system has

---

41 On March 7, 1966, President de Gaulle, in private messages to his counterparts on the North Atlantic Council (NAC), informed them of the decision to pull French forces out of NATO's integrated command structure and to request, which he subsequently did on March 29, the withdrawal from French territory of NATO headquarters, apparently fearing that French forces would be dragged into the war in Vietnam. At the same time, de Gaulle made clear his intention to remain on the Alliance's political councils and to seek a new "entente" with "Russia," France's historic ally. Subsequently, on June 21, 1966, de Gaulle embarked on a historic trip to Moscow, where he announced that France would be "placed" between the two great-power blocs and, belonging to neither, would be better positioned to mediate between the two (Williams 1993, 445-457).

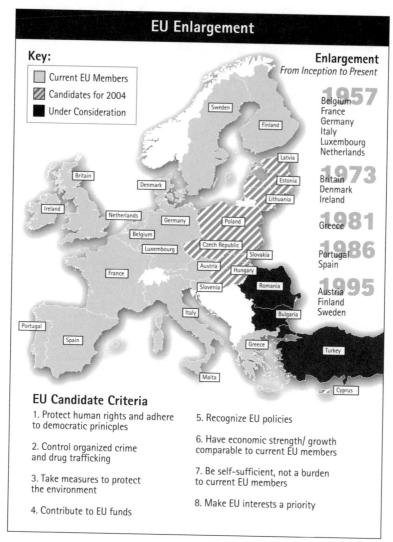

EU Enlargement

Key:
- Current EU Members
- Candidates for 2004
- Under Consideration

Enlargement
From Inception to Present

Sweden
Finland
Latvia
Britain
Denmark
Estonia
Lithuania
Ireland
Netherlands
Germany
Poland
Belgium
Luxembourg
Czech Republic
Slovakia
Austria
Hungary
France
Slovenia
Romania
Italy
Bulgaria
Portugal
Spain
Greece
Turkey
Malta
Cyprus

1957
Belgium
France
Germany
Italy
Luxembourg
Netherlands

1973
Britain
Denmark
Ireland

1981
Greece

1986
Portugal
Spain

1995
Austria
Finland
Sweden

EU Candidate Criteria

1. Protect human rights and adhere to democratic prinicples

2. Control organized crime and drug trafficking

3. Take measures to protect the environment

4. Contribute to EU funds

5. Recognize EU policies

6. Have economic strength/ growth comparable to current EU members

7. Be self-sufficient, not a burden to current EU members

8. Make EU interests a priority

been an important feature of French security policy, providing impetus for the Conference on Security and Cooperation in Europe (CSCE) in the 1970s, and leading to the establishment of the Organization for Security and Cooperation in Europe (OSCE), which continues to this day to be an important framework, from the French perspective, for crisis management and conflict resolution in Europe.[42]

The preceding discussion identifies four themes that have influenced French consideration of European security cooperation from the time of de Gaulle to the present. These encompass

---

42 The role of the OSCE in crisis and conflict management is elaborated in IFPA (2000, esp. 117-143, 144-172).

efforts to: stem the tide of American unilateralism; reach out to Russia; constrain the rising power of Germany in Europe; and undermine the Anglo-American special relationship in NATO. To empower these efforts, France has variously sought to use the Western European Union (WEU) and, more recently, the European Security and Defense Policy to challenge the primacy of NATO as the preeminent framework for European security.[43] It was not until the European Union emerged as a concrete political entity, however, that the French challenge to NATO was so well positioned and calculated. The fall of the Soviet Union and the emancipation of Eastern and Central Europe from Soviet domination created a new European political landscape, one that erased the Yalta-inspired East-West frontier, and that gave rise to the very real possibility of a pan-European security system. Coming under discussion at the same time as the convergence of the economies of the major West European powers, prompted first by the EEC's monetary agreements and subsequently by renewed discussion of "Europe as a single space," a variant of the French desire for an integrated European pole in a multipolar international system, establishment of a "common" foreign and defense policy for the Europeans seemed to be well on its way with the signing of the Maastricht Treaty in 1991.

French aspirations for a common European security and defense identity have long been a theme of French diplomacy. Astute observers of the French scene have attributed this to three factors: first, France, since the Second World War, has sought to contain any prospect of German re-militarization and even its reemergence as the most formidable power in Europe. Second, the French have viewed European foreign policy and defense collaboration as a way to compete with the "Anglo-Saxons" and in particular as a means of eroding the strength of the special relationship between the United

---

43 The Western European Union (WEU) was created in 1948, as part of the Brussels Treaty of Economic, Social, and Cultural Collaboration and Collective Self-Defense. Its signatories included France, Belgium, Luxembourg, the Netherlands, and Great Britain. Later, under the Paris Agreements of 1954, Germany and Italy joined the Brussels Treaty and the organization was renamed the Western European Union. As clearly indicated in the WEU Charter, its original intention was to foster European defense cooperation within NATO, although in later years the French, in particular, sought to use the WEU framework to rival NATO planning through the creation of alternative force structures and command headquarters for use in non-(NATO) Article 5 contingencies, such as the Yugoslav wars. The demise of the WEU came very quickly after the establishment of the European Union and the codification at the Berlin (NATO) ministerial in 1996 of a European Security and Defense Identity (ESDI), which has since evolved under the EU's Common Foreign and Security Policy (CFSP) to become today's European Security and Defense Policy (ESDP).

States and the United Kingdom. Finally, and probably a more important factor for French politicians, ESDP was, and is, viewed as a way to project and channel French power on the international stage. Taken together, these considerations have focused French governmental efforts on the EU and, despite a brief period in the 1990s when the first Chirac government made a concerted effort to bridge French differences with the United States and Britain over NATO reform, there is no question now of a French change of heart on the NATO reintegration issue.[44]

During the period from 1993 to 1996, U.S. and French thinking appeared to converge about ways to modify the Alliance to meet future security challenges. Of particular importance during this time was the 1996 NATO Summit, held in Berlin. First, it recognized the growing impetus toward "Europeanization" within the Alliance by referencing the WEU's new and growing role in parallel with that of NATO. Second, and just as important, it noted the significance of British and French nuclear forces and the prominent contribution that they make to European security. And, finally, the Berlin communiqué opened the door for reform of NATO structures, the long-held objective of the French bureaucracy and a principal source of controversy with the Americans for what this implied in terms of an Alliance division of labor. However, after the Berlin Summit, events in the Balkans took center stage, U.S. and French convergence on European security issues halted, and, as discussed in chapter 4, relations between the two reverted to their more familiar, contentious pattern. The United States correctly posited that with the demise of the Soviet empire, NATO reform had, of necessity, to embrace a redefinition of NATO roles and missions, to include consideration of action beyond Alliance borders. The

---

44 After the March 1993 National Assembly elections in which President Mitterrand's Socialist Party suffered a landslide defeat, the conservatives formed a government, and Alliance reform was one of its priority agenda items. With the crisis over Bosnia a coalescing event for the French political establishment, Ministry of Defense proposals for closer French collaboration with NATO operational planning, in part to induce the United States to intervene in Yugoslavia, gave rise to the perception that officials in Paris were ready for France to reintegrate into the Alliance's integrated command structure. After what were perceived in Washington and elsewhere in Alliance capitals as several false starts, two changes in government in France (from cohabitation to a Chirac presidency, first with a center-right government under Alain Juppé and later with a Socialist Jospin government) and recriminations (between France and the United States) over NATO reform, the chance was lost, and the French focused their energies on ESDI/ESDP.

French, alternatively, were more concerned with process and mechanisms and, accordingly, sought to emphasize NATO's structural reform, in a not too transparent effort to erode American power in the Alliance.

Now that the Soviet Union and its Warsaw Pact appendage no longer existed, the Americans were convinced that the time had come to focus Alliance attention on a number of pressing issues, including tools for reacting to crises on NATO's periphery and ways to meet new challenges, such as missile proliferation, that threatened to infringe upon Europe's security. In addition, means had to be found to help solidify and build upon the victories of the late 1980s, in which the nations of East and Central Europe had come out from under Russian domination and begun to build new democracies in the heart of Europe. NATO enlargement emerged as an important political imperative for the United States, although there was no consensus either at home or across the Atlantic on how far and how fast NATO should evolve. However, before dealing seriously with NATO expansion, NATO members had to come to grips with the Alliance's raison d'être in the new era. To that end, Alliance members agreed that a new security concept was needed to address the new political and strategic realities in and outside of Europe, and with it the reform of Alliance decision-making structures to deal with crises and issues that could have an impact on members' security and strategic stability on the Continent.

In the run-up to the Berlin Summit, and indeed in the years immediately following the 1993 parliamentary elections, the French government, according to one authoritative source, was genuinely prepared to move closer to NATO, and even to re-associate itself (via a dual-hatted formula) with operational decision-making in the Alliance. This was provided, however, that NATO's political authorities, represented in the North Atlantic Council (NAC)—and not its military leadership, headed by the Supreme Allied Commander, Europe (SACEUR)—had the ultimate decision-making authority.[45] Over the years, the French apparently had come to the view that SACEUR, largely because of his dual role as commander of all U.S. forces in Europe

---

45 The French continue to feel strongly on this point, as was reiterated during interviews in Paris in 2002.

(EUCOM) and the person who is charged with implementing the NAC's operational decisions, exercised unparalleled power and influence in NATO political councils. Very often, SACEUR was invited to NAC sessions, and over time, because the Alliance in the post-Soviet era found itself increasingly engaged in peace-support missions, not to mention a hot war over Kosovo, SACEUR's authority was seen in Paris to be taking on a larger, political dimension. The French saw the convergence of political and military operational authority under SACEUR's auspices as unacceptable and as perpetuating American heavy-handedness with respect to all Alliance decision-making, including in areas that were, and are, exclusively under the purview of the NAC.

As a result, the French for years have attempted to curb SACEUR's powers, more recently through proposals for the reform of NATO's headquarters and decision-making structures. In the 1994-95 time period, French proposals for Alliance reform centered on NATO's major regional command (MRC) structures. Theoretically, French proposals for reform of NATO were justified as necessary to accommodate new thinking about the roles and missions of the Alliance in the post-Cold War era. In reality, however, they had much more to do with French efforts to dilute the power of SACEUR, and with it that of the United States in Alliance decision councils to accommodate the French desire to "Europeanize" the Alliance.

Even in the United States, there was hesitant support for arguments in favor of reforming Alliance structures to make NATO more relevant to the challenges of the new era, but there was virtually no support—neither in U.S. military circles, nor in Congress—for agreeing to any reform that would erode the power of SACEUR, particularly as a reflection of his role as commander of all U.S. forces in Europe. In practical terms, however, French proposals for NATO reform were seeking to do just that by focusing on an effort to increase the power and decision authority of SACEUR's deputy (DSACEUR) to act in non-Article 5 crises, that is, in humanitarian or policing interventions outside of NATO proper. More worrisome for the United States was the blatant French attempt to transform Allied Forces South (AFSOUTH) from a command that, traditionally, had been set aside for the Americans because of the U.S. Navy's large (Sixth Fleet) presence in the wider Mediterranean region, to one that would be assigned, on a rotational basis, to a major European ally.

Even today, French officials vehemently deny that their ulterior motive was to gain control of AFSOUTH for themselves. Rather, the French contend that it was always their intention to create a headquarters command that resembled that of Allied Forces Central Europe (or ACE), which had a European commander and whose assets included the ACE Rapid Reaction Force—a capability that had been developed for crisis interventions, but that has since been disbanded for lack of available troops.[46] Specifically, France's then-chief of Defense Staff (CHOD), General Jean-Philippe Douin, proposed the creation of a special strike force from the European Maritime Force (EUROMARFOR), which was newly established to give substance to European efforts to strengthen the WEU. Together with a land force component (EUROFOR) headquartered in Florence, Italy, French government officials presumably also saw this as a means to bolster support for their proposal for reform of the NATO command structure.

For the Americans, this was, and is, a non-starter, primarily because of AFSOUTH's coterminous assignment as commander-in-chief of U.S. Naval Forces in Europe. Not that this duality of command authority could not have been sorted out and accommodated, even were AFSOUTH no longer assigned to a U.S. military leader. The more important issue, from the U.S. perspective, was, and is, the inequality of NATO military assets assigned to AFSOUTH, the growing gap between U.S. and European capabilities assigned to NATO, and forces' interoperability. Washington is also concerned over the implications of changes to AFSOUTH for U.S. staging for Middle East contingencies. To the extent that

---

46 Subsequently, the NATO command structure was refined, leaving in place (for the moment) three strategic commands (Atlantic, Northern, and Southern Regions) and numerous major sub-regional commands (MSRs), in part to satisfy national political leaderships and to spread headquarters commands to virtually all members of the Alliance. There are, however, proposals on the table to downgrade SACLANT, making it a subordinate command to U.S. EUCOM, much like AFSOUTH currently is, and to restructure the MRCs and cut out several of the major sub-regional subordinate command components (MSRCs). There is also discussion of creating a NATO transformation command, focusing it on NATO transformation, experimentation, and exercises, and a decision was taken in 2002 to disband the ACE mobile force after Britain withdrew its forces from the command to make UK troops available for future operations in the war on terror (Smith 2002). Subsequently, in September 2002, U.S. Secretary of Defense Donald Rumsfeld proposed the creation of a NATO Rapid Reaction Force, to be composed of up to twenty-one thousand troops and ready for action with no more than thirty days' notice.

the Southern Region remains a critical transshipment hub for U.S. forces, as well as a potential base of operations, the American stake in NATO transformation in this area is huge, and its contribution to U.S. global strategy is not lost on the French, who aspire to influence that planning in a more systematic fashion.

Controversy over NATO reform, as manifested in debate over the leadership of AFSOUTH, culminated at the NATO defense ministerial in December of 1996, when neither the French nor the Americans backed away from their positions. It was only in early spring of 1997, after intensive negotiations, that the issue was more or less put to rest, based on a British proposal for creation of a European deputy to the AFSOUTH commander, who, in effect, would operate as the force commander during a non-NATO, European operation. While prominent observers of the French scene have recently suggested that the AFSOUTH controversy "overshadowed the fact that the two countries' divergent conceptions of what the Alliance was for and of how it should be managed had come closer," there is no doubt that it had soured Alliance efforts to reintegrate French military forces into NATO's integrated command structure (Brenner and Parmentier 2002, 55).

More than this, the AFSOUTH controversy re-opened other, old wounds, including French criticism of SACEUR's role in the Alliance, and more fundamentally, NATO's role in the broader European security landscape. Harkening back to a now common theme in French diplomacy, French government officials, after the AFSOUTH debacle, resumed their posturing for a common European defense identity and added to that cacophony by arguing the case for establishing a new relationship with Russia. With respect both to SACEUR and to forging a new relationship with Russia, the French penchant to see the Alliance as a political entity informed French thinking about NATO and its reform. Thus, regarding operational planning as well as crisis decision-making, the Alliance's member states, through the North Atlantic Council and the machinery of the International Staff, should, from the French view, take precedence over any recommendation or input from the SHAPE (Supreme Headquarters Allied Powers Europe, SACEUR's military component) staff.

While the United States accepts the principle that the North Atlantic Council is the Alliance's final decision authority (with members getting directions from their national capitals), Washington has great concerns about the politicization of military-operational issues, and on that basis was initially reluctant to open the door too wide to NATO reform. However, once it became evident, after the failure of the United Nations Protection Force mission in Bosnia (UNPROFOR), that the new circumstances demanded a different kind of NATO intervention and capability, the United States was galvanized to support that end. This began with consideration of a new strategic concept to meet new and emerging security challenges, followed by NATO enlargement to embrace the fledgling democracies in East and Central Europe, and by significant, structural reform of the Alliance to enhance its operational effectiveness.

At the 1999 Washington Summit, NATO adopted a new strategic concept and announced a Defense Capabilities Initiative (DCI) that included reference to the ESDP and an intention to further reform NATO command structures. This was a particularly important event for the French, who, earlier in 1998, at Saint Malo had secured a commitment from the United Kingdom to consider a formal role for the European Union in the defense and security field.[47] However, President Jacques Chirac's earlier decision to dissolve the National Assembly and call for elections in 1997 brought a disastrous result for the conservatives in France, and with the creation of a new cohabitation government with Socialist leader Lionel Jospin at its helm, further progress in this direction languished. Defense cooperation between France and its European partners stalled, in part because the new prime minister had little interest in security issues.

Jospin's lack of interest notwithstanding, Chirac was still president of France, and his tenure in government had another five years to run. This unhappy state of affairs resulted in another French cohabitation government, and it provided the catalyst

---

47 The so-called Saint Malo accords are significant for a number of reasons. For one, they established a formal basis for practical Anglo-French defense cooperation across a number of areas. Second, they paved the way for closer consultation on crisis management and provided a means for such consultation by allowing French representation at Northwood, the UK's Permanent Joint Force Headquarters. Various regimes for operational collaboration were established, beyond that which had originated in 1996 with the creation of the Franco-British Air Group at RAF High Wycombe. The French contend that Saint Malo set in motion the forces that culminated in institutionalization of the ESDP at the EU Helsinki Summit in December 1999.

for limiting the term of the French presidency to five years, renewable by election for a second five-year term. The dynamics of the Chirac-Jospin cohabitation were never comfortable and became downright hostile by the time new elections were held in 2002. For domestic political reasons, then, the French had very little maneuver room on NATO and EU issues during this period, and, predictably, this had a marked effect on U.S. perceptions of France as an ally. Ironically, though, during this period there was significant movement on operational planning for contingencies in which the United States had opted not to become involved.

Saint Malo: A Turning Point?

Through a British initiative at Saint Malo, the French agreed to tie ESDP to Alliance planning, though not exclusively, and with that provision brought the UK closer to consideration of a more formal role for the European Union in defense and foreign policy. From all appearances, the French were willing to compromise on the British insistence that ESDP be tied to NATO because they realized that most of the European members of the Alliance would insist on just that in order to rationalize force structure. Germany's force structure, for one, was completely integrated into NATO, while other allies lacked an ability to generate a separate force structure and command chain for EU-only purposes. France itself also required a "dual-hatted" approach in order to retain capabilities for use in national contingencies. Thus, the Saint Malo compromise appeared to suit most of the European nations, the sole exceptions being Greece and Turkey, both for reasons related to their historic enmity.

The Saint Malo accords and an accompanying agreement that outlined concrete proposals for intensifying Franco-British defense cooperation were always viewed in Paris in the broader political context. From the French perspective, improved military cooperation between the two would add to the credibility of the EU's Common Foreign and Security Policy (CFSP), which in turn would be boosted by the successful evolution of practical collaboration in the defense field. In order for this to happen, however, the French military had to reform its own structures and planning concepts. Apart from taking on the difficult task of moving away from conscription to create a professional

The 1994 *Defense White Paper*

The 1994 *Defense White Paper* indentified six scenarios for the employment of French armed forces. The following are excerpts from the six scenarios outlined in the White Paper:

Scenario I – Regional Conflict Which Would Not Threaten France's Vital Interests

Regional powers equipped with considerable conventional assets can be expected to further strengthen their forces in the future, despite the enforcement of arms control agreements. Conflicts between regional powers might directly or indirectly threaten France's strategic interests; by the same token, international interventions aimed at restoring peace and international law might induce confrontations with these powers [...]. The regional threat would be constituted of conventional forces, often similar to those of Western nations in strength and at least partly in nature [...]. French participation in an international action could also trigger retaliation against our national territory or towards our nationals abroad. This could mainly take the form of terrorism [...]. In the case of an intervention, our forces would act under international mandate within the framework of NATO, the WEU and, in the longer run, of the EU or a coalition [...].

Scenario II – Regional Conflict Which Could Threaten France's Vital Interests

This assumption takes into account the possibility, in the twenty years to come, of seeing European security seriously threatened by a regional conflict involving a nuclear power and, as a consequence, running the risk of threatening France's vital interests in the escalation [...]. To the threats listed in the previous scenario, one would add an increase in the risks run by our forces, including the nuclear ones. Whatever the qualitative and quantitative level of the threats, the difference with the first scenario lies in the risk of destabilization and of the increasing power of extremism which could denigrate and possibly even threaten France's vital interests, especially on the national territory. For the international community, the aim should be, as at the beginning of the crisis, to prevent the situation from escalating out of control. France would then act within a multinational framework, be this NATO, the WEU or, in the longer run, the European Union.

Scenario III – Attack on the Integrity of the National Territory Outside Mainland France

This assumption considers a threat against France's overseas departments and territories, which can take several shapes involving e.g. direct aggression for territorial reasons (which is an unlikely case) or indirect destabilization actions. France must be able, acting independently and despite possible international pressure, to control and settle this type of conflict.

Scenario IV – Application of Bilateral Defense Agreements

This type of intervention is considered in the context of low-intensity regional conflicts such as those taking place in Africa. France will keep the capability to act alone. An increased participation of the United Nations could however be looked for, while the definition of a common security policy with the European Union members could lead in the future to combined EU deployments, although France must retain a capacity to act on her own.

Scenario V – Operations in Support of Peace or International Law

Operations in support of peace or international law will take multiple shapes, such as the interposition between belligerents with or without a genuine end to hostilities, the control of borders (land, air, sea), the conduct of strictly humanitarian operations, the restoration of secure communications, the surveillance of a ceasefire, etc. [...] The likelihood of France being obliged to take part in these operations, and even in several of them around the world at the same time, is already very strong. France's participation in the settlement of this type of situation is only considered in an international political framework (UN, CSCE, etc.) and in a multinational military framework (NATO, EU, coalitions).

Scenario VI – Reappearance of a Major Threat Against Western Europe

The aim of this scenario is to take into account the possible reappearance, in the twenty years to come, of the threat of major aggression against Europe committed by a state or a coalition of states with large nuclear and conventional forces, and showing hegemonic ambitions. The actual development of this scenario would largely depend on the evolution of Europe's security structures. In any case, France must keep, for the considered time-frame, the assets needed to preserve its vital interests. This scenario is highly unlikely today and will remain unlikely for the next twenty years. It cannot be completely discarded, however, since it represents a lethal threat.

military force, the French, not unlike the Germans, adhered to a defense culture that was decidedly different from that of the UK and other European states that were in the process of modernizing their force structures. Until quite recently, the French had continued to emphasize an approach to European defense that embodied territorial defense rather than force projection, although in 1994, with the publication of the first French *Defense White Paper* (France 1994) in twenty-two years, it was apparent that the French had begun to think very seriously about expeditionary force development, in part as a means of offsetting troop withdrawals from Africa and French overseas territories, while at the same time maintaining options for crisis interventions in these regions.[48]

So, too, the French had also tended to concentrate on structures rather than capabilities, assuming that in the final analysis their nuclear deterrent would suffice, together with NATO's extended deterrence guarantee, to handle virtually any and all threats directed against the French homeland, or "sanctuary" as it had been called.[49] In this context as well, the French were more interested in developing headquarters assets, for example

---

48 The 1994 *Defense White Paper*, produced during Balladur's term as prime minister, was significant in its emphasis on conventional deterrence, contrasting markedly with previous consideration of the priority role of nuclear weapons in French security planning. Also of importance was the *White Paper*'s consideration of the role of advanced non-nuclear weapons in crisis and contingency planning. The underlying assumption of this *White Paper* was that France no longer faced an immediate or direct threat to its territorial integrity, but was confronting new security challenges outside of its borders that might require intervention by French military forces. Accordingly, the *White Paper* elaborated six operational scenarios, including a combined arms threat to Europe at one extreme and a humanitarian contingency in Central Africa at the other, to evaluate capabilities, missions, and force structures for modernizing French conventional forces. In a significant departure, the 1994 *White Paper* elaborated the need for interoperability of French and Allied forces and it established priorities for funding in certain areas, notably in space, command and control, and sensor-netting. Significantly, the *White Paper* also discussed the prospective French development of a more useable nuclear capability for regional crisis management, and while it maintained support for the deployment of the IRBMs on the Albion Plateau—in part because of President Mitterrand's unconditional support for these systems—the Balladur government hinted at its intention to move toward a strategic dyad of SSBN/SLBMs and nuclear-dedicated aircraft platforms, which, subsequently, the French did after Mitterrand left office, and as part of a 1996 nuclear forces review.

49 To a certain extent, the credibility of French security strategy has always rested on the credibility of the collective defense concept of the Atlantic Alliance, certainly with respect to a major attack against Europe, but also even with respect to a direct threat against France itself. That said, however, the French have long relied on their own national deterrent capabilities to ensure French freedom of action in contingencies directly affecting French national interests, and to underscore France's status as a major power. There is no question that Paris would invoke French nuclear forces if the country were deliberately and directly threatened by another nuclear-armed nation. There is debate over the use of French nuclear weapons in regional planning contingencies, particularly in the context of what François Heisbourg has termed "hyperterrorism," or against non-nuclear-armed states that also possessed a chemical or biological warfare capability. See Heisbourg (2001a).

for the Franco-German Brigade that very quickly evolved into the EURO-CORPS,[50] rather than ready, useable capabilities that could be mobilized and deployed outside of France in a timely fashion. From this, the French appeared to be more interested in the trappings of European defense integration than in confronting the shortcomings of French force structure, which in any case would have entailed

Helsinki Headline Goals

- Focused military forces for use in implementing the Petersberg Tasks and not territorial defense.

- Creation of a European Rapid Reaction Force (ERRF) composed of up to 60,000 troops with appropriate air and naval support, for deployment within 60 days, and sustainable in theater for up to 12 months. The ERRF should be operational by 2003.

- Priority procurement in the key areas of strategic transport, air-to-air refueling, amphibious capabilities, joint multinational headquarters, satellite communications, and space-based sensors; tactical transport, AGS, SEAD, data fusion and ground links, and all-weather, precision-strike forces.

- A standing Political and Security Committee (PSC) composed of national representatives, EU military committee and military staff to provide planning and assessment of the member nations' efforts was commissioned to assess progress in EU military collaborating and modernization.

the difficult and painful task of moving away from conscription and toward creation of a professional all-volunteer armed forces structure. Without question, the way in which French forces were manned and equipped was heavily influenced by political considerations, which above all else emphasized autonomy of decision-making and independence of action. Reconciling this approach with that of the UK and the other NATO members would be no easy task, though that is precisely what the French military had hoped to do. For its part, the United Kingdom sought to use Saint Malo and later the Helsinki Headline Goals[51] to move the French political establishment in a direction that did not discriminate against the United States, decouple European security from the transatlantic link, or duplicate American capabilities at great and needless expense.[52]

---

50 The EUROCORPS had its origins in a Franco-German initiative, dating back to the Elysée Treaty, signed on January 22, 1963, by President de Gaulle and German Chancellor Konrad Adenauer. The treaty was intended to enhance cooperation and reconciliation between France and Germany, particularly in the defense and foreign policy sectors. In 1988, President Mitterrand and Chancellor Helmut Kohl decided to further that cooperation, and announced the establishment of the Franco-German Security and Defense Council, which, in turn, resulted in the creation of the Franco-German Brigade. Operational since 1991, this brigade was quickly identified by both parties as a mechanism for broader European defense collaboration, and on May 22, 1992, at the La Rochelle Summit of European leaders, the EUROCORPS was formally launched. On July 1, 1992, a headquarters was established in Strasbourg, and to date, the EUROCORPS comprises troops from France, Germany, Belgium, Luxembourg, and Spain.

51 The Helsinki Headline Goals were established in December 1999, at the European Union's Helsinki Summit.

52 Former Secretary of State Madeleine Albright is credited with conceptualizing American concerns about ESDP in this way.

Above all else, ESDP offered the French a means of transforming their military forces in a more cost-effective manner. Their recent experiences in Bosnia and Kosovo had yielded some painful lessons in this regard, and provided further impetus, if any was needed, to the political desire to "Europeanize" decision-making on issues affecting Europe's security. Operation *Allied Force*, the U.S.-inspired and (largely) -implemented air campaign over Kosovo and Serb territory had clearly demonstrated the widening gap between American and European military technologies and capabilities. It also served to illustrate the ineffectiveness of diplomacy without force, the approach that the Europeans had favored to cover the disagreement in the European Union on whether and how to implement the Petersberg tasks in support of the Kosovar Muslim population.[53] Once it had become apparent that NATO, led by the United States, would have to intervene militarily to separate the warring factions in the beleaguered province, the transatlantic allies agreed to try to forestall another war by convening another Dayton-like conference. The result was the abortive Rambouillet Summit, which was doomed to failure by a confluence of factors, including U.S. ambivalence about another Balkan war, divisions in the Alliance over NATO's use of force in an offensive mode, and most importantly, an apparent Serb impression that like the *Desert Fox* operation over Iraq, another NATO intervention in the former Yugoslavia would be limited and so could be "withstood."[54] Whatever the train of events that led to war,

---

53 Meeting on June 19, 1992, in Bad Godesberg, Germany, WEU foreign and defense ministers took a major step forward in defining the WEU's operational role. WEU member states declared their "willingness to make available military units from the whole spectrum of their conventional armed forces for military tasks conducted under the auspices of the WEU." The types of military tasks were defined: "Apart from contributing to the common defense in accordance with Article 5 of the Washington Treaty, and Article 5 of the modified Brussels Treaty, military units of the WEU states, acting under WEU authority, could be employed for peacekeeping, humanitarian and rescue tasks, and for crisis management." These tasks have come to be known as the Petersberg tasks.

54 The Rambouillet Summit was convened as a last-ditch effort to get Serb agreement on deployment of a NATO peacekeeping force on the ground. Without Serb acquiescence, NATO air strikes were inevitable, as discussed further in chapter 4. So, too, David Halberstam in *War in a Time of Peace*, describes Assistant Secretary of State for European Affairs and chief U.S. negotiator (at the Dayton Conference that resulted in the Bosnian peace settlement) Richard Holbrooke's views that with respect to Kosovo, "Milosevic was oddly fatalistic and much less afraid than he was back in October [1998] when the Americans had [first] threatened to bomb...Perhaps it was the bombing that had taken place during *Desert Fox* [that had changed Milosevic], when the United States had attacked Iraq for seventy-two hours and then stopped, and Milosevic believed that he could withstand that kind of bombing. Or perhaps he had received from sources within NATO some sense of the limited nature of the NATO bombing orders and believed that he could withstand that, too" (Halberstam 2001, 421-22).

Kosovo, more than any other single event in the recent past, provided an important catalyst to French efforts to bring the ESDP into being. To all appearances, the Kosovo experience of having once again had to depend on American military capabilities to save Europe from itself profoundly affected the French psyche, and renewed French determination to establish a

Petersberg Tasks

Meeting on 19 June 1992 at Petersberg, Germany, WEU foreign and defense ministers took a major step forward in defining the WEU's operational role. WEU member states declared their preparedness "to make available military units from the whole spectrum of their conventional armed forces for military tasks conducted under the authority of the WEU." The types of WEU military tasks were defined: "Apart from contributing to the common defense in accordance with Article 5 of the Washington Treaty and Article 5 of the modified Brussels Treaty respectively, military units of WEU Member States, acting under the authority of WEU, could be employed for:

- humanitarian and rescue tasks
- peacekeeping tasks
- tasks of combat forces in crisis management, including peacemaking."

European defense identity and capability independent of NATO and its American-dominated decision chain.

Without *Tomahawks* You Have No Power

In the immediate aftermath of the air war over Kosovo, the French concentrated their efforts on building a framework to give substance to the European Security and Defense Identity, with an eye toward getting agreement at the upcoming December (1999) Helsinki EU Summit on policy guidance to do just that. At Helsinki, the ESDI was transformed into the European Security and Defense Policy (ESDP) and a series of so-called Headline Goals was established to give the Europeans a military capability to implement future decision-making, as necessary. Viewed from Paris, the ESDP was a natural extension of the 1996 Berlin agreements outlining the relationship between NATO and the now-moribund WEU. For the French, it was a simple matter of substituting the EU and its ESDP for the WEU, in effect legitimizing the option to establish a distinct European-based decision chain for security planning in the event that NATO decided not to act. While it is extremely difficult to conceive that the Europeans would decide to act outside of NATO parameters if there were no Alliance consensus on the use of NATO forces, in theory, there may be circumstances, like those pertaining to Bosnia in 1995, where individual European nations might consider it necessary to intervene, using combat forces, as provided for in the Petersberg tasks that were enunciated by the WEU just for this purpose. The unhappy reality, however, is that Europe is unable to do that, except in very limited circumstances, because of years of neglect in defense spending and because European forces are generally structured for their own territorial defense. As noted earlier, the expeditionary mindset was alien to most Europeans until quite recently, and even the French, who have had an active record of intervention in Africa since their colonial rule in Central Africa, relied heavily upon fixed bases and established infrastructure. Key capabilities were lacking, notably air transport and intelligence assets, but even more damaging, its conscripted force base restricted France's ability to deploy forces outside of the "Hexagon," or French national territory. This was a problem that constrained French operations in *Desert Storm*, and it vexes France even today, after conscription has been phased out.[55]

European deficiencies in defense capabilities led to a consensus among the EU nations that any autonomous European defense entity could never really be totally independent of the United States—at least in the foreseeable future and certainly not until glaring capability shortfalls were redressed. Because European governments, in general, remain unwilling to commit the necessary resources to defense spending, collective European defense efforts will still need to rely on the United States in certain key areas, such as space, transport, and precision weapons. One way out of this dependency box would be to revolutionize European defense planning, far beyond anything that has been suggested so far by the French, or for that matter by any other

---

55 Shortly after his election in May 1995, Chirac, with the support of his center-right government headed by Alain Juppé, set out to reform the French military. Chirac, from his own time in service during the Algerian war, has always had a vested interest in the welfare and effectiveness of French military forces. After the fall of the Soviet empire and the realignment of power on the European continent, marked by German unification and discussion of EU enlargement, the Chirac-Juppé government decided to create a professional force, along the lines of that which had been established in the United Kingdom, while retaining a percentage of conscripted soldiers for special duties and to help alleviate France's unemployment problem. The phasing out of conscription and the creation of a professional force was central to the government's defense guidance for its military programs for 1997-2002. With the change in government that resulted from the 1997 National Assembly elections and the coming to power of the Jospin government, plans for professionalizing the armed forces were accelerated, and Chirac's initial decision to retain a certain percentage of conscripted troops to help alleviate French unemployment problems was overruled by the Socialists, who opted to bring forward the timelines for professionalizing France's military, to 1999 instead of 2002.

European government.[56] The problem is that force structure modernization entails new spending, and base and logistical infrastructure re-alignment incurs costs and, quite often, political penalties, as the United States has found in its own base re-alignment and closure (BRAC) process. From all appearances, the political will to take the difficult decisions necessary to create a viable European defense entity is lacking in major capitals in Europe today, so from that perspective, the need to make a virtue out of necessity brings us to the inescapable conclusion that the transatlantic tie remains indispensable to European defense-planning efforts, even to the creation of an autonomous European defense identity.

To the extent that the crisis over Kosovo drove that point home to most Europeans, it also increased their frustration over America's leading role in European security decision-making and their hostility to what they perceived as an increasing American penchant to bypass them during operational deliberations. In the context of U.S.-French relations this led to recriminations and charges of American unilateralism and French obstructionism with respect to Alliance consideration of rules of engagement, not to mention the use of force as a tool of coercive diplomacy.[57] It may be trite to observe that the United States tends to emphasize the use of force as an important tool in its diplomatic toolkit, in contrast to the French, who pride themselves on their diplomatic prowess—perhaps again making a virtue out of necessity.[58] And,

---

56 That said, various prominent European defense analysts have offered some ambitious proposals for force specialization, rationalization, and a capabilities-based approach to security planning. Rob de Wijk (1997) of the Netherlands has written extensively on these issues and has proposed some important, if radical, solutions to Europe's defense dilemma. Currently, defense analysts in the United States and at NATO Headquarters are focused on identifying national "niche" capabilities, or those technologies or operational areas where certain countries are more proficient than others, and in which they may excel in terms of deployable capabilities.

57 For an in-depth analysis from a U.S. perspective of transatlantic differences over these and other issues pertaining to NATO and the EU, see Clark (2001).

58 Indeed, this is Robert Kagan's very point in his article "Power and Weakness" (2002a). From recent interviews, it is evident that many French analysts reject the Kagan formulation as too simplistic. One even suggests that it is wrong on two counts. First, he contends that Kagan fails to appreciate the extent to which the so-called Vietnam syndrome is still operative in American policy circles, manifested in the Powell doctrine of overwhelming force and the political imperative of casualty aversion. Secondly, this analyst contends that the French and the British are much more willing to embrace military power as a component of policy than are the other Europeans. By considering all Europeans in the same manner, Kagan, he contends, fails to take into account important differences and nuances among the Europeans. It seems clear that the French are contradicting themselves and want to have it both ways. In this example, the United States is accused of being both unwilling and unable to use force. As discussed at length in the concluding chapter, this reveals that although they criticize the United States for an excessive willingness to use military power, the French would be deeply concerned if the U.S. were unable or unwilling to use force in the Hobbesian world described by Kagan in his article.

yet, this philosophical difference has come to exacerbate U.S.-French relations across a broad spectrum of issues. It has shaped the two nations' world views and the ways in which each seeks to manage crises. Former U.S. President Bill Clinton's resort to "cruise missile diplomacy" was especially irksome to the French, not least to the current French president who actually was surprised shortly after taking office in 1995 by the U.S. employment of cruise missiles on September 10 of that year, in an effort to bring the Serbs to the negotiating table.

From Chirac's perspective, the use of force against the Serbs was legitimate since it was sanctioned by a UN mandate and because it fell within the boundaries of a specifically defined political mandate for a negotiated settlement. The point here is that on the night of September 10, 1995, just as the French president was on television addressing his nation, and noting that a "pause" had been introduced in the NATO air campaign to allow the Serbs time to consider their options, U.S. cruise missiles were striking Serb targets. To say the least, this embarrassed Chirac and, more importantly, contributed to French anger over what Paris considered to be the high-handedness of U.S. actions. The failure to consult them was a particular source of irritation for the French, who believed that they were left out of the decision loop because France lacked its own cruise missile capability.

America's "cruise missile diplomacy" was, and remains, a source of particular French frustration. This U.S. weapon, which was used so effectively during the Gulf war, has come to be viewed in some French circles as the new currency of power politics. The U.S. has cruise missiles, the British are in the process of acquiring them from the United States, and the Russians and others are trying to develop *Tomahawk*-like capabilities. France, on the other hand, lacks such a capability, at least of a status comparable to that of the Americans and the British, and without a corresponding cruise missile capability, French officials perceive that they have been left out of important decisions, including those pertaining to planning for the operations in Afghanistan. One influential French defense journalist, Jacques Isnard, writing in July 2002 in *Le Monde*, reflected this view, writing: "Afghanistan has shown that either you are in the club, or you are not, and when you are a member, you can claim the

French Capability Shortfalls		
Operational Capability	**Situation Assessment**	**Command, Control, Communications**
Deterrence		• Stategic transmissions
Command, Control, Communications Intelligence (C³I)	• Optical space observation • Radar imaging (SAR-MTI) • Sensors • Drone system architecture	• Data merging • Battle-space digitization • Space telecommunications (EHF)
Deep Strike		
Preparation	• Geophysical environment • Man/machine interfaces	• Large-system architecture, simulation tools
Air/Land Environment	• Robotics	• Integrated modular combat systems
Air/Sea Environment		
Aerospace Environment		

right to take a full part in strategic planning, which is a prelude to the launch of operations" (2002b, 2).

Indeed, one of the lessons learned from *Desert Storm* was the broad-based utility of cruise missiles, particularly those like the American *Tomahawk*, which possess great accuracy potential and thus could limit collateral damage and so be used surgically as a strategic weapon. France has several cruise missile programs in train, including *Apache* and *Storm Shadow*, but both were air-launched and were not strategic systems. Apart from the aging *Exocet*, anti-ship cruise missile, the French lacked a long-range (strategic) surface-to-surface cruise missile capability that could strike from great distances, from the relative invulnerability of a submarine or sea-based cruiser/destroyer, and destroy its objective with the pinpoint accuracy afforded by satellite guidance and advanced targeting systems. Clearly, from France's perspective, to be a major power player it needed to invest in a *Tomahawk*-like cruise missile capability, because, in the words of one Ministry of Defense staff member, "events always start with cruise missiles. If you are not equipped with

French Capability Shortfalls (cont.)		
Operational Capability	**Strike**	**Hedging Technologies**
Deterrence	• Penetration aids • Ballistic missile propulsion and architecture • Air-breathing missile propulsion and architecture	• Anti-submarine warfare
Command, Control, Communications Intelligence (C³I)		• Computer network defenses • Critical infrastructure protection
Deep Strike	• Cruise missiles • Turbojets for missiles and drones • Precision guidance and navigation • Unmanned air vehicles (UAVs)	• Non-cooperative target identification • Offensive jamming
Preparation		• Medical combat support • BW protection
Air/Land Environment	• Intelligent munitions • Directed-energy weapons	• Balanced protection for armored vehicles and helicopters • Land-mine detection/neutralization
Air/Sea Environment		• Underwater detection • Stealthy platforms • New propulsion systems
Aerospace Environment	• High performance motors • Open architecture for avionics	• Integration of shared UAVs • Anti-stealth air detection & interception • Ballistic missile defenses • Cruise missile defenses

this capability then you are excluded from the game" (Isnard, 2002b, 2).

Once they perceived the importance of cruise missiles to modern-day power calculations and decision-making, the French determined to press ahead in this area, seeking to build a collaborative European effort to offset program costs, but also to ensure that a European-oriented capability was in place. After having first approached the British and, being spurned by them in favor of their preferred technological partnership with the Americans—at least with respect to *Tomahawk* acquisition and *Tactical Tomahawk* development—the French decided to force the issue with the United Kingdom by presenting their proposal as part of a broader effort to enhance EU industrial collaboration in the face of the American technological challenge. Indeed, upon coming to office in 1995, Chirac had announced his intention to stimulate European defense collaboration by establishing concrete projects in which European industries could participate, and even challenge America's superior defense technology base. Thus, if the unfolding situation in the former Yugoslavia was a defining moment for post-Cold War Europe, it was also the rallying call for the Organisation Conjointe de Coopération en Matière d'Armament (OCCAR), or the French initiative to organize and create a consolidated European defense industry that could compete on a more level playing field with the mega-companies in the United States.

Much of the French activity surrounding NATO and United Nations debates over the Implementation Force for Bosnia (IFOR) and later the Stabilization Force for Bosnia (SFOR), the Kosovo Intervention Force (KFOR), was designed to give substance to the ESDP and to French efforts to create a Europe-wide defense industry, capable of supporting the ESDP, and more importantly, of challenging American technological supremacy and hence arms sales all over the world. As the French see it, defense-industrial issues have always been an important incentive for security integration in Europe; now, with the emergence of a transatlantic technology gap in terms of U.S. and European defense capabilities, they could open the door to new collaborative opportunities in the security arena, or they could further exacerbate Allied differences over the implications for NATO of the ESDP. The jury is still out as to whether France and the United States can set aside their political differences about NATO and establish a defense-industrial partnership that benefits both the Alliance and EU aspirations in the security arena, but one thing is eminently clear, and that is that defense-industrial collaboration is central to operational planning. Without it, Allied interoperability and forces pooling will never be achieved.

Combined Joint Task Forces and NATO/EU Coalitions

For the French, the capacity to operate with the United States remains an important—if unacknowledged—attribute of their global power. Apart from French nuclear weapons holdings and France's seat on the UN Security Council, the French have come to see themselves as having fallen behind the British in military capabilities and deployment potential and thus have determined a need to match them in these areas. This is not just a matter of pride for the French, but a real political imperative, if Paris is to retain any pretension to influence events in Europe or in distant theaters. On its own, France struggled to do so, but always with the view toward galvanizing the EU nations, and in particular

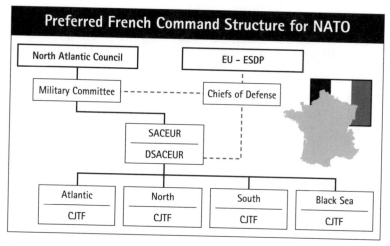

Preferred French Command Structure for NATO

- North Atlantic Council
- EU – ESDP
- Military Committee ---- Chiefs of Defense
- SACEUR
- DSACEUR
- Atlantic — CJTF
- North — CJTF
- South — CJTF
- Black Sea — CJTF

the nations of southern Europe, with which the French share a common heritage and security outlook, to augment their defense collaboration and always for the purpose of enhancing Europe's voice in transatlantic debates.

Outside of Europe, this has proved to be increasingly difficult given the growing ethnocentrism of the Europeans and, more particularly, in light of Germany's resistance to such efforts. Germany, the other part of de Gaulle's "indispensable couple," has changed dramatically over the years, and, after unification, became much more introspective and hence less willing to consider an activist role outside of Europe. Even within Europe, this new, reunited Germany was preoccupied with the attendant problems brought about by unification, and its center of gravity very clearly was moving toward the East, with a foreign policy to match. Thus, when the Yugoslav wars broke out, and the French sought to energize the Europeans to take the policy lead, they were restrained by their German partners, who had to deal with their own legacy in the Balkans, and the British, who had a decidedly different view of what was needed to enforce a settlement among and between the warring factions.

Peacekeeping, along with EU and NATO debates over peace enforcement of the UN Charter, informed French positions on the Balkans, as discussed in Chapter 4, but at the time, neither France nor the West European Union had virtually any capacity to intervene on its own, and certainly not without logistical and intelligence support from the United States and NATO. French efforts to redress this situation were concentrated on getting European agreement on a framework for organizing their military forces to perform an array of so-called peace-support tasks, which were formally enunciated in the Petersberg declaration of June 1992, discussed earlier. The tasks set out in the declaration had particular relevance to the emerging situation in the former Yugoslavia, which many in France had singled out as the practical focus for French efforts to galvanize defense collaboration under the EU umbrella. A WEU planning cell was set up in Brussels, and a series of "joint" deployments comprised of national forces from WEU member states were carried out, but it would not be until the creation of the EUROCORPS, out of the Franco-German brigade, that actual forces and a headquarters were earmarked for WEU taskings. Inevitably, this caused considerable consternation at NATO Headquarters because of the perceived dangers associated with creating competing European and transatlantic force structures. Accordingly, because most European NATO assets were national capabilities and could be assigned to "European" missions if national governments approved, there was a need to create overlapping planning staffs and cooperative structures in Brussels to ensure that resources were being expended wisely. More importantly, these structures were necessary to ensure that the evolution of the WEU did not come at the expense of NATO, specifically its modernization programs and the ability of Allied forces to operate seamlessly in coalition deployments.

For the French, this was precisely their objective, as subsequent controversy with the United Kingdom over operational planning for this force was to demonstrate. Whereas the British and other NATO partners regarded this force, and its successor, formally dubbed the European Rapid Reaction Corps at the 1999 EU Helsinki Summit, as the kernel of Europe's peacekeeping capabilities, the French had always conceived of it as the core of a European army. This became eminently clear at the 2002 NATO Prague Summit when the French attempted to derail the American proposal for creation of a new NATO Rapid Reaction Force that would be capable of deploying to crisis spots in seven to ten days to perform a variety of war-fighting tasks.

In 1992, however, none of this was yet apparent, except perhaps in the minds of Quai d'Orsay planners, and the maturation of the WEU was heralded as a political triumph. Still, in the early years of the Bosnian wars, WEU forces were constrained in what they could do, lacking adequate capabilities and suffering from European divisions over how far to go in emphasizing its independence from NATO. Operationally, as the Bosnian experience was to show, European forces lacked coherence as well as the capabilities to enforce the peace in a non-permissive environment where the sides continued to snipe at and war against each other. Differences over whether the European forces were "peacekeepers" or "war-fighters" plagued their employment in Bosnia, and until the American intervention as part of the Implementation Force (IFOR), and later in the Stabilization Force (SFOR), they suffered the embarrassment of being held hostage by the Serbs, failing to protect the UN safe havens, and, ultimately, of threatening withdrawal unless the Americans put "boots on the ground." As explored in greater depth in the next chapter, Bosnia proved to be a disastrous experience for the Europeans and their efforts to create a separate European defense identity, ending as it did with the fall of Srebrenica, the failure of the UN mission, and its inevitable consequence of pushing the Americans to the forefront to resolve the crisis. UN and European failings in Bosnia were a bitter pill for the French to swallow, particularly after the Dayton meeting and the American success in devising a peace settlement for Bosnia.

In 1997, with Dayton behind them and a crisis looming over Kosovo, the Europeans faced another Balkan nightmare as the Albanian economy teetered on the brink of collapse as a result of a pyramid scheme that had triggered a run on the banks and the devaluation of its currency. Italy was particularly worried about the prospects for a refugee crisis that had the potential to overwhelm Italian social services and perhaps even contribute to the fall of the Italian government. But the EU, with its attention diverted to Kosovo and the reconstruction of Bosnia, had little interest in intervening in Albania. However, at French insistence, the EU did encourage individual member states to take action, based on the development of a so-called coalition-of-the-willing deployment of military forces. Led by the French, who had belatedly perceived in the situation an opportunity to spotlight the WEU, and with it Europe's capacity to act without recourse to U.S. or NATO assistance, Operation *Alba*, as it was called, was, by all accounts, a military failure. The operation came too late in the crisis, and was hampered by European disagreements over the scope, purpose, and rules of engagement for this coalition-of-the-willing deployment. As originally conceived, *Alba* was intended to stanch the flow of Albanian refugees onto Italian shores. Prodded on by the Italians, who were bearing the brunt of the crisis, the EU encouraged individual nations to do what they could, but, as an organization, refrained from providing a collective response. Lacking a mandate and an institutional cover, Italy, as the lead nation, and France, whose MoD was deeply involved in the planning, were forced to act on an ad hoc basis, without the benefit of WEU assets. This caused innumerable problems, and by the time that forces could be earmarked and deployed, the situation in Albania had begun to improve, thanks in large measure to the activities of the Organization for Security and Cooperation in Europe (OSCE).[59]

Even as the French reject the characterization of *Alba* as a disaster, they readily admit that it was far from perfect, though they also contend that it taught them important lessons with respect to the future of European security collaboration. Notable in this regard is the need for an institutional framework, to provide an operational mandate, and to enhance forces interoperability through combined training, exercises, and force planning. Perhaps *Alba*, more than anything else, gave rise to French interest in the U.S.-conceived Combined Joint Task Force (CJTF) concept, which had been advanced in 1994, principally by Admiral Paul-David Miller (now retired) when he served as Supreme Commander Atlantic, and adopted at the Berlin ministerial as the way ahead for NATO planning and headquarters development for crisis action (see Miller 1994, 81).

The intent of the CJTF, as agreed at NATO, is to provide flexible command arrangements within which Allied forces could be organized on a task-specific basis for non-Article 5 missions. This appealed to the French, who also saw it as a way to retain national sovereignty, since the CJTF depended on member governments' agreement to participate in a specific operation, and could be organized on a lead-nation basis wherein the nation providing the bulk of the forces would automatically be assigned its headquarters command. From the French perspective, the CJTF concept could also usefully bridge the organizational

---

59 For an in-depth analysis of operation *Alba*, and the role of the OSCE, see IFPA (2000, esp. 99–116).

firewalls of NATO and the WEU, though on this latter point there was no consensus either in NATO or in WEU circles. In fact, there was some concern at SHAPE that the French might try to use the CJTF concept to duplicate Alliance force structure, specifically the assets of the ACE Rapid Reaction Corps.

Concerns in this area opened considerable intra-European debate as well, culminating in an agreement, reached at the EU Helsinki Summit in December 1999, on creation of a European Rapid Reaction Force (ERRF), to be established out of the EUROCORPS. Thanks to the British initiative at Saint Malo, the Helsinki Summit communiqué explicitly tied the European development of a rapid reaction capability to NATO, thereby creating consensus that in any non-Article 5 crisis, NATO would, in effect, have the right of first refusal, and only if NATO refused to intervene would the EU be free to decide to intervene using NATO assets. This is an important provision for the Europeans because of their lack of certain capabilities, but also for NATO since the decision to earmark forces for the European reaction force stipulates that they be available first to the Atlantic Alliance, and then to the EU. By making these capabilities available to the EU, the agreement reduced the risk of expending scarce resources on duplicative structures. At the same time, however, a danger exists in that the memberships of the EU and NATO are not identical, and one NATO member can block the use of Alliance assets for European missions and even for combined planning and joint training.[60]

---

60 The long-standing dispute between Greece and Turkey over Cyprus and Aegean island sovereignty issues is an example of this imbalance and has long confounded Alliance planning. For the EU it presents an even greater challenge because Turkey is not a member of the European Union. *Amber Fox*, currently led by NATO in Macedonia, was supposed to have been taken over by the EU in the autumn of 2002, based on the "Berlin plus" arrangements, which provide for EU access to, and use of, NATO assets in a non-Article 5 emergency in which NATO does not participate. Berlin-plus takes one step further the understanding reached between the United States and its European allies at the 1996 Berlin (NATO) ministerial that gave formal recognition to the EU desire to create a European Security and Defense Identity (ESDI), independent from, but supportive of, NATO. Greece and Turkey both have held up agreement on Berlin-plus "by insisting that it should also include a general code of conduct. 'It should set out how allies and partners see each other,'" according to Greek Foreign Minister George Papandreou, quoted in Jack Dempsey's "EU Military Operation in Macedonia at Risk" in the *Financial Times* on May 16, 2002. For its part, Turkey has resisted the use of NATO assets in the EU's planned Macedonian operation (to supersede NATO's *Amber Fox* deployment) because of the unwillingness of the Europeans to commit to a date to begin EU accession talks for Turkey. Consequently, at the 2002 Prague NATO Summit, the United States proposed an extension to the *Amber Fox* mission, in effect undercutting the French who had sought to deploy (to Macedonia) without using NATO assets. Subsequently, in December 2002, at the EU summit in Copenhagen, Turkey lifted its veto on EU access to NATO forces and planning capabilities for peacekeeping missions, in exchange for EU agreement to consider Turkey's application in 2005, one year after Cyprus gains membership, in 2004. This accord addresses U.S. fears that the EU might use the ERRF to siphon off funds from NATO and to challenge Alliance primacy in defense planning for European security.

In December 2000 at the EU Inter-governmental Conference held in Nice, the French used their presidency of the European Union to push the ESDP agenda forward. Accordingly, the Nice conference set for itself some ambitious goals, none more so than in the security arena. Among them were very specific French proposals for crisis management procedures, including the interface between NATO and the EU, as well as elaboration of the Helsinki Headline Goals, and options for meeting current shortfalls in areas affecting the EU's ability to deploy crisis intervention forces (Rutten 2002). Unfortunately for the French, however, European debate over models for enlargement and integration overwhelmed all other considerations, and the Nice conference left open key questions about the future direction that the evolution of security collaboration would take in the European Union.

From the French perspective, enlargement threatens to weaken the EU's potential to develop a coherent foreign and security policy, and that is why, even at Nice, the French have been less than enthusiastic about adding new members just now, before fundamental issues revolving around the EU's structural reform are resolved first. On this issue, the French have been strong proponents of a federation of states, as described both by Dominique de Villepin and Prime Minister Raffarin in their respective books (Villepin 2002a and Raffarin 2002). From their perspective, it is absolutely necessary to reform the EU to ensure that even with enlargement the decision authority of the larger nations will be sustained, although each appears to be unprepared to accept the implications of this position when it comes to a unified Germany, which is the EU's largest member. That said, without the appropriate institutional reforms that would lend greater weight to the larger European countries, France's ability to position the EU as a viable counterweight to U.S. power inevitably would be compromised. Trade and economic collaboration across European borders is one thing, contend the French, but real and exploitable military power is the currency of great-power politics. The efforts of France to "bring its aspirations in line with its capabilities," as Dr. Kissinger has observed, is at the center of its views of the ESDP, and it is the formative element of its vision of Europe, as noted throughout this study.[61]

That the French aspire to great-power status once again is apparent in their efforts to mold the EU into a vehicle for maximizing their and Europe's weight in discussions with the United States. What is less clear is the path that they will ultimately take in an effort to attain this objective. In the wake of September 11, 2001, there has been a resurgence of national identity, and in some European countries—France included—popular support for controls on immigration and in some instances a reversion to national—as opposed to European—policy solutions. In France this is manifested in the Chirac government's rationalization for higher defense spending, as well as in French efforts to reform EU institutions to ensure that the smaller countries of Europe, and the aspirant countries, do not have undue influence over EU policies and decision-making.

Within French policy circles doubts about EU enlargement are likely to influence the Chirac government's approach to EU development, strengthening the case for revitalizing the Franco-German relationship, which the late President Mitterrand had identified as the essential element in the emergence of a European power. As reflected in their October 2002 agreement on the EU's Common Agricultural Policy (CAP), French officials set out to court the Germans in an effort to achieve closer coordination between Paris and Berlin. Even as the Chirac government had hedged its options with respect to Chancellor Schroeder's re-election in the fall of 2002, by the beginning of 2003, the Franco-German "engine" appeared to be on-track in the security field, with their controversial pronouncement that they, speaking for Europe, were opposed to a U.S.-led military intervention in Iraq. Even as this initiative appears to have backfired, leading eighteen other

---

61 Among others, Dr. Henry A. Kissinger has documented French views of power throughout France's history. Writing in *Diplomacy*, Dr. Kissinger observes: "Since the end of Napoleon III's reign, France has lacked the power to impose the universalist aspirations it inherited from the French Revolution, or the arena to find an adequate outlet for its missionary zeal. For over a century, France has been finding it difficult to accept the fact that the objective conditions for the preeminence that Richelieu had brought it had disappeared once national consolidation had been achieved in Europe. Much of the prickly style of its diplomacy has been due to attempts by its leaders to perpetuate its role as the center of European policy in an environment increasingly uncongenial to such aspirations. It is ironic that the country that invented the raison d'état should have had to occupy itself, for the better part of a century, with trying to bring its aspirations in line with its capabilities" (1994,120).

European leaders to declare in print that neither France nor Germany spoke for them, it served once again to illustrate Chirac's cynicism about using the EU to serve narrower French national interests. German-American differences over Bush administration policies could embolden France in this regard, particularly if French officials believed that by doing so they could incur more favor with the Germans and, in so doing, get their commitment to put the ESDP on a fast track. Not only would this serve French interests with respect to enhancing the position of the European Union in the face of American power in NATO, but it would also serve to put the British and the other Europeans on notice that the Franco-German "motor" was once again igniting European aspirations. That said, organizational fixes without adequate military forces or defense spending commitments will do little to forward French goals in the defense and security realms. As NATO Secretary General Lord (George) Robertson has observed, you cannot go to war with a "virtual" capability. As the record of French efforts to galvanize European intervention in the Balkans attests, the absence of adequate military capabilities, coupled with fundamental European differences over rules of engagement, and the role of force itself, served to stymie all of the European initiatives, particularly when they were taken without the active support of the United States or the use of NATO assets and infrastructure. As the next chapter illustrates, the Balkan wars carry important lessons for both U.S. and French policy-makers in this regard.

CHAPTER 4

Balkan Futures and
Peace-Support Operations

French views of NATO and EU enlargement have far-reaching implications for European security and crisis stability in the broader Mediterranean region. Arising from the French penchant for the three Ms—multilateralism, multipolarity, and a mission mandate—it was perhaps inevitable that France and the United States would differ over approaches to handling the successive crises that emerged in the former Yugoslavia. Not only did the two allies clash over the framework for intervention in both Bosnia and Kosovo, they could agree neither on the form that any intervention should take, nor on the extent of their involvement. For the French, the situations in Croatia, Bosnia, and Serbia proper were never perceived in terms of stark alternatives, with one side or the other having the moral high ground. Rather, Paris saw the situation in the former Yugoslavia as very complex, and there was a substantial pool of French sympathy for the Serbs, though this was tempered by scenes reminiscent of Nazi concentration camps and massed refugee movements across southern Europe.

Still, the Serbs had been French allies in two world wars, and pro-Serb sentiments unquestionably influenced the contours of French policies in the Balkan crises. Quite often, they were also the source of bitter disputes between France and the United States, which, in any case, had determined very early on that the Balkans were a European problem, better left to others to sort out. For the French, the prevailing American view was both welcome and troublesome, since, on one level, it acknowledged the potentially important role that should be played by the Europeans, while on another level it forced the Europeans to confront their own impotence in dealing with the emerging Balkan crises. Jacques Poos, from Luxembourg and a former head of the Council of the West European Union and rotating president of the Council of the European Union, publicly proclaimed that this was Europe's hour. Indeed, the French generally regarded the crises as such, although in France there was very little domestic support for an active interventionist policy, certainly not for one that would put French forces in a position from which casualties might occur.

Also, a French decision to intervene in the early years of the Balkan crises had the potential to disturb the close affinity that the French had shared with the Serbs. This was an issue as well for others in Europe, who maintained that any intervention under EU or OSCE auspices must be impartial and serve the need for a political settlement, not the objectives of the warring parties on either side. It was, in any case, a moot point in the early years of the crises, since there was no EU consensus either on what to do or on the advisability of using military forces to separate the warring factions. For François Mitterrand in particular, EU dissention on policy vis-à-vis the former Yugoslavia created a dilemma for France, especially after Germany recognized Croatia's and Slovenia's independence. Notwithstanding his own attachment to the principle of self-determination, from Mitterrand's perspective, as Princeton professor Ronald Tiersky described, self-determination had its limits. "Without reasonable, practical limits, national self-determination becomes self-destructive by creating economically unviable, politically threatened states in dangerous neighborhoods" (Tiersky 2000, 205). Thus, as the French government saw it at the time, no good would be served by creating new states that lacked the capacity to sustain their own independence, let alone their economic viability or their own defense. Very soon, it became apparent that Milosevic's Serbs had no intention of allowing Bosnia, or even more importantly Kosovo, to follow that route. Shortly thereafter, the French and the rest of Europe were confronted with the need to intervene to forestall a growing humanitarian disaster.

While technically the United States also preferred to keep Yugoslavia unified, competing domestic constituencies in the United States very soon stigmatized the Serbs, whose relative strength and brutality in their dealings with the Bosnians and Croats brought greater U.S. sympathy to those ethnic minorities. However, in the early years of the Balkan crises, American attention was diverted from the storm clouds gathering over

Yugoslavia, and was instead focused on Somalia, Haiti, and more importantly the dissolution of the Soviet empire. When, via CNN or some other news outlet, the new Clinton administration was forced to confront the Balkan crises, the preferred U.S. response was that these were issues on which Europe should take the lead, more so now that they were trumpeting the centrality of their Common Foreign and Security Policy. However, it was soon very clear that the EU was unable to act decisively in the Balkans, and from this, with the French in the lead, the Europeans sought from the United Nations a means of resolving the mess. UNPROFOR[62] was the result, and though its mandate was restricted to humanitarian support and protection of the UN-designated safe havens, the French, at least, had convinced themselves that they had done something useful both to moderate the ethnic violence and to establish that the EU was prepared to act in its own backyard.

Thus, in Bosnia, French intervention was just as much, in the first instance, a test for the new Europe as it was a humanitarian impulse conceived by the Mitterrand government. After 1995 and Chirac's election, it became more an issue of pride, as the new president, in contrast to his predecessor—who by this time was close to dying—tended to view the crisis more through the lens of power politics, with concern registered about the inability of the peacekeepers to effect demonstrable change on the ground. From 1995 onward, the French government sought to employ military power in the Balkans as a means to an end, namely, the establishment of a political settlement that would be enforced by the threatened use of military power. However, lacking the appropriate capabilities, they knew that their only recourse was to entice the Americans to join them by deploying "boots on the ground." At no time was the Clinton administration prepared to do

---

62 UNPROFOR, or the United Nations Protection Force, was dispatched to Bosnia in 1992 to provide humanitarian aid and to act as a peacekeeping force, as described in UN Security Council resolution 770, passed on August 13. Resolution 770 authorized the use of "all measures" to ensure the safe passage of humanitarian relief but did not sanction the use of force to intervene in the fighting between or among combatants. This mandate was passed under Chapter 7 of the UN Charter on peace enforcement. Subsequently, on June 4, 1993, the UN Security Council passed another resolution, designated UNSC resolution 836, also under Chapter 7, authorizing UNPROFOR to use force if necessary to deter attacks on six UN-designated safe havens (Sarajevo, Srebrenica, Gorazde, Tuzla, Bihac, and Zepa), and to protect the withdrawal of paramilitary forces, other than those of Bosnia and Herzegovina. It also provided for the employment of air power to support the protection of the safe havens, and to deter attacks against the UN forces themselves.

that, certainly not without a clearer understanding of the political objectives to be obtained, the so-called endgame, and
the rules of engagement by which American forces would be
enabled to use force to protect themselves and to attain specific mission objectives, much less under UN authority.

Mandate Issues and Rules of Engagement

The related issues of a mandate for so-called lesser contingencies
and rules of engagement for the employment of military forces
in peace-support operations would continue to vex U.S.-French
collaboration throughout the Balkan crises. In the early stages of
the war in Bosnia, French insistence on a broad political mandate from the United Nations resulted in an uneasy partnership
between NATO and the UN, based on the Europeans' desire to
emerge from under the American wing and to undertake an initiative on their own, as had been envisaged by the WEU's Petersberg formulation. As early as June 1992, at the Oslo ministerial,
NATO had accepted an expansion into the peace-support area,
and certified for use some NATO assets for peace-support missions (non-Article 5 operations) in Europe beyond NATO's borders. This was a significant step for NATO, and a monumental
one for France, which had only reluctantly accepted the idea of
NATO involvement in OSCE or UN operations.

By all accounts, the experience of UNPROFOR, whose
deployment was supposed to protect the UN-designated safe
havens as spelled out in UNSC resolutions 770 and 836, was
a defining moment for both the French and NATO. Its procedures proved wanting, none more so than the dual chain of
command that had been established at French insistence and
that depended upon UN compliance with operational decision-
makers on the ground who were "double-hatted" to NATO
because Alliance assets were being used. Furthermore, the mandates for UNPROFOR did not adequately reflect the reality on
the ground, exposing the UN troops to force protection issues
that had not been contemplated by the Security Council resolutions. By 1993, the French were among the loudest in urging
the United States to intervene with military forces in Bosnia, but
they were hesitant about operating outside of the legal framework of the United Nations. To ease this concern, the French
had devised the so-called dual-key concept, whereby air strikes
against the Bosnian Serbs could be implemented only upon the

joint approval of NATO's North Atlantic Council (NAC) and the UN secretary general, who was to receive his advice from the UNPROFOR leadership. The first test of this concept came in the late summer of 1994, when one of the UN-designated safe havens, Bihac, erupted in conflict.

Begun at the Bosnian initiative and initially intended to defeat the forces of renegade Muslim leader Fikret Abdic, who eventually retreated into Croatia, the battle for Bihac soon was joined, and the Bosnian Serbs, firing artillery from Udbina air base in the Krajina, were close to seizing the city. After protracted debate, the United States succeeded in getting NATO and UN approval for air strikes against the Krajina outpost. However, the UNPROFOR leadership on the ground, after having misrepresented the extent of the threat to the city, authorized bombings against the airfield, but not the Serbian aircraft, which were allowed to escape by flying off base. The fiasco almost torpedoed NATO as an institution, and it certainly created an even bigger fissure in U.S.-UK relations, which were already on shaky ground over the rules of engagement governing the use of force in Bosnia. Paradoxically, however, the evolving situation in Bihac did serve to focus French attention on the shortcomings of the dual-key arrangement, and it stimulated wider debate in Paris over whether to withdraw French forces from UNPROFOR.

Yet, it would not be until some six months later that this debate would open a new chapter in French policy vis-à-vis Bosnia. Several intervening events were crucial in hardening both American and French resolve that these latest Serb atrocities should not go unanswered. Among these were the Republican victory in the 1994 U.S. Congressional elections, bringing to the Congress a majority in support of the "lift and strike" policy;[63] the French election of Jacques Chirac; the hostage-taking crisis; and the Srebrenica massacre, during which Bosnian Serbs killed more than six thousand Muslim men and boys while UN (Dutch) peacekeepers stood by and did nothing. Taken together these events were critical in galvanizing American support for widening the air campaign to strike Belgrade and other strategic

---

63"Lift and strike" referred to the need to lift the arms embargo against the Bosnian government, while supporting the provision of training aid for Bosnian and Croat military forces. The "strike" element of the equation referred to the U.S. preference for developing a massive bombing campaign against the Serbs, including, after 1994, strategic targets in Serbia.

targets. For the French, they provided a convincing rationale for revising their earlier position on the use of military force to coerce a peaceful settlement over Bosnia.

While the French, under Chirac, were far less reluctant to support the use of military power to deter, compel, or dissuade the Bosnian Serbs, French policy elites were still unwilling to sanction a wider use of force, one that would be directed against Belgrade, for fear of widening the war. From the French perspective, there is a delicate balance between peacekeeping and peace enforcement operations, although French officials are quick to point out that in the case of the UN mandates for Bosnia, this was an artificial distinction. Indeed, all of the crucial UN resolutions relevant to the situation in Bosnia fell under Chapter 7 of the UN Charter, which addressed enforcement of UN decisions to provide humanitarian aid and to designate specific areas as safe havens for ethnic populations.[64] There was no question, from this perspective, of arming the Muslims, as many proponents in the United States wished to do, and there was very little enthusiasm for deepening the Western commitment with no endgame or exit strategy in sight. Thus, in September 1995, after the fall of Zepa and Srebrenica, the French finally drew the line at Gorazde and announced their support for more substantive measures to protect the beleaguered enclave. However, they stopped short of endorsing the American approach, which by this time had evolved to include a massive air campaign, including strikes against Serb strategic targets in wider Yugoslavia.

Instead, the preferred French response amounted to a renewed call to augment the European Rapid Reaction Force with the provision of artillery systems, to protect the UNPROFOR troops. The French did not intend for these forces or those of UNPROFOR to go beyond the UN mandate to protect the aid convoys and the safe havens. Nor did they have any change in mind with respect to arming the Croats or the Bosnians to level the playing field against the Serb forces. However, because this was not a step that would take immediate effect, the French agreed to new instructions that would allow a limited employment of air power, but only for what euphemistically came to

---

64 The crucial UN resolutions included those of May 1992 (757), August 1992 (770), and June 1993 (836). All fell under Chapter 7 of the UN Charter, though UNPROFOR's interpretation of the mandates was in many cases different from the intended mission.

be known as "close air support." The French, and more so the British acting on the advice of then-UNPROFOR commander General Sir Michael Rose, remained vocal in their opposition to a strategic bombing campaign directed against Belgrade. Still, as events on the ground deteriorated, the French gradually inclined toward the U.S. view, and they were very helpful at the London conference, following Srebrenica's fall, in getting the other European allies to accept the necessity for more substantive action in the face of the continued Serb aggression.

As previously noted, just days after coming to office in 1995, President Chirac was faced with a crisis in which the European peacekeepers in UNPROFOR were taken hostage by the Bosnian Serbs in retaliation for the first round of NATO air strikes. French and other UN troops were publicly humiliated and shown not to be up to the task of enforcing the UN mandate. Chirac, in particular, appears to have taken this incident personally, whereupon he adopted an aggressive stance on the need for a more credible Western intervention in Bosnia, including the U.S. provision of ground forces—a position that was hardened several months later, as a result of the shelling on August 28, 1995, of the Trznica market in Sarajevo. Otherwise, Chirac warned that France would be forced to withdraw its troops from UNPROFOR, spelling certain failure of the mission.

In the aftermath of the UNPROFOR hostage taking and the Serb shelling of Trznica, NATO resumed its air campaign and began making preparations for a substantial ground force intervention. By that time, however, Milosevic had seen the handwriting on the wall and by the fall had agreed to participate in the U.S.-brokered Dayton peace talks, which, ultimately, led to an uneasy settlement that was to be presided over by a peacekeeping force composed of NATO, French, and Russian forces. For the French, who were assigned the Sarajevo sector to police, interoperability with the other NATO forces proved to be an issue, and by all accounts, this factor, as well as their UNPROFOR experience, was said to have marked a watershed in French thinking about NATO, its relationship to the ESDP, and broader peace-support operations. From the outset, it was readily apparent to most independent French defense analysts that without NATO, UNPROFOR was destined to fail in Bosnia, and that with NATO, UNPROFOR's cumbersome decision procedures were unworkable. Indeed, they proved deadly in Bihac, Gorazde, and Brčko, as exhaustive UN debates on mission taskings and rules of engagement left these safe havens vulnerable to Serb attacks. Thus, from 1995 onward, French government officials sought to bypass the cumbersome decision procedures of the United Nations, though they remained committed to using the UN framework, in part as a means of diminishing the relative importance of NATO councils in political decision-making.

For its part, the Clinton administration had vacillated between an active role in the Balkan crises and an inclination to step aside to let the Europeans sort out the problems of the region. After the military disaster that accompanied U.S. intervention in Somalia, and with a questionable record with respect to Haiti, the U.S. military had no appetite for intervening in the Balkan wars, and resorted to Vietnam analogies suggesting the potential for mission creep and a progressively deeper and broader commitment of U.S. forces without any clear idea of how long they would have to remain in theater. Moreover, it was readily apparent that whatever the nature of the deployment, U.S. forces would be confronted with more than just humanitarian missions; there was no doubt that they would face a non-permissive environment in which they would have to separate factions, enforce a political settlement, and deter and contain the outbreak of further violence.

In this respect, prominent differences exist between French and American views of peacekeeping operations, not the least having to do with the legal basis for peace-support and crisis-stability operations and the application of international law to specific contingencies. This difference in views has implications for a broad range of issues, from crisis management by NATO, to the detention of prisoners of war in Guantanamo, and now to intervention in Iraq. As seen from Paris, the a priori need for a political mandate directing military intervention is necessary for most contingencies, the clear exceptions being operations that are precisely defined as defensive under the Washington Treaty establishing NATO. Since the core function of the Atlantic Alliance is collective defense, as spelled out in Article 5 of the Washington Treaty, in the face of a direct threat to the territorial integrity of the NATO nations, and because NATO was established in accordance with international law, the right of self-defense already is codified by the UN Charter.

On the other hand, when NATO went on the offensive over Kosovo in 1999, the French maintained that a separate empowering UN mandate was needed, since the Washington Treaty only covered the use of force for self-defense or collective defense purposes. Given their view of the situation, the French were strongly inclined to tie NATO military operations to the territorial defense of Alliance territories, although this was a view that was slowly evolving as a result of the so-called out-of-area deployments of NATO forces during the Gulf war. So, too, there was less clarity on the French position on a NATO member request for Alliance intervention, under Article 7 of the Washington Treaty. In some circumstances, such as when a member state itself was under direct threat, some French policy officials were willing to consider an intervention based only upon European Union agreement to act, or, failing that, an OSCE directive. In all other situations, the French maintained the need for a broader UN Security Council mandate, in part to ensure that nations do not act at will in crises; Russian intervention in Chechnya is frequently cited by French analysts to be a case in point. When the crisis over Kosovo erupted, and the United States and Great Britain began planning for an offensive air operation to support the beleaguered enclave, the French were adamantly opposed to a "unilateral" NATO operation that had not been sanctioned by the United Nations, and on this issue the French were unyielding, though when it had suited their purposes, they, too, had opted for unilateral action.[65]

---

65 Notable in this regard, operation *Turquoise* was a unilateral French initiative, taken in order to establish a "humanitarian protected zone" in the Cyangugu-Kibuye-Gikomgoro triangle in southwest Rwanda. The Rwandan crisis began as an ethnic and tribal conflict between the Hutu majority in Rwanda and Tutsi rebels. In October 1990, President François Mitterrand decided to support Rwandan President Juvenal Habyarimana's request for French aid in fighting the rebels, on a national-bilateral basis and not in conjunction with UN activity in the region. When the UN force, authorized under Chapter 6 of the UN Charter, came under attack, the French stepped in until UN forces could be reinforced, and a force protection mandate passed, authorizing peace enforcement missions under Chapter 7 of the UN Charter. UN resolution 929, passed on June 22, 1994, by the UN Security Council, determined that the conflict in Rwanda constituted a broader threat to regional stability, and on that basis, endorsed the French-led intervention to help alleviate the humanitarian crisis until such time as the United Nations contingent could be reinforced. Operation *Turquoise* ended with the withdrawal of French forces from Rwanda on August 21, 1994, though not before Médecins sans Frontières (Doctors without Borders) accused the French government of complicity in the genocide of the Tutsis. An internal French parliamentary committee ultimately absolved the French government of responsibility in this regard, but noted that in future, all military interventions should be authorized by a decree that specifies the mandate, the role of force, and the exact nature of the mission.

Thus, from the beginning, the U.S. and French perspectives differed on how to deal with the emerging Kosovo crisis. If Dayton's failure to address the simmering crisis over Kosovo made a new confrontation between Milosevic and the West inevitable, it also foretold new problems in Franco-American relations. This was particularly true after the failure of the Rambouillet conference of February 1999, during which the French government hosted a U.S.-supported effort to broker a peace settlement between the Kosovo Liberation Army (KLA) and Milosevic's Serbs to try to forestall NATO's use of force. The French believed that the best way to achieve that end was to get a UN mandate for an intervention force that was designed to meet certain explicit political objectives. According to the French, these included crisis management forces to reinforce the Kosovo border, supervise the withdrawal of Serb internal security forces from Kosovo proper, and facilitate negotiations to give Kosovo greater autonomy within the Yugoslav federation. The French view was that an independent Kosovo should not, however, be the ultimate goal of the UN-mandated intervention, as this would create an unviable entity, while unfairly penalizing the Kosovar Serbs.

However, French objections to the use of force to coerce Serb behavior changed rather dramatically after the Serb massacre of Kosovar Albanians in the village of Racak in the fall of 1998. In early 1999, after Racak and before the NATO air operations were to begin, President Chirac traveled to Moscow to lay out the West's position on Kosovo, assuming that the Russians would have to become involved in any ensuing peace settlement. He returned after having received the tacit support of the Russians to use the threat of force to get the Serbs and the Kosovo Liberation Army to the negotiating table. Thus, while the French continued to promote the need to obtain UN legitimacy before initiating any action, they were resigned to the fact that the United States and the United Kingdom had passed the point of no return in that regard and were now in the midst of serious planning for a U.S.-led NATO military intervention.

"Foot Soldiers for American Knights"

In several important respects, beyond the issue of a mandate for operations, Kosovo brought to light fundamental differences between France and the United States on their respective conceptions of the evolving world order and the role of force in contemporary international relations. As they had been with Bosnia, the French were initially reluctant to consider the use of force unless and until all political and diplomatic options had been exhausted. In Bosnia, as we have seen, the May 1995 peacekeeper hostage crisis provided the first evidence that a French government under Jacques Chirac was prepared to consider options for a deeper French military involvement in Bosnia. Indeed, on Bastille Day (July 14) 1995, Chirac called for a more active Western military campaign, including the provision of American ground forces to help protect the UN-designated safe haven of Gorazde.

Up to that point, the United States had refused to table its option for using ground forces, preferring to coerce the Serbs to the negotiating table via a strategic air campaign that could be augmented by the use of cruise missiles, launched from sea-based platforms, if need be. For his part, Chirac let it be known that the UNPROFOR deploying countries had no intention of becoming "foot soldiers for the American knights."[66] Moreover, the French were convinced that the use of airpower had gone on long enough and was about to become counterproductive, emboldening the Serbs to be even more defiant. NATO's employment of U.S. cruise missiles on September 10, 1995, was too much for the French, who claimed that they had been excluded deliberately from NATO's decision process—a charge that was untrue, but perhaps a telling reflection of France's on-again, off-again relationship with NATO. From the U.S. perspective, the *Tomahawk* strikes fell squarely within the so-called Option Two strike package that NATO's North Atlantic Council had earlier approved. As a party to the deliberations in both the Contact Group on Bosnia and the NAC, where all NATO strike options were reviewed and passed on to member capitals for comment and approval, the French were intimately involved in decision-making on the general parameters involving the use of force in Bosnia. However, misreporting by General Bernard Janvier, Chirac's representative on the ground, and/or failure to understand the nuances of the NAC process may have led the French president to believe that the NAC had endorsed the French proposal for a bombing pause.

---

66 For a more in-depth treatment of the politics surrounding the U.S. interventions in Bosnia and later in Kosovo, see Clark (2001) and Halberstam (2001).

There can be no question that the U.S.-led NATO air campaign was decisive in bringing the Serbs to Dayton, and in securing their agreement in the subsequent negotiations for a cease-fire and the introduction of UN-mandated peacekeeping forces. In Bosnia, the French were prepared to authorize the use of force for specifically defined ends (the protection of the UN enclaves—UN resolution 836) or in support of the UNPROFOR troops on the ground. On three occasions between July 1993 and April 1994, France joined with the United States in supporting the threatened use of air strikes against the Bosnian Serbs, first to dissuade them from tightening the noose around Sarajevo in August 1993 and again in February 1994, and in April 1994 to protect Gorazde's safe-haven status. Ultimately, in the face of this unified Western stance—which also encouraged Russian acquiescence—the Bosnian Serbs retreated, but not before the historic Anglo-American relationship suffered deep strains and the French had extracted British support for creation of a European Rapid Reaction Force (ERRF) for use in future crises.

In many respects, French and American perspectives on the need to employ military force to coerce a diplomatic solution in Bosnia, and even ultimately in Kosovo, were closer than those of the United States and the United Kingdom. In point of fact, during the crisis over Bosnia, French and American positions were converging, just as Anglo-American ties reached their lowest point since Suez. What had been conceived in the aftermath of World War II as a triangular Alliance of like-minded allies—Britain, France, and the United States—had now become a zero-sum triangular relationship, much as it had been in the formative years of the United States' creation. Richard Perle, chairman of the Defense Policy Board, noted that Anglo-American friction over Bosnia was "certainly convenient from a French point of view, because it enabled the French to renew the charge ... that the United States was going to be unreliable or appeared to be unreliable ... the French made it a point to use almost any American behavior that could be characterized as a failure or otherwise to drive that agenda, which is to diminish the United States in Europe" (Simms 2001, 110).

After the fall of Srebrenica on July 11, 1995, Chirac pushed the United States to agree to a plan to use French troops flying in American helicopters to re-take the town. When the American military shot down the plan, which had been devised in Paris, Chirac made his fiery Bastille Day speech during which he hinted that France was being forced to consider withdrawal from UNPROFOR.[67] Srebrenica, very clearly, was a turning point for the French with respect to the use of force in Bosnia beyond those missions that had been specified in the UNPROFOR mandate. For the United States, this was a decisive event as well, since it gave credence to arguments in favor of a massive air campaign to take out Serb air defenses and to interdict important elements of their command and control. With Chirac of the view that more force was needed, the British were forced to reconsider their position, and now, finally, there was growing European support for a policy of lift and strike, that, in 1993, had been soundly opposed when Secretary of State Warren Christopher first promoted it.

However, where the French did differ from the Americans was on the precise instruments to be used and the framework for decision-making on operational matters. Whereas the United States was clear in designating NATO as its chosen tool, the French preferred the WEU, acting under UN supervision. At the beginning of the Yugoslav crises, François Mitterrand was still president of France, though he had had to endure the constraints of a cohabitation government under the premiership of Edouard Balladur, the centrist leader who had engineered the defeat of the Socialist Party in the National Assembly elections of 1993. The impulse of the Balladur government was to develop a closer, if pragmatic, relationship with NATO, but the unwillingness of Mitterrand to challenge the Gaullist orthodoxy on NATO provided a major restraint on just how far the French were willing to go in collaborating with the formal Alliance structure. A compromise was struck in which France would participate in NATO Military Committee consideration of peace-support operations in the Balkans, but anything more would have met with Mitterrand's opposition, as did Defense Minister François Léotard's participation in the 1994 NATO defense ministerial in Travemuende, Germany. Even as the Balladur government had tried to keep Léotard's participation a low-key affair, when

---

67 Chirac actually said, "We cannot imagine that the UN force will remain only to observe, and to be, in a way, accomplices in the situation. If that is the case, it is better to withdraw" (2001a).

Mitterrand found out what had occurred, he prevented his chief of staff, Admiral Jacques Lanxade, from participating in a subsequent Military Committee session on Bosnia.

Shortly thereafter, the French presidency passed for the first time into the hands of Jacques Chirac, and for two years, from 1995 until 1997, when the Socialists were returned to power, the French government, as we have seen, appeared to be on the verge of reintroducing its forces into the integrated NATO command structure. For unlike Mitterrand, whose world view had been shaped by the staggering loss of life at Verdun, followed by his World War II experiences as a member of the French underground and subsequently as a German prisoner of war, Chirac's defining experiences had been in Algeria. Consequently, Chirac never felt drawn to support the Serbs to the degree that Mitterrand had. Neither did he view German power in Europe in the same way that Mitterrand did. This made it much easier for Chirac to contemplate a revival of ties to NATO, which had effectively integrated German forces into the fabric of the Alliance in a way that had adverse implications for Mitterrand's concept of European defense collaboration. That is not to say that Chirac lacked a vision for the new Europe; he very clearly had one, and it too included the need to create a separate European defense capability for use in contingencies in which the United States or NATO as an alliance had refused to participate.

Chirac's vision was a pragmatic one, however, tied explicitly to the performance of the Europeans in Bosnia, and to ways of leveraging U.S. and NATO capabilities for the ESDI. One of the outcomes of the London conference was, as suggested above, the drawing of a "red line" around Gorazde, even as the participants seemed to write off Srebrenica and Zepa, both of which had fallen to Serb forces, and to turn a blind eye to the fates of Bihac and Sarajevo, whose situations were rapidly changing. With respect to Gorazde, however, the conference participants agreed to lift the "dual key" arrangement and allow NATO greater latitude in deciding when and how to implement various air strike options, including the possibility of further cruise missile attacks. The target list was expanded to include Bosnian Serb strategic targets, though few in French military and political circles were convinced that this type of coercion would check the Serb offensive.

In the United States, the fall of Srebrenica led swiftly and decisively to a call for measures to end the immediate crises. Led by the Republican majority in Congress, but supported by a bipartisan group of legislators, media pundits, and analysts, the U.S. administration made clear its intention to support the arming of the Bosnian government, which it apparently had already begun to do via covert means and through third parties.[68] No less than the future of the Atlantic Alliance was on the line, as more than one U.S. analyst pointed out.[69] On July 26, 1995, the U.S. Congress passed, by overwhelming vote, a resolution to lift the arms embargo against the Bosnian government, precipitating calls in Europe for the withdrawal of UNPROFOR and for NATO planning to cover that contingency. Shortly thereafter, the United States pressured the Alliance into agreeing to extend the protection formula for Gorazde to all the safe havens, including Sarajevo, in effect ending once and for all the dual-key process, and relegating the UN to a back seat in what was quickly becoming a NATO-focused operation.

At the same time, a coalition of Croatian regulars and Bosnian Croat forces launched a new offensive against the Serbs in Glamoc and Bosansko Grahovo in Herzegovina, followed several days later by an offensive against Serb-occupied territory in the Krajina. Taking the West by surprise, coalition forces were able to eject the Serbs and set the stage for the final act in this conflict, with the Serb shelling of Sarajevo in mid-August, followed by a concerted Western response in the air and on the ground, using NATO assets. The siege of Sarajevo was lifted, as Bosnian and Croat forces regained major pieces of territory in the northwest of Bosnia, and the Serbs were forced to the negotiating table. The ensuing Dayton peace settlement confirmed the success of the American strategy of lift and strike and established the credibility of U.S. efforts to work with indigenous forces to attain strategic objectives. This is a similar strategy to the one that was executed in Afghanistan.

---

68 French officials contend that from 1994 onward, the U.S. government was engaged in covert operations to arm and train Croat and Bosnian Muslim forces. News stories to that effect proliferated in early 1995, and whether or not they were true, they contributed to and even exacerbated the deterioration in relations between the United States and the UNPROFOR deploying countries. See, for example, Beaumont and Villiamy (1994) and Barber and Usborne (1995).

69 See, for example, William Odom's "Send in the Troops," in the *Pittsburgh Post-Gazette* of June 4, 1995. According to Odom, "If the Alliance cannot deal effectively with Bosnia, questions will arise about its effectiveness in the face of the challenges of potential instability in Central and Eastern Europe."

Peacekeeping or Policing?

Notwithstanding its success in bringing the warring parties to the negotiating table, the employment of U.S. and NATO military forces to implement the peace in Bosnia has proved to be controversial in the United States. During the transition from the Implementation Force (IFOR) to the Stabilization Force (SFOR), the absence of a clear exit strategy gave weight to opponents' arguments that Bosnia was becoming an open-ended commitment from which the United States should extract itself. The U.S. view, particularly after the Bush administration came to office, was that stability in the Balkans is the responsibility of the Europeans, and that enforcement of the Dayton accords amounts to a policing action and not a formal military function. This position actually corresponds with the EU desire to take responsibility for the Petersberg tasks, as well as with specific French aspirations for the Europeans to assume a more active, higher-profile role in European crisis management and stability operations. Thus, as U.S. forces transitioned out of the Stabilization Force, and those of the European nations assumed a more prominent role, both U.S. and French interests appeared to have been satisfied, although differences persisted with respect to force protection and rules of engagement, with the Americans much more cautious and less inclined to mix with the locals.

Philosophically, the Europeans and the United States have always approached peace-support operations from differing perspectives, although the French have been more willing to use force as a coercive instrument of power than have, say, the British, whose experiences in Northern Ireland have conferred a perspective that favors police-type operations rather than combat tactics in undertaking peace-support missions, particularly those established by the consent of the (formerly) warring parties. Thus, in Bosnia and later in Kosovo, after the submission of the Serbs following the NATO air campaigns, the types of missions necessary to establish order and stability on the ground were very different from those that had been central to bringing the parties to the negotiating table in the first place. In the case of UNPROFOR, the UN-mandated troops intervened in a nonpermissive environment where one of the warring parties—the Serbs—refused to acknowledge the UN mission, and indeed challenged its enforcement at every turn. The capabilities that had been required in this situation embodied the full array of combat forces, including in several instances the need for heavy tanks and artillery systems. Force protection in these circumstances also required combat-capable troops, and even in the early days of the SFOR deployment, after Dayton, these skills were still needed to guard against renegade operations. There still remains some need for specialized military forces in Bosnia, since over the last year remnants of Al Qaeda have taken refuge in the country.

Generally speaking, French and American perspectives on the types of capabilities needed for the post-conflict operations in Bosnia and Kosovo converged, although the United States has tended to operate with tighter rules of engagement in both areas, given the potential for terrorist threats against American forces. However, for the most part, policing of the Dayton settlement has proved to be just that kind of an operation, leading Bush administration officials to conclude that it is time to extract American forces from their peace-support operations in the Balkans, not just to be available for action in the war on terror, but to move aside and let the Europeans handle this responsibility, now that the hot war has ended. The French, then, should regard this as an important opportunity to display EU capabilities. Instead, it has become an issue of U.S.-European controversy, largely because the Europeans, on their own and without U.S. help, remain unable to fulfill various important missions. More than this, it has created an impression in Europe that while the United States makes war, it is up to the Europeans to pick up the pieces. This view prevails with respect to Afghanistan, where the International Security Assistance Force (ISAF) is composed largely of European forces, with post-war reconstruction of the country perceived to be of little interest to the Americans.

In point of fact, so-called nation-building has never enjoyed American support, although the United States has been extremely generous with its provision of aid in countries where it has intervened for a larger good. The United States has committed funds for the recovery of both Bosnia and Kosovo, but the American view is that the Balkans are the responsibility of the EU. In Afghanistan, the story is somewhat less clear, and there is dawning recognition in Washington that the inherent instability of that country will require a longer-term American military presence and commitment of funds to ensure stability in the broader Central Asian region. So, too, a longer-term U.S. presence in Afghanistan would have important implications for U.S. relations with neighboring countries, from Iran to Russia to China. Thus, as the French muse about American intentions in the Central Asian region, the realities of power politics, not to mention an ongoing war, require a continuing American commitment, one that goes far beyond the immediate goals of defeating Al Qaeda. Certainly in this circumstance, peacekeeping requires capabilities well beyond those of European police forces; it requires a formidable array of combat assets to which sophisticated intelligence capabilities are central, as they were in Bosnia and Kosovo, and the Gulf war before them.

During *Desert Storm*, the U.S.-led coalition relied heavily on NATO infrastructure and procedures. To the eternal frustration of the French, the coalition also had to rely on U.S. space and intelligence capabilities. But the American practice of providing only the fruits of American intelligence assessments and not the raw intelligence data that American technical capabilities had generated was a constant source of friction between the United States and its French ally. Then as today, there was a deeply held and abiding suspicion among French defense officials that the United States withholds important intelligence information from its allies and only selectively shares with them that information needed to support the American position. Ever since the Gulf war, the French have been determined to create their own space-based intelligence sensors and satellites, offsetting the expense of these programs by collaborating with their European partners. To date, the French have had moderate success in this area, finally getting German support for some cooperative projects, but the ongoing need to rely on American capabilities in this and other selected areas, such as transport, continues to vex the French and has opened a new area in the two countries' industrial competition.[70]

---

70 In the late 1990s France and Germany had agreed to develop jointly a high-resolution imaging satellite, designated *Horus*. However, the project was abandoned in 1997 when the German government pulled out because of its expense. Subsequently, the Germans decided to build a cheaper alternative, called *SARLupe*, a synthetic aperture radar program, consisting of five satellites, to be launched between 2004 and 2006. France has decided to contribute financially to this German program, but will not participate in its actual development, preferring to concentrate its own technological efforts on the *Helios-2* project, in cooperation with Spain. *Helios-2* is to be composed of two satellites, orbiting the earth in low-polar orbits, and having an infrared imaging capability and an improved resolution over *Helios-1*, which only has a 1.5-meter resolution capability and a daily revisit rate. In addition, France deploys two electronic transmission information-gathering satellite platforms, *Cerise*, which was launched in 1995, and *Clémentine*. The EU has a global positioning system program in train, called *Galileo*, which is planned to be in service by 2008.

The Gulf war first highlighted the centrality of command, control, computer, and communications technologies to modern combat, especially for timely intelligence, surveillance, and reconnaissance missions (C^{4}ISR). It also demonstrated, very starkly, European shortcomings in this regard—deficiencies that were further revealed when the Europeans tried to intervene on their own in the Balkans in the early 1990s. For the French the Gulf war was a wake-up call with respect to the need to invest funds in this particular area, but it was only after the Balkan crises began and the Rwandan intervention was contemplated that their dependence on American space-based capabilities forced the French government to address this particular shortfall in a much more focused manner. First in Bosnia, and later over Kosovo, the French undertook to find operational alternatives to relying on U.S., or even NATO, space assets, preferring to find ways to use the WEU framework, and later the nascent EU military capability, to leverage American assets, but from the UN pedestal to cushion the reality that it was American capabilities that were necessary to make the operations a success.

To varying degrees, the French have been successful in gaining access to U.S. imagery under various defense and intelligence cooperation agreements. However, the denial, as noted above, of raw data has been a powerful motivation for the French in their own national developmental efforts in this arena, as well as an important rallying call to the other Europeans on the need to create an autonomous EU capability in this area. Though time will tell as to their seriousness in this regard, this is one area where the British have demonstrated some ambivalence about their reliance on the United States, arising in part from their irritation over being cut off from American intelligence data in 1994, during U.S. covert operations in Croatia and Bosnia. For U.S.-French relations, this could emerge as another irritant, however, especially if the French government uses its own intelligence images to contest American positions or assessments, as it did in 1996, when French *Helios* images allegedly did not show the massive Iraqi troop movements that the U.S. had asserted were taking place.

The subsequent failures of the EU to act in Bosnia and Kosovo—at least until after the United States had intervened—created new momentum, certainly among the French, to address European shortcomings in the security arena, and with the Helsinki Summit decisions, the EU took a major step in this direction. In the future, assuming that the Europeans commit the necessary resources and political will to the tasks ahead, the EU could reach that objective, while fulfilling a fifty-year-old objective of U.S. foreign policy: namely, the creation of a viable European defense entity that can work in partnership with the United States and help to alleviate the burden of security planning in areas where the Americans and the Europeans have similar interests. At the same time, this would inject an element of credibility into French and European aspirations for Europe's emergence as a major pillar in a transforming international system.

CHAPTER 5

Strategic Stability
and the Bush Doctrine

O f all the areas where there is potential for confrontation in U.S.-French relations, none is more controversial in France than the Bush Doctrine, the emerging U.S. national security strategy that embraces strategic defenses and espouses the concept of military preemption. The major tenets of the Bush Doctrine trouble the French because they call into question established "rules of the road" for dealing with rogue nations, and because they disregard preferred European constructs for operational planning, creating, in turn, potentially profound implications for force structure decisions, strategic and crisis stability, and even the ESDP.

Bush Doctrine: A New Paradigm for Force Planning

Concepts
- Engagement • Prevention
- Detection • Preemption • Denial
- Coercion • Dissuasion • Deterrence

Implementation
- Interoperable C^{4}ISR for rapid decision-making
- Mission-driven HQ structures
- Accelerated national restructuring of European armed forces

Missions

Article 5	Peace Support Operations (PSOs)	Counter-Terrorism (CT)	Counter-WMD	Cyber Warfare
Professional armies, mechanized armor and maneuver units	Infantry forces	SOF	Passive/active defenses, SOF, early warning	Computer network defense/attack
Stealth and precision strike	Special Operations Forces (SOF)	Interagency intelligence	Antibiotic and sera stores	Critical infrastructure protection
Critical infrastructure protection (CIP) and homeland defense	Combat medical and combat support	Stealth and precision strike	Stealth strike	
Border security/air defenses	Civil affairs	Maritime intercept	Real-time sensors for NBCR detection	
Medical/consequence management	Intelligence	Early warning	Precision strike/PGMs	
Civil affairs	Transport	Consequence management	Nuclear?	
	Stealth and precision strike	Nuclear?		

The Bush Doctrine has received wide attention in the French press. On the whole, the attention is highly critical, which is hardly surprising given French perceptions of the Bush administration. What is somewhat disconcerting, however, is their apparent lack of precision when it comes to identifying just what the Bush Doctrine entails, and more significantly, the dangers it is designed to address. For example, most French probably would be pleasantly surprised to learn that the three major tenets of the Bush Doctrine, namely the promotion of democracy, anticipatory self-defense, and establishment of a new formula for strategic stability based on the development and deployment of defense technologies, are entirely consistent with the protection of French interests. Certainly, the promotion of democratic values is a shared interest between France and the United States, and is probably the least controversial aspect of the Bush Doctrine for the French, though here, too, the French have voiced some concerns over perceived U.S. efforts to shape the world in its own image.

Indeed, these themes cut to the heart of French concerns about America's unbridled power in the twenty-first century. And, they make no distinction between the employment of U.S. military power and its soft power, which in the era of globalization is equated in France with the pervasiveness of American ideas, culture, and institutions, as promoted by the Internet and in the global economy. To the extent that American soft power is derived from its military prowess and its global reach, one reinforces the other, a point that is made by Dr. Joseph Nye, dean of the Kennedy School of Government at Harvard University. Expressing a view similar to that of the French, Nye suggests that "how others react to American power is equally important to the question of stability and governance in this global information age" (Nye 2002, 12).[71] In this respect, many in France contend that the United States has set itself up to be the target of groups with disparate causes precisely because it has chosen

---

71 According to Nye, "Soft power rests on the ability to set the political agenda in a way that shapes the preferences of others ... The ability to establish preferences tends to be associated with intangible power resources, such as an attractive culture, ideology, and institutions ... Soft power is not merely the same as influence, though it is one source of influence ... [It] is also more than persuasion or the ability to move people by argument. It is the ability to entice and attract. And attraction often leads to acquiescence or imitation. Soft power [also] arises in large part from our values. These values are expressed in our culture, in the policies that we follow inside our country, and in the way we handle ourselves internationally" (2002, 9).

to operate unilaterally and without regard to the legitimate concerns of others.

Thus, in many respects, these concerns are amplified by the second tenet of the Bush Doctrine, namely its emphasis on preventive action. In several respects, those in French policy circles consider this as an unveiled attempt to combine the raw attributes of American power with a specific values structure mired in a religious outlook based on a clear-cut delineation between good and evil. In this context, the French point to President Bush's remarks before the joint session of Congress, following the September 11 attacks. "Either you are with us, or you are with the terrorists," the president remarked. For many French analysts, this American outlook is too simplistic for an increasingly complex world. More than this, however, the French perceive that the Americans are possessed of a messiah complex, where every intervention is a crusade, and all U.S. enemies are the devil incarnate. From Reagan's "evil empire" to Bush's "axis of evil," U.S. foreign policy is perceived as centered on a new Manifest Destiny based on a belief that "you can solve problems by a missionary activity" (Schultz 2001). In the cases of Iraq, Iran, and North Korea, this is to be accomplished by provoking forces to overthrow the ruling regimes and installing in their place democratic governments that support liberal economic principles.

This alleged American tendency to view the world in stark alternatives was in many ways for the French the defining reality in President Bush's "axis of evil" speech. To the French, the abiding American focus on regime change in Iraq, Iran, and North Korea has the feel of a new-age crusade steeped in right-wing religious fervor and colored by a messianic vision of a world conforming to American dictates and principles. The Bush Doctrine's call for what they see as the illegal use of force to effect regime change in these sovereign states is particularly contentious for the French, who hold that even if these states are home to terrible regimes, international law forbids outside intervention, unless or until the United Nations agrees to the need for using military forces to compel a change in government in a legally recognized sovereign entity. Thus, absent a UN resolution or a specific incident that flies in the face of international law, the French oppose the use of force to remove Saddam Hussein, the Iranian ayatollahs, or Kim Jong-il from power. Furthermore, the perception that the United States is prepared to violate the sovereignty of one or more of these states reinforces a general French impression that America is an imperial power, and one that has little regard for playing by anyone's rules but its own. An even less sympathetic view suggests that the United States is itself a rogue power, willing to act outside of internationally accepted legal norms to get what it wants, no matter the consequences for the rest of the world community. This view of the United States was substantiated in the September 2002 Sofres poll, which found that close to two-thirds of those polled "feel that Washington's first intentions are to 'protect and extend American interests and investments in the world' (64 percent), and 'impose America's will on the rest of the world' (63 percent)." As assessed by Sofres, "this represents a significant 11 point increase from two years ago" (Courtois 2002).

Considering the issue in this way, many French analysts contend that it is inevitable that coalitions will form against the United States precisely because of its unmatched power. For this reason, they caution that the United States had better be more receptive to the complaints of its allies, because it is only a matter of time before its adversaries unite to constrain U.S. actions, and when they do, the great superpower will sorely need friends. Already, many in France argue that this is the most prominent lesson of September 11. In its campaign to eradicate terrorism, the United States has been forced to work with other nations, since the nature of globalization demands a collective and transnational response. This may be true, but the broader meaning of the Bush Doctrine is its intention to provide the United States with a framework for action when and if American interests are threatened. Stated differently, there is no apparent intention to jettison time-honored U.S. alliance relationships—although there is a clear intention to redress the inefficiencies of multilateral or alliance mechanisms and, when necessary, to establish the basis for U.S. unilateral action, just as the French themselves have been prepared to do, most notably in Africa but also when they opted to withdraw French forces from NATO's integrated military command structure.

To all appearances, the French are schizophrenic about unilateralism and multilateralism as a basis for effecting action.

As with most nations, France is prepared to act unilaterally when its interests are compromised or under threat, although it would prefer, as would the United States, to act in conjunction with its allies when circumstances permit. Thus, it is not the concept of unilateralism to which the French object so much as it is the fact that it is a concept that has been implemented by the United States, and there is nothing that France seems to be able to do to influence the American decision process when the unilateral option is under consideration, apart from drawing out the deliberation process when given an opening, as has been the case with respect to UN deliberation of a mandate for action in Iraq. Conversely, it is not multilateralism per se to which the United States objects, but precisely how it is to be developed, and toward what end. To paraphrase U.S. Secretary of Defense Donald Rumsfeld, "It is the mission that must determine the coalition, not the reverse" (2002, 31).

The French contend that American notions of multilateralism fall short of their criteria for collaboration, and suggest that what passes for multilateral diplomacy or operational planning is nothing more than an impulse for coordination on specific aspects of policy or its implementation. America's brand of multilateralism has no theoretical underpinning, in contrast to that of the Europeans, who always tie it to universal principles and the rule of law. Robert Kagan called this "principled multilateralism," as opposed to the U.S. version, which he termed "pragmatic multilateralism" (Kagan 2002b). Accordingly, from the French perspective, true multilateralism involves a commitment to an international order, marked by full participation in global treaties and compromises on national positions for the benefit of the larger world community. The United States is generally perceived as unwilling to surrender any of its sovereignty to attain that higher goal (Heisbourg 2002), and worse still, it allegedly pursues its interests at the expense of others, as was apparent in its rejection of the Kyoto Treaty (on gas emissions and environmental standards), the International Criminal Court, and more recently with its insistence that Iraq must be disarmed. As President Chirac expressed it in an interview with Elaine Sciolino for the New York Times, "A few principles and a little order are needed to run the affairs of the world ...

I can't say both 'the Security Council must decide' and then, once it has decided, 'I'll do what I want'" (Chirac 2002b). This view of American motivations imbues the French with a sense of moral superiority, which manifests itself in criticisms of American policy positions, but also in efforts to promote a deepening of the European Union, to provide a more effective means of challenging U.S. policy positions.[72]

European concerns over U.S. unilateralism, which are perceived in France as an expression of the United States' unparalleled power at this moment in history, are closely related to Europe's objections to the Bush Doctrine's emphasis on a preventive strategy that singles out the strategic concept of preemption for its centerpiece. Preemption, and the right of "anticipatory self-defense," as provided for in Article 51 of the UN Charter, is considered the essence of what Secretary of Defense Donald Rumsfeld has called "forward deterrence." Writing in the May-June 2002 issue of *Foreign Affairs*, Secretary Rumsfeld noted that:

> Our challenge in this new century is a difficult one: to defend our nation against the unknown, the uncertain, the unforeseen, and the unexpected ... to accomplish it, we must put aside comfortable ways of thinking and planning—take risks and try new things—so we can deter and defeat adversaries that have not yet emerged to challenge us (23).

Most Europeans are extremely uncomfortable with adopting offensive action as an option, as was the case in Kosovo, so it is hardly surprising that U.S. talk of preemption is making them uneasy. On this issue, the French are no exception, having in 1981 been at the forefront of critics who condemned Israel's interdiction of Iraq's Osirik nuclear power reactor, although their criticism may have been somewhat self-serving since it was France that was helping Iraq to build the reactor in the first place.

Shortly after September 11, President Bush warned that America and its friends could not be protected from this insidious enemy by remaining on the defensive. As he put it in his remarks at the U.S. Military Academy at West Point on June 1, 2002, "If we wait for threats to materialize fully, it will be too

---

72 For a perceptive analysis along these lines, see Joffe 2002.

late." Thus, Mr. Bush continued, from the U.S. administration's perspective, "[w]e must take the battle to the enemy, disrupt his plans, and confront the worst threats before they emerge." For the United States, the war on terrorism and the rollback of rogue-actor WMD proliferation justifies radical, new thinking with respect to strategy and its attendant rules of engagement. That said, however, the American penchant to believe that the best defense sometimes is a good offense remains an uncomfortable concept for most Europeans, although, paradoxically, this is the foundation of French deterrence theory, based as it is on offensive nuclear weapons deployments and an employment policy that is tied exclusively to the protection of vital national interests, as defined by the French president, who has the ultimate decision authority on the use of French nuclear weapons.

French Nuclear Weapons and the "Non-use" Strategy

As we have seen, the French decision to develop nuclear weapons stemmed from two major events, first from the Suez crisis in 1956, followed in 1957 by the Soviet *Sputnik* launch, which demonstrated the limits of French autonomy and raised questions about the U.S. extended deterrence commitment to Western Europe. The *force de frappe* was a defining element of French strategy, reflecting a fundamental choice—which remains valid today in terms of the defense of French vital interests—to reject the notion of the conventional defense of France in favor of a deterrence concept that embraced nuclear weapons to "prevent war." At the same time, as originally conceived and as it pertains today, the French concept of nuclear deterrence does not accept the idea that nuclear weapons can be used for coercion or for war-fighting purposes, and emphasizes that nuclear weapons are

Evolution of French Nuclear Forces (1990–2010)

1990	2000	2010
18 IRBM S-3D (TN-61) *Pluton* (AN-51)		
Mirage IV-P – ASMP (TN-81) *Mirage* -2000N – ASMP (TN-81) *Jaguar* (AN-52) *Super-Étendard* (AN-52)	*Mirage* 2000N – ASMP (TN-81) *Super-Étendard* – ASMP (TN-81)	*Rafale*-Air – ASMPA (TNA) *Rafale*-Marine – ASMPA (TNA)
2 SSBN – M-20 (TN-61) 4 SSBN – M-4 (TN-71)	2 SSBN – M-4 (TN-71) 2 SSBN-NG – M-45 (TN-75)	4 SSBN-NG – M-51 (TN-75)

political instruments, deployed only for the purpose of safeguarding vital French national interests. As such, they are weapons of "non-use," designed to demonstrate that France is reliant on no other power for its survival. In this sense, they also are intended to perpetuate the French notion of (French) *exceptionalisme* that has long defined France as distinct from other states. Unlike Great Britain, whose deterrent posture and nuclear weapons evolved from the unique Anglo-American political and technological association, the French, largely on their own, but with a little U.S. help,[73] developed and deployed their own strategic path and weapons options. These centered around a deterrence strategy, during the Cold War years, of proportional deterrence and a variant of the U.S.-Soviet "assured destruction" strategy.

To be sure, France has, over the years, refined its deterrence concept and nuclear force postures. It developed its first, "pre-strategic," forces in the 1980s, to test Soviet intentions and to warn the Soviet leadership that if it persisted in threatening French strategic interests it would open the USSR to the prospect of an all-out French nuclear attack against its cities and industrial infrastructure. More recently, the French have articulated concepts for dealing with the proliferation challenge. However, French deterrence thought has always rejected the "no-first-use" doctrine, while embracing the concept of "first strike non-use." Essentially, what this means is that France set aside the right to use its nuclear weapons in any contingency that directly placed French strategic interests at risk of destruction. On this basis, the French made no distinction among the various types of weapons of mass destruction, and reserved for French leaders the right to use nuclear weapons against any and all enemies who threatened those interests.

---

73 In 1989, Princeton Professor Richard Ullman, writing in *Foreign Policy*, raised the lid on the nature and extent of U.S. assistance to France in its nuclear weapons programs. Belying the notion that France had independently developed its nuclear capability, Ullman wrote that Franco-American collaboration had been extensive, beginning in the Nixon administration and marking a clear departure from U.S. policy during the Eisenhower, Kennedy, and Johnson years. According to Ullman, this collaboration was highly compartmentalized and few people inside the U.S. government knew of its existence, so as to protect the myth of French independence and to ensure, on the U.S. side, that American help did not become subject to criticism because of conflicts with American non-proliferation efforts. Ullman also asserted that, "(a)ll presidents on both sides since Nixon and Pompidou have endorsed the nuclear collaboration, but it was probably at its most intense when Jimmy Carter was in the White House and Valéry Giscard d'Estaing was in the Elysée Palace" (Ullman 1989,18). Not everyone who was in the know supported this effort, and several have commented that the United States has suffered in the bargain. The French were less than forthcoming, and one U.S. official even felt that, in the Carter years, the U.S. "had given away the store" (Ullman 1989, 20).

In the regional planning context this clearly implied that the use of French nuclear weapons was not directly tied to a conventional force engagement. Rather, in a regional crisis, nuclear weapons could be invoked at will, to give the French president greater freedom of action, and in particular, to ensure that France was not subjected to blackmail involving threats to its vital interests. By this conception, French nuclear weapons were considered political instruments, and not operational weapons whose use was contingent upon the ebb and flow of conventional force operations. In other words, French nuclear weapons use was never viewed as a war-fighting option, either in the context of deterring the Soviet threat in Europe or, more recently, as a means of prevailing in a conventional war outside of Europe. It was, and continues to be, justified in the context of Article 51 of the UN Charter, which provides for a nation's right of self-defense.

Consistent with the rejection of any war-fighting role for the *force de frappe*, French nuclear deployments have conformed to a doctrine of "sufficiency," which President de Gaulle attempted to measure in terms of the "catastrophic damage" that French forces would inflict against an aggressor. During the Cold War years, sufficiency was closely tied to an anti-cities (or counter-value) targeting strategy intended to devastate Moscow and much of Soviet society, in proportion to the devastation that a Soviet attack would levy upon France in a major military campaign against Western Europe. Over time, however, as their nuclear weapons technologies matured, the French adopted precision targeting options, both to lower collateral damage and to target Soviet industrial infrastructure and command and control networks. Still, as was made clear in the 1972 French *Defense White Paper* (France 1972), the destruction of a major portion of the demographic and economic base of the Soviet Union remained the objective of French deterrence strategy, but for the first time, publicly at least, the French had moved away from the notion of proportionality as a basis for French deterrence planning.

By 1994 and the publication of a new French *Defense White Paper* (France 1994), the proportional deterrence concept was firmly rejected, and the French nuclear posture review of 1996 showed signs of an attempt to reconcile French nuclear strategy with the emerging threat of proliferation and the emergence of Europe as an integrated political entity. Whereas both issues became immediately apparent after the Gulf war, each had also been previously alluded to, if not spelled out, in French strategic thought; the former in the context of the *tous azimuts* strategy,[74] and the latter in the context of de Gaulle's far-sighted vision of a European union of states.[75] President de Gaulle obviously understood the extent to which French security rested upon that of its European neighbors. Reportedly, he once declared that "France ought to feel threatened if the territory of the Federal Republic of Germany and the Benelux countries were violated" (Isnard 1997).

The French *Defense White Paper* published in 1972 explicitly raised the possibility of a French deterrent capability for Europe (France 1972, vol. 1, 12-14),[76] although at the time there was a great deal of doubt as to how far beyond West Germany this could credibly apply. In the words of the 1972 *Defense White Paper*, "Crossing the threshold of the atomic threat can only be justified in a really critical situation" (France 1972, vol. 1, 13). There was, in this context, considerable discussion of "the forward battle" and the adoption of a French strategy very much like that of NATO's Flexible Response Strategy in which a conventional forces engagement would precede the threatened use of Alliance nuclear weapons.[77] To go down this road, however,

---

74 General Charles Ailleret, de Gaulle's chief of the defense staff, wrote in his 1967 article for the *Revue de Défense Nationale* of the need for an omni-directional nuclear capability (*tous azimuts*) that would "deter those who might wish, from whatever part of the world, to use us or to destroy us in order to achieve their war aims" (Ailleret 1967b, 428-9).

75 De Gaulle's Grand Design included a vision of Europe as a potent political entity, based on the "interdependence" of France and Germany. On May 15, 1962, de Gaulle referred to that interdependence during a press conference, stating, "On that interdependence depends the immediate security of both peoples. One has only to look at the map to see this. On that interdependence depends any hope of uniting Europe in the political field as also in the defense or economic fields. On that interdependence depends, consequently, the destiny of Europe as a whole" (de Gaulle 1962).

76 Published during the presidential tenure of Georges Pompidou, de Gaulle's immediate successor, when Michel Debré—a Gaullist—was defense minister, this document made some interesting refinements to French deterrence theory. As stated in the *White Paper*, "France lives in a network of interests which go beyond her borders. She is not isolated. Therefore, Western Europe as a whole cannot fail to benefit indirectly from French strategy that constitutes a stable and determining factor of security in Europe" (13).

77 When, on June 16, 1962, American Secretary of Defense Robert McNamara gave his now-famous Ann Arbor speech, in which he announced the adoption by the United States of the Flexible Response Strategy, tying nuclear weapons use to the forward engagement of NATO conventional forces, de Gaulle determined that the unconditional American promise to defend Western Europe was in doubt, especially as the United States increased its engagement in Vietnam. This line of reasoning contributed to several courses of French action, one of which was France's subsequent withdrawal from NATO's integrated military structure in 1966; another was consideration of France's role as Europe's protector, now that the country had developed its own nuclear weapons capability.

would have posed a fundamental dilemma for French deterrence strategy, since that would have meant moving closer to NATO, a notion with which then-president Georges Pompidou was extremely uncomfortable.

It would thus take another French President, Valéry Giscard d'Estaing, to move in this direction, based upon his vision of a "confederal" Europe in which France was destined to play a leading role. Accordingly, in 1976, the concept of the "enlarged sanctuary" was articulated by General Guy Méry, President d'Estaing's close military advisor, and later army chief of staff, to mean the inclusion under the French nuclear umbrella of territory outside of France, particularly along the approaches to France. Giscard d'Estaing's thinking was rooted in a desire to come closer to NATO without rejoining its integrated command structure; this would have been too much for the Gaullists to accept, and it conceivably could have undermined the much vaunted French defense consensus that generated bipartisan support for French defense policies. Still, in a move controversial for its implications for defense spending, Giscard d'Estaing slowed down some important nuclear weapons-related spending programs, and raised the priority of conventional forces modernization. Presumably, this was done so that France could participate with NATO forces in the forward battle to the east, though d'Estaing stopped short of renouncing the Gaullist doctrine of reliance on nuclear weapons for the direct defense of France itself (Frears 1981, 89-91). Doing so would surely have undermined France's defense consensus and opened the door to controversy over efforts to work more closely with the Atlantic Alliance.

Years later, when Charles Hernu, a Socialist and President François Mitterrand's first defense minister (in the Pierre Mauroy government), employed the term "pre-strategic," he used it in a context that recognized the growing importance of Europe to French security strategy and, specifically, to underscore the intensifying relationship between France and Germany, which Mitterrand himself had characterized as the indispensable duo for European security and defense collaboration. There was never any intention to convey a French acceptance of the operational use of nuclear weapons.

The term "pre-strategic" was intended to replace "tactical" when describing the category of shorter-range nuclear weapons, in an effort to underscore the close operational linkage between those weapons and France's strategic arsenal. And, while there is evidence that Mitterrand, early on, did subscribe to the notion of the ultimate warning, where tactical nuclear weapons would be employed to warn an enemy from advancing further or against breaching French borders, there is also evidence that later in his tenure, notably during the 1986-88 cohabitation with Jacques Chirac as prime minister, his doubts about the operational utility of nuclear weapons of any kind were paramount. In Mitterrand's own words, "I do not believe at all in the utility of *pre-strategic* weapons. To tell the truth, they should rather be called *post-strategic* weapons, because their use would necessarily signify that the Russians were already in Germany and one would find oneself beyond the moment when strategic deterrence should have worked" (Mitterrand 1987, 645).

In 1989, the fall of the Berlin Wall and Germany's subsequent unification caught the French by surprise, to a certain extent because of the quick pace of events, but more because of the strong will of Chancellor Helmut Kohl to move in this direction and the considerable support given to Kohl in this endeavor by the United States. A unified Germany within NATO changed the balance of power in Europe, particularly in light of the internal collapse of the Soviet Union, and challenged the planning assumptions underlying French nuclear strategy. In the broader context of European unity and security planning, the relevance of French nuclear forces needed to be reestablished, especially with respect to Russia's reemergence as a potential French partner in the new European landscape. Accordingly, in a landmark speech, President Mitterrand unveiled a new deterrence strategy, aptly called "existential deterrence," where French nuclear forces were to be held in trust for a uniting Europe and focused on global threats outside of Europe that might emerge to challenge European security. In this context, Pierre Joxe, Mitterrand's minister of defense from January 1991 to March 1993, reprised the phrase *tous azimuts* when referring to French deterrence policy, reinforcing the notion that any nuclear threat to Europe could be met by the threatened use of French nuclear weapons. At the time, members of the Jacobin left wing of the French Socialist Party interpreted this to mean that the United States, too, had been targeted by French nuclear forces. This fit nicely with their Marxist political philosophy and with their leadership's pro-Arab, anti-U.S. policy stances. It will be recalled that Jean-Pierre Chevènement, French defense minister at the time of Iraq's 1990 invasion of Kuwait, resigned rather than support French participation in *Desert Storm*.[78]

To operationalize the notion of a deterrent held in trust for a European entity now under construction, Defense Minister Joxe undertook various practical measures to give substance to the concept of a European deterrent capability, among them efforts to foster nuclear cooperation with Britain and offers to consult with other allies on nuclear deterrence and employment issues. During the period from 1991 to 1993 discussions with the United Kingdom moved substantially forward on practical, operational matters relating to such issues as submarine patrols. The French also held consultations with Germany on strategic doctrine and on France's role in the defense of Germany, now that the Soviet Union had ceased to exist. As the French saw it, development of a European deterrent force had to be predicated on agreement among Europeans on a single doctrine and on the establishment of an appropriate political structure. From this point on, Mitterrand conceived of French nuclear forces in the context of European unification and as an attribute of the EU's power on the rapidly changing international stage.

After his election as president in May 1995, Jacques Chirac introduced several important changes to French deterrence theory, while honoring the constants of previous French policies. During the 1986-88 cohabitation, when Chirac was prime minister, he and his defense minister, André Giraud, had attempted to introduce limited employment options into French nuclear thinking. But they were always opposed by President Mitterrand, who refused to sanction any change in the operational philosophy of French deterrence thought, other than to extend the French deterrence umbrella over

---

78 Chevènement subsequently went on to reclaim the leadership mantle of this leftist wing of the Socialist Party. He also campaigned from this base in the 2002 presidential election, only to be defeated in the first round by Jean-Marie Le Pen, who championed an anti-immigration platform. However, like Le Pen, Chevènement is an ardent nationalist and a Gaullist in his conception of French deterrence strategy, although his views of Europe differed considerably from those of the late president, who had a far-sighted vision of Europe and France's role in it.

Germany. Now, in the aftermath of the Gulf war and with new concerns about WMD proliferation, Chirac was free to resume nuclear testing (which Mitterrand had terminated in 1992), and to make his own mark on French deterrence theory, which he did with the articulation of the concerted deterrence concept.

As outlined by Prime Minister Alain Juppé on September 7, 1995, in a major speech before the Institute for Higher Defense Studies, European security collaboration could be based on what he called concerted deterrence. As described, concerted deterrence takes into account the interests of Germany by giving the German government a role—which to date has remained undefined—in the employment of French nuclear forces. Without doubt, this was an effort to influence German policy orientation, particularly as the French had begun to sense a shift to the east in Europe's center of gravity. At the same time, aware of the growing frictions in the Anglo-American relationship, essentially over the Balkans but also with respect to Russia, the French sought to exploit the situation by leaning further forward on nuclear collaboration with the United Kingdom than they had ever done before.

Thus, for a period of time in the mid-to-late 1990s, the French engaged in an intensive effort to identify concrete areas for cooperation, including in the areas of cooperative targeting, joint submarine patrols, and collaboration on anti-submarine warfare (ASW) defenses. They even considered joint development of a common missile, based on the UK Tactical Air-to-Surface (TASM) project that had been discarded in the early 1990s when the Royal Air Force had decided to retire all of its dual-capable aircraft (DCA) *Tornado* platforms. In this context, too, the French proposed development of a *Tomahawk*-like system, which still is possible as an outgrowth of their current collaboration on the *Scalp-EG* cruise missile.[79] As noted earlier, *Tomahawk* cruise missiles

---

79 France, Italy, and the United Kingdom are partners in the *Scalp-EG* program, which is designed to produce an air-launched cruise missile, having a range capability of six hundred kilometers and a warhead capable of penetrating buried or hardened targets. The French would like to develop a longer-range (thirteen hundred kilometers), naval-launched *Scalp* variant, for launch from submarines and frigates using torpedo tubes and vertical launchers, similar to the American SSN/SSGN and *Aegis* deployment concepts. However, the United Kingdom has resisted participation in this project since it had earlier opted to purchase American *Tomahawk* cruise missiles and currently is a U.S. partner in *Tactical Tomahawk* development.

have become the new currency of power politics, and without a corresponding cruise missile capability, France perceives that it has been excluded from important decision-making in the Atlantic Alliance, as well as U.S. operational planning. It also perceives that the United Kingdom's procurement from the United States of its own cruise missile capability ties that country more solidly to the Americans and makes it difficult to pry it loose to support European-launched technology initiatives.

Nevertheless, from time to time, the French have also flirted with the notion of British collaboration on a new ballistic missile-launching submarine platform to serve as the basis for a European deterrent capability. In truth, however, there never was any real chance that this would be pursued—at least for the time being—because of the UK's *Trident* development (based on technology sharing with the United States), and more importantly because neither the French nor the British have any desire to forego their own national development of nuclear reactor technologies, although this could change if the two countries do manage to collaborate on the development of a common aircraft carrier platform, if not on the aircraft themselves. With respect to the latter, in theory, the Royal Navy has the option of choosing either a fixed-wing aircraft, similar to the French *Rafale*, for deployment on its new-generation carriers, or a variant of the Joint Strike Fighter (JSF), which from the British perspective makes eminent sense since the UK is a partner in the American-proposed JSF collaboration. Until quite recently, the French believed that this represented their best chance for turning UK defense policy away from the United States and toward Europe. However, once the British government decided to move ahead with a JSF-compatible carrier, French expectations in this regard have been dashed.

The accelerated French efforts to entice the British into European defense collaboration during the first Chirac presidency, while Juppé was prime minister, primarily involved offering irresistible projects for industrial collaboration and using defense industries to make their case for defense collaboration. To the extent that the concerted deterrence concept provided the context for exploration of new nuclear weapons technologies, it was also used as a lure to open a dialogue with the United Kingdom on issues that heretofore had been exclusively the domain of the Anglo-American relationship. From collaboration on intelligence, to development of low-collateral-damage, surgical-strike nuclear weapons, nothing was beyond discussion.[80]

For two and a half years, the French vigorously pursued options for nuclear collaboration with the United Kingdom. By all accounts this activity was scaled back once the Socialists were returned to government in 1997. Defense issues, not to mention nuclear deterrence, were a decidedly low priority for the Jospin government, and even though the president retained his authority on security policy matters, as provided by the Fifth Republic's constitution, the constant internecine political warfare between the president and the prime minister on all issues was extremely disruptive to French security policy from 1997 to 2002, when Chirac resoundingly won in the second round of voting in the presidential election and his party did likewise in the parliamentary elections that followed.

Deterring Proliferation and WMD Threats

Throughout the decade of the 1990s and right up until the elections of 2002, external events exacted a high toll on French security and defense policies, making clear the need for new thinking with respect to deterrence planning. Beginning with the Gulf war, the expert community in France had begun to address what was widely referred to as the "identity crisis of French deterrence doctrine." As time went on, this exercise was made all the more urgent by the fallout from the Balkan wars, the escalation in violence between Israel and the Palestinians, simmering crises over Iraq, particularly after Baghdad refused, on August 5, 1998, to allow further weapons inspections by the United Nations Special Commission (UNSCOM), and, more recently, the war against terrorism.

When Chirac first came to power in 1995, he made a concerted effort to examine the implications of global proliferation threats for French security concepts and force posture.

---

80 This course of action marked a significant departure from Mitterrand's thinking about nuclear weapons. In particular, it contrasted starkly with his evolution with respect to *Hades*, France's "pre-strategic" system that had replaced the shorter-range *Pluton*, and which was dismantled and stored in bunkers when Mitterrand feared that nuclear weapons were actually being readied for operational use in non-strategic contingencies.

This took place at a time of great momentum in the European Union, and a key question that the Chirac government sought to resolve was how the concept of French defense autonomy could be reconciled with the political objective of a common European foreign and security policy. In effect this was resolved with the articulation of the concerted deterrence concept, discussed earlier.

A second, more contentious issue had to do with the employment of nuclear weapons to forestall enemy action to destroy France or to ensure the protection of vital French interests in the face of nuclear blackmail or even the employment of some other type of "weapon of mass effect." While the French have never viewed nuclear weapons as instruments of war, they must have operational coherence if they are going to be credible as a deterrent. For the French, the question became one of how, when, and where nuclear weapons should actually be employed if they had failed to deter the outbreak of war in the first instance.

As previously noted, the French had based their nuclear planning on an assured destruction paradigm. Second-strike forces that were more or less invulnerable because of their basing mode aboard French nuclear submarines would ensure that the French president had at his disposal the means to threaten the destruction of an adversary's territory and societal institutions. From the first, French nuclear doctrine rejected any no-first-use pledge and relied largely on counter-value capabilities to implement France's nuclear employment plans—although, in the 1980s, France had begun to explore options for limited counter-force targeting against high-value industrial aim-points and infrastructure in the Soviet Union as a means of injecting even greater credibility into their concept of deterrence "of the strong by the weaker." During the Jospin years, there was some thought given to the changing context of deterrence, that is, to explore the notion of relying on French nuclear weapons to deter chemical or biological weapons. However, consideration of using French strategic systems in the regional planning context proved to be controversial and of little relative interest to the Socialist government, which maintained that French nuclear forces must be closely linked to a political outcome and diplomatic objectives. Thus, while nuclear war-fighting options were once again clearly rejected, the role of French nuclear weapons in deterring weaker states, irrational leaders, or even non-state actors such as Al Qaeda was tabled for further consideration, since this was an area that was viewed in some quarters as central to the future of deterrence planning.

Although the French continued to maintain that nuclear weapons can never be viewed as ordinary instruments of war, for fear, among other things, of lowering the nuclear threshold, there was some consideration, in MoD circles, of updating French nuclear thinking to take into account growing proliferation challenges, particularly as states on Europe's periphery demonstrated attempts to gain access to fissile materials and the means of their delivery. For the French, this created a fundamental dilemma for their deterrence construct. On the one hand, as noted earlier, the French considered their nuclear weapons to be strategic instruments whose use would be dictated by the French president when he assessed that vital French interests were in danger. On the other hand, nuclear weapons were also regarded as weapons of non-use, too terrible to consider using in most circumstances but a necessary evil in terms of protecting the capacity of French forces to operate in foreign theaters. In a delicate and semantic compromise, MoD planners opted to take the safer road. Emphasizing their role as political instruments, French nuclear weapons were said to have a potentially important role in regional contingency planning, but that role was limited to dissuading hostile action against French vital interests, which might be threatened by (state or non-state) weapons of mass destruction. Earlier, during the Gulf war, François Mitterrand had firmly rejected any consideration that French nuclear weapons would be used in the regional context, including against a non-nuclear Iraqi WMD threat. Now, at least, there was a crack in the French line of thought on regional WMD use, although there was still no consideration given to amending French nuclear doctrine to consider an employment concept that had some connection to conventional force operations. Nor was there any consideration of bridging the conceptual gap between WMD use, nuclear retaliation, or non-nuclear, advanced technology weapons, such as the precision-guided munitions that had been used so spectacularly by U.S. forces during *Desert Storm* and later in the Balkans.

In one of his last speeches before his retirement, the former French chief of defense, Air Force General Jean-Philippe Douin, reiterated this view, contending that nuclear weapons and deterrence concepts have reduced utility in the regional planning context, especially against state and non-state actors whose decision calculus and communications channels with the West differ significantly from those that existed between the West and the former Soviet Union.[81] Douin's views notwithstanding, there emerged in France an extended debate over the notion of deterrence "of the crazy by the strong." Already, by 1994, in the *Defense White Paper* of that year (see chapter 3), the French explicitly had acknowledged that a regional nuclear power outside of Europe could possess the means to threaten French vital interests. At that time, French analysts struggled to define their concept of vital interests, and came to the conclusion that French vital interests could no longer only be understood in terms of French territory or the approaches to France. In fact, it was established that they were not even territorial in nature. As expounded in the 1994 *White Paper*, the Balladur government defined those interests to include "the integrity of the national territory of France and the Overseas Departments and Territories, its air and sea approaches, the free exercise of our sovereignty and the protection of the French population" (France 1994, 49).

Subsequently, in the 1996 Chirac-Juppé nuclear posture review, French analysts reaffirmed that view, and went on to imply that nuclear weapons might be used in "untraditional" scenarios in which French vital interests were at risk. From this, the Juppé government endeavored to take into account potential regional proliferation risks, marking a distinction between WMD use in theater against operational forces, and adversary targeting of French vital interests as delineated by no less than the French president himself. Conceptualized in this way, and as part of the Chirac government's nuclear posture review, the French president observed no distinction can be made, either in the nature of a threat to French vital interests, or in the source of that threat, when it comes to considerations affecting the possible use of French nuclear forces. In other words, if French national interests are threatened, then

---

81 See Douin (1996) for more on his views in this regard.

nuclear forces will be used; if less-than-vital French interests are at stake, then they will not. It is up to the discretion of the French president to assess whether French vital interests are at stake in any particular contingency, but the assumption, widely shared among French strategic analysts, is that the use of nuclear, chemical, or even biological weapons against French forces operating outside of Europe would not pose a threat to vital French national interests.

Conversely, however, non-state, transnational terrorists employing WMD against certain targets in France conceivably could be viewed as falling within the established criteria for a deterrent response, although, as one prominent French strategist has pointed out, there are no geographic coordinates against which to plan an attack (Heisbourg 2001a, esp. 201-11). This line of thinking, which was reiterated in President Chirac's June 2001 speech before the Institute for Higher Defense Studies, comes precipitously close to the Bush Doctrine's consideration of preemption as a means of dealing with emerging WMD threats, although most French analysts would most emphatically deny this.

In a close reading of recent French statements about the evolution of nuclear weapons planning, it is even possible to infer that preemption is possible using French nuclear weapons, if the French president determined that vital national interests were under threat. After all, this is why the French have maintained their first-use policy. Recognizing the growing dangers posed by WMD proliferation, and concerned about the use of such weapons by state and non-state actors alike, this French government, at least, seems to be prepared to consider nuclear weapons employment in the regional planning context and outside of the engagement of conventional forces. However, in contrast to the Bush administration's emphasis on the operational utility of advanced nuclear weapons (together with new-generation conventional munitions and missile defenses) to shore up planning against emerging state and non-state threats, the French remain committed to their non-use strategy, bolstered by a legal-diplomatic framework of arms control constraints to combat the proliferation of weapons of mass destruction and their ballistic and cruise missile launchers.

Moreover, in recent discussions about the Bush Doctrine, French defense experts made it very clear that for the French to consider preemption as an option, very precise intelligence, indicating that an adversary was about to mount a devastating attack on Western interests, would be necessary to justify military action, especially nuclear weapons use. At the same time, these experts reiterated that the use of French nuclear weapons would only be considered as a last resort when the danger to French vital interests was readily apparent. Thus, for certain regional contingencies in which an adversary state actor can be defined, French nuclear forces have the potential to guarantee freedom of action for conventional forces. This stands on its head French deterrence thinking as delineated in the 1972 *Defense White Paper*, which specified a strategic role for French Army forces, tying their defense of France to a "test" employment of nuclear weapons to demonstrate that France was prepared to use its nuclear arsenal to protect its vital interests.[82] In the context of the Bush Doctrine's dual emphasis on prevention and forward deterrence, there may be a convergence with evolving French nuclear thought, although the French clearly part company with the United States in discussions of the development of small-yield nuclear weapons that might have greater operational use in such a regional planning setting.

That said, the employment of French nuclear weapons in the regional planning context is not the preferred French approach to the proliferation challenge. From the French perspective, a more appropriate response to emerging proliferation threats is to strengthen arms control regimes, while seeking to engage potential proliferators in constructive political dialogues. In many respects, or so the French contend, the United States has overstated proliferation risks, basing its assessments on worst case or overly pessimistic intelligence estimates of emerging threats. In contrast, French analysts tend to believe that "real threats" will be less serious and emerge over a longer time period than

---

82 On April 6, 1995, Alain Juppé, the former French prime minister and a member of Chirac's political coalition, testified before the French Senate on the Chirac government's views of refinements to French deterrence thought, particularly with respect to previous assurances (relating to the non-use of French nuclear weapons) that had been provided to non-nuclear states. According to Juppé, "It goes without saying that our deterrence covers any challenge to our vital interests, regardless of the means or origin of the threat, including, to be sure weapons of mass destruction produced and used in violation of the international ban on them. To borrow the terms used by the 1994 *White Paper*, no one should doubt our resolve and ability to subject any adversary, in such circumstances, to unacceptable damage."

those foreseen by U.S. analysts, thereby opening the prospect for effective political engagement and the creation of a network of reinforcing arms control frameworks to forestall the emergence of these "real threats."

This is a widespread European view that is firmly established in policy and analytical circles, and one that remains unchanged, despite the weighty evidence that Secretary Rumsfeld presented to his counterparts at the June 2002 NATO ministerial in Brussels. At least with respect to the French, the basis for their assessments of emerging proliferation threats lies in the technological challenges associated with development of ICBMs and miniaturized warheads, down-playing U.S. arguments that the greater danger comes from an off-the-shelf procurement from a known proliferator. While the French concede that this indeed is a real concern, French analysts also contend that the political and military context in which a regional state actor would seek to employ WMD is unlikely to arise given the retaliatory power of any Western coalition. From this, French elites stress the value of a diversified deterrent posture, in which sea-based capabilities provide the ultimate protection, given their relative invulnerability to enemy interdiction.

For France, the more difficult problem is deterring non-state terrorists—called non-governmental criminal organizations (NCOs) by French security experts—whose ultimate objective is to destroy Western civilization at any cost. Since these non-state actors operate in loosely organized structures built around redundant and self-sufficient operating cells that are largely independent from each other, the ability to place at risk fundamental assets or high-value infrastructure is virtually non-existent. The exception, perhaps, is the extent to which host-country assets could be targeted, as was the case with respect to Al Qaeda's reliance on the Taliban government in Afghanistan.

In general, however, French elites appear to reject an operational role for French deterrent forces in counter-proliferation planning, except, perhaps, when it comes to the possibility of blackmailing French leadership to support or adopt a particular course of action. Within expert circles there also are reservations about the use of non-nuclear forces for this purpose, particularly with respect to preemption, although the specifics of a particular contingency would influence the French decision calculus in this regard. In cases where a nation's sovereignty was involved, the French would have a difficult time justifying preemptive action, unless they perceived a clear and present danger. The problem, according to the French, is the subjective nature of intelligence on proliferation matters, leaving contending intelligence assessments open to interpretation.

Having made a conscious decision to approach proliferation issues from a political and legalistic standpoint, the French argue that the most effective way to deal with proliferation concerns is through multilateral arms control arrangements and the establishment of both negative and positive security guarantees, which are given substance by French security policy. In other words, French deterrence forces together with binding defense agreements and political arrangements can reassure allies or warn off adversaries, thereby reducing the incentives for regional proliferation.

Missile Defenses and Crisis Stability

This brings us to French concerns about another aspect of the Bush Doctrine, namely its reliance on national missile defenses (NMD) to counter the increasingly dangerous and lethal challenges posed by missile and WMD proliferation. There are essentially two major aspects to French opposition to the Bush Doctrine in this area. The first relates to its potential implications for the French deterrent posture, although the French maintain that because their deterrence concept is based on the non-use of nuclear weapons, the U.S. development of national missile defenses will not affect the credibility of French deterrent forces since there is neither an expectation that the United States will target France nor any confidence that a "leak-proof" missile defense shield can be built cost-effectively.

Without question, French officials continue to hope that the whole idea of national missile defenses will be overtaken by events, including the change in U.S. funding priorities established after September 11, 2001. Notwithstanding the Bush administration's intention to press ahead in the missile defense arena—having just reorganized and expanded the program to take advantage of the absence of the ABM Treaty constraints—the French apparently hold out some hope that domestic opposition in the United States may slow or moderate the program to accord with their strategic preferences. Underlying this perspective is a tendency to underestimate the technological progress that the United States has registered in the missile defense area and to play up the highly publicized failures in the Missile Defense Agency's (MDA) testing programs.

Apart from arguments maintaining that a determined adversary will find a means to penetrate a missile shield, just as the Germans did with respect to the Maginot Line, French officials appear to be persuaded that "defenses will not work; that they will siphon off dozens of billions of defense dollars from more sensible applications" (Heisbourg 2001b); and even one "leaker" would suffice to create unimaginable devastation and terror. French and European critics further point to more effective options for a determined adversary, including terrorist threats and employment of the suitcase bomb to discount the utility or cost-effectiveness of missile defenses. Whatever the specific nature of their contention, the truth is that most European political and strategic affairs elites have very little knowledge of, or even interest in exploring, the technological advances that have enabled missile defenses to mature over the last two decades since President Reagan announced the Strategic Defense Initiative in 1983.

U.S. proponents of missile defenses point out that the layered defense architecture that forms the basis of the American missile defense program is designed to address the "leaker" issue. Moreover, the American approach is to pursue parallel paths of development, to include more conventional ground-based intercept technologies and the development of very advanced technology concepts, including kinetic energy boost-phase and, potentially, satellite-based technologies. To this, French critics of the missile defense concept fall back on one of several arguments. Either they contend that the technologies may work only in specific cases (for example, a limited attack scenario, generally based on the employment of one or two missile warheads); or they suggest that the development of offensive systems will inevitably outpace defensive technologies.

Critics pursuing this line of reasoning tend to fall back on cost-effectiveness arguments, asserting, as Heisbourg suggests above, that other military priorities, including readiness and conventional force modernization, will be adversely affected, making missile defense funding a zero-sum calculation. When confronted with the promise afforded by space-based mid-course intercept technologies such as *Brilliant Pebbles*—a concept developed by scientists at the U.S. Lawrence Livermore Laboratory, which entails the deployment of hit-to-kill vehicles ("pebbles") from space-based platforms, using space-based sensors ("brilliant eyes")—French and European critics revert to their "weapons in space" arguments, and contend that this approach to missile defense is destabilizing and even harmful to European security.

In the past, some French analysts have argued that a U.S. national missile defense deployment would be destabilizing because of its potential effects upon Russia and China, either of which could decide to rekindle the arms race to defeat the American defensive deployments. Others contended that a U.S. national missile defense capability would loosen the ties that bind the United States to its European allies, since it would protect America, but not its allies, thereby making Europe more susceptible to blackmail threats and less secure than it is today. Holding to this view, French analysts suggest that because nations of the West tend to be viewed homogeneously by Middle East state and non-state actors, enemies of the United States may seek to target Europe or U.S. assets based in Europe in an effort to circumvent an American missile defense deployment. In other words, Europe could emerge as the projected target of anti-American sentiments, while the United States itself, because it was protected by a national missile defense architecture, would be left alone. This line of argument is somewhat disingenuous when we recall that the motivating factor in France's national nuclear development was based largely on the rationale that the American extended deterrence guarantee over Europe was not credible. Indeed, French politicians at the time suggested that the United States would never endanger its security just to defend Europe, and this was enough, together with the Suez crisis and other perceived slights, to propel the French firmly on the path toward development of their own nuclear capability. It also is true that successive U.S. administrations from Reagan to

George W. Bush have considered the protection of Allied inter-ests to be a central aspect of their missile defense planning. In the face of existing and emerging proliferation challenges, and because two European countries (the United Kingdom and Den-mark) host facilities and radar capabilities that may be central to U.S. missile defense architectures, the obverse is in fact true, and the United States is engaged in a major effort to work with its allies in developing a missile defense capability that protects NATO-Europe as well as the United States.

That said, in France there is apparent concern that the U.S. pursuit of NMD will perpetuate an "unequal security zone," especially in the face of blackmail threats, which, it is alleged, would transfer the risk to Europe in a "quasi-zero sum game." (See, for example, Tertrais 2001, 31.) Apart from blackmail, the emergence of a ballistic missile threat from the Middle East could threaten Europe to a much greater degree than the United States, depending on the capabilities in play, and this could have dire consequences for Europe if the United States were not similarly targeted. Of course, now that the United States is free of any ABM Treaty constraints, it is able to pursue develop-ment of a host of new missile defense technologies, including boost-phase intercept (BPI) systems, which have equal potential to handle short-range and longer-range ballistic missile threats, depending on their deployment modalities and the sensor-net-ting of interceptors. Thus, the demise of the ABM Treaty should be viewed as a positive development for European security, one that remains to be exploited through the establishment of a sys-tems architecture that provides for redundant and reinforcing layered technologies.

Indeed, central to the Bush administration's missile defense concept is the notion of Allied participation. This, too, was not possible before the demise of the ABM Treaty, which prohibited the transfer of missile defense technologies to third parties. French industry officials are interested in missile defense collaboration, and NATO has under study an assessment of future requirements in this regard. These realities have served to undercut much of the French and European criticism of the Bush administration's decision to adopt a new strategic paradigm that includes missile defense development. The very fact that President Bush tied the U.S.

withdrawal from the ABM Treaty to a decision to reduce dramatically U.S. offensive nuclear weapons holdings served to mute French criticisms in a rather substantial way. Above all else, the president's vision for a new strategic paradigm should have struck a resonant chord in European arms control circles, because it reinvigorated the U.S.-Russian strategic arms control process that had been stalled since 1993.

It was Russia's acquiescence to the new U.S. strategic paradigm, however, that virtually silenced all of France's remaining criticisms of the ABM Treaty's demise. By the end of 2002, it was very difficult for the French to sustain their objections to the Bush administration's approach to missile defenses, once the Russians accepted the American decision, which was formalized on June 13, 2002, to withdraw from the ABM Treaty. "We cannot be more Catholic than the Pope on this matter," commented French analyst Henri Conze in a June 2002 interview. Moreover, as another French analyst, Bruno Tertrais (2002) of the Foundation for Strategic Research in Paris, pointed out, the U.S. ABM decision was accompanied by the U.S.-Russian agreement to lower offensive warhead inventories dramatically, a position that the French strategic affairs community has long advocated. More importantly, however, at least with respect to their concerns about missile defenses, the French have concluded that even the Bush national missile defense program (as compared to the Clinton administration's pursuit of theater missile defenses, or TMD) is not as robust as they had originally feared.

It is clear, then, that the French position on missile defenses was never absolute, although the distinction between NMD and TMD remains an important—if artificial—one in French strategic thinking. While the consensus view in France was that the Reagan vision of missile defense was too ambitious and politically infeasible with respect to the large Soviet nuclear force, government officials gradually came around to the position that limited deployments of so-called point defense systems around key installations and platforms might have some operational value, and perhaps even a limited deterrence value if they complicated adversary attack calculations and so long as those defenses relied on non-nuclear interceptors. French officials have been careful to point out that a tactical deployment of non-nuclear missile defense systems has an operational value, but it still neither adds to nor detracts from the French conception of deterrence that depends for its implementation on offensive strategic nuclear weapons employments.

That said, several prominent French analysts, among them Bruno Tertrais, concede that the Bush administration's desire to develop missile defenses can be seen as a logical response to the challenges posed by missile and WMD proliferation (Tertrais 2002). In this context, Tertrais notes the importance of President Chirac's speech before the Institute of Higher National Defense Studies (IHEDN) on June 8, 2001, three months before the Al Qaeda attacks against the United States. According to Chirac:

> We do not refute the dangers of ballistic proliferation, although our analysis differs as to the scale of the threat and how it might evolve over time. There can be no single answer to this problem which should be viewed within a broader debate on new security requirements ... As a Frenchman and a European, I am convinced that in the long run our security will rest on three fundamental and complementary pillars: respect for the rule of law, the modernity and Europeanization of our defense capability, and the permanence of nuclear deterrence ... New avenues must be explored to prevent ballistic proliferation through better control of technology transfers ... In parallel to these priority efforts to enhance arms control, we do not rule out the possibility of seeking military answers to certain challenges posed by proliferation. But this must not upset the equilibria that are crucial to international security. Space must not be militarized (2001b, 2-4).

Chirac thus opened the door to French consideration of the missile defense concept, although, as he subsequently made clear, French interest in missile defenses is tied almost exclusively to the protection of expeditionary forces operating in theaters outside of France (and presumably outside of Europe), with some latent interest in the protection of specific assets on French territory, such as nuclear power plants, post-September 11 (Chirac 2001b, 8).

For this reason, French government and industry experts have embraced the notion of missile defenses, specifically to protect operational forces and limited point assets on national territory, including civilian nuclear power plants, that

French analysts believe to be a target of terrorist planners. Additionally, French security analysts identify an emerging operational requirement to defend southern Europe and European troops—in particular the European Rapid Reaction Force—operating in remote theaters against both short-range and medium-range ballistic missiles (SRBMs and MRBMs, respectively), and against a growing cruise missile threat. With these types of contingencies in mind, the French Ministry of Defense has included funding for research and development of two types of theater missile defense capabilities in its new five-year defense plan, set to run from 2003 to 2008. Building on the on-going French-Italian collaboration on a family of missile defense systems, of which the *Aster* (surface-to-air missile system) and the *Arabel* radar are arguably the most important, at least from the French perspective, the French are seeking to develop a series of missile defense capabilities, including a naval variant of the *Aster* (15), which was test-fired on October 30, 2002; a land-based version, designated *Aster Mark I* , for use against SCUD-class missiles; and an *Aster Mark II* capability roughly equivalent to the U.S. *Patriot* PAC 3 system. The *Mark I* missile and its naval variant are slated to be operational by 2005, while the *Mark II* will not be available until 2010. Each of these capabilities is envisaged as complementing French efforts to project military power abroad, and both are likely to be offered for export in the international market, to compete directly with U.S. arms sales in this area.

As for national missile defenses, however, the French remain skeptical. As characterized by President Chirac, "In the struggle between sword and shield, there is no instance in which the shield has won." Consistent with this logic, the French government has invested considerable funds in enhancing the reliability and destructiveness of its nuclear forces. French nuclear forces are based on a strategic dyad of nuclear submarines and aircraft platforms. Their missiles are equipped with MIRVs (multiple independently-targeted re-entry vehicles) and employ sophisticated decoy systems. Maneuverable (MARV) warheads have been investigated, and although this program was put on a back burner, new funds may be invested in this area if and when needed to meet the changing dynamics of the international security setting.

As they are currently configured, French government officials contend that their strategic forces have been modernized to penetrate state-of-the-art defensive technologies. Though small, with about three hundred warheads on its survivable SSBN/SLBM force, and sixty more on three *Mirage* 2000N and two *Super-Etendard* squadrons, each platform of which deploys the ASMP missile (see figure, p. 117), the size of the French arsenal is said to be less important than its reliability and destructive potential.

Arms Control and a "Paradise Lost"

By far a more devastating critique of the Bush administration's strategic paradigm concerns its implications for arms control, which has long been regarded by the French as the centerpiece of European security. From this perspective, arms control, and the deterrence concepts to which it gave rise, were associated with both strategic and crisis stability in the Cold War bipolar international system. Although France was not an ABM Treaty signatory, the French had viewed the U.S.-Soviet decision to prohibit the development of national missile defenses as the sine qua non of the mutual assured destruction (MAD) paradigm that also lent credibility to France's independent deterrent posture, and to the notion of sufficiency that had allowed Chirac to dismantle the French land-based Intermediate-Range Ballistic Missile (IRBM) force in 1996 and move to a dyad, based on sea-based and aircraft platform deployments.

Even with the dissolution of the Soviet Union, the value of the Cold War arms control agreements endures in European strategic thinking. Frameworks such as the Mutual and Balanced Force Reductions (MBFR), the Conventional Forces Europe (CFE) Treaty, and very particularly the Intermediate Nuclear Forces (INF) Treaty, which resulted in the dismantling of NATO and some Warsaw Pact tactical nuclear forces deployed in Europe, were credited with adding significantly to the transparency and predictability of the East-West competition during the Cold War. Thus, it was not at all surprising when the Bush administration decided to withdraw from the 1972 ABM Treaty that the French, together with other Europeans, were openly critical and even hostile to this U.S. decision, notwithstanding that in 1991, President George H. Bush had ordered the unilateral destruction of thousands of American tactical

Major Arms Control Frameworks

Treaty Name	Date Entered into Force	Provisions	U.S. & French Positions
Anti-Ballistic Missile (ABM) Treaty	Oct. 3, 1972	U.S. & U.S.S.R. agree to limited deployments and constraints on ABM technology, enhancements, and technology transfers.	U.S. withdrew June 13, 2002; France was not a signatory.
SORT (Strategic Offensive Reductions Treaty)	May 24, 2002	Reduces nuclear forces to between 1700 and 2200 deployed warheads.	U.S.-Russian treaty, which will remain in force until Dec. 31, 2012. Either party, however, may withdraw upon three months' written notice. France is not a signatory.
Non-Proliferation Treaty (NPT)	Mar. 3, 1970	Five nuclear weapons states will not transfer nuclear weapons, technology, or devices to non-nuclear states. These states accept safeguards ensuring nuclear materials are not diverted to production of weapons.	Both nations, as nuclear powers, are NPT signatories. France views the NPT as key to counter-proliferation planning, while the U.S. sees limitations in relying solely on arms control to constrain proliferation incentives.
Comprehensive Test Ban Treaty (CTBT)	Dependent on ratification process	Prohibits all nuclear explosions, either for weapons testing or peaceful purposes. Establishes organization to ensure implementation.	U.S. signed treaty but did not ratify it; France was a late adherent to the cause, joining CTBT after completion of the French nuclear testing program in 1998.
Nuclear Suppliers Group	Jan. 1978	Seeks to manage flow of nuclear materials, technology, and equipment. Prohibits transfer of dual-use items to non-nuclear states or NCOs.	Both nations are members.
Missile Technology Control Regime (MTCR)	April 16, 1987	Restricts exports of delivery systems and technologies for carrying 500+kg payloads at ranges of 300+km, as well as WMD delivery systems.	U.S. and France are signatories.
Intermediate Nuclear Forces Treaty (INF)	June 1, 1988	Eliminates nuclear-armed, ground-launched ballistic and cruise missiles with ranges between 500 and 5500 kilometers, and their infrastructure.	Inspections ended May 31, 2001, 13 years after treaty's implementaion. U.S. was a party; France was not.
Chemical Weapons Convention (CWC)	Apr. 29, 1997	Bans production, stockpiling, acquisition, and use of CW. Signatories must destroy CW and CW production facilities.	U.S. endorses CWC and provides large proportion (22%) of the operating budget for the Organization for the Prohibition of Chemical Weapons, the body charged with enforcing the CWC.
Biological Weapons Convention (BWC)	Mar. 26, 1975	Bans production, development, acquisition, and use of BW. Bans weapons and delivery systems intended to use such agents.	France and the U.S. are parties to the convention, but the U.S. is seeking stronger enforcement mechanisms and has concerns about privacy issues pertaining to the pharmaceutical industry.
Conventional Forces in Europe Treaty (CFE)	Jul. 17, 1992	Establishes military balance between Warsaw Pact and NATO on specific weapons systems and inventories stationed in Europe.	Both France and the U.S. allowed the inclusion of their national forces based in Europe in the overall ceiling for the Atlantic Alliance.

nuclear warheads, and his son's decision to disband the ABM Treaty was accompanied by another providing for deep cuts in U.S. and Russian offensive nuclear inventories.

For much of the Cold War era, U.S. and French approaches to arms control differed in several important respects. Above all, the United States conceived of arms control as one component in a comprehensive security strategy, whose frameworks were important to creating transparency and hence were indispensable as confidence-building measures, designed to avert crises. For the French, however, arms control was a means of sustaining the credibility of French deterrence, and of increasing the size of their arsenals to come closer to that of the two superpowers. Successive French governments during the Cold War years held to the position that the United States and the Soviet Union must scale back their offensive weapons deployments quite significantly before France would allow its deterrent forces to be the object of arms control negotiations.

Proliferation of nuclear weapons was always a worry for both the United States and France, but unlike the Americans, who sought to reduce proliferation incentives among their allies by extending a security guarantee—the so-called nuclear umbrella, in the context of established alliance frameworks—the French preferred to rely only on themselves, creating their own nuclear deterrent and rejecting the concept of U.S. extended security assurances. After German reunification and in the face of the dramatic changes that were taking placing in the post-*Desert Storm* security environment, the French, like the Americans, sought to tighten existing arms control frameworks, notably the provisions of the 1968 Non-Proliferation Treaty (NPT), and to create new forums for discussion of proliferation issues, including those addressing a fissile materials cut off, and the Missile Technology Control Regime (MTCR). Unable in some instances to influence proliferation incentives, both France and the United States determined that another route, that of working together with potential suppliers of nuclear-related materials and technologies, would also benefit non-proliferation objectives. And, each has devoted resources to establishing export controls and has invested in the development of physical protection systems to ensure stockpile safety.

Nevertheless, the French have been very critical of what they call a lack of honesty with respect to America's commitment to non-proliferation and counter-proliferation efforts.

This lack of honesty is seen in America's rejection of the ABM Treaty, its failure to agree on provisions to strengthen the Biological Convention, its lack of support for the Comprehensive Test Ban Treaty (CTBT), and even in its opposition to the establishment of a nuclear-free zone in the Middle East, which the French attribute to America's complicit support for the Israeli nuclear program. Washington assesses such French criticisms as disingenuous, especially when comparing them to French arms sale efforts, notably to the Gulf Arabs.[83] The facts belie the assertion that the United States has not been committed to strengthening NPT mechanisms. But, and this is an important caveat, the United States, like France as a matter of fact, has never been prepared to rely solely on the goodwill of others when it comes to U.S. security. And, as set out in the Bush Doctrine, the United States is prepared to act unilaterally to defend its interests when directly threatened.

The American decision to jettison the ABM Treaty was never viewed in France in that context. Similar to other Europeans, the French had held the ABM Treaty in particularly high regard, no doubt because, as alluded to above, it stifled U.S. and Soviet development of missile defenses, which if pursued would have challenged the traditional Gaullist orthodoxy of deterrence. Perhaps of even greater importance, as conceived in France, the concept of mutual assured destruction to which this treaty gave support had established a firm basis for East-West crisis management by diminishing the opportunities for misunderstanding and foreclosing the possibility of a "strategic surprise," or so it was alleged. But predictability and transparency were never assured, at least with respect to Russian programs, and strategic stability was compromised when, shortly after Germany's reunification, Moscow announced that it was raising the profile of nuclear weapons in Russian defense planning. Europeans then began to worry about the large, residual Russian tactical nuclear warhead holdings and Moscow's apparent lack of accountability with respect to fissile materials and warhead stores from Soviet times.

---

83 For example, according to one analysis, the French decision to sell its stealthy *Apache* cruise missiles to the United Arab Emirates (UAE) violates the provisions of the MTCR and has legitimized cruise missile proliferation, a new and serious threat that the U.S. secretary of defense has recently flagged for members of Congress. For information about the French sale, see Gormley (1998).

To meet this challenge, the Europeans, led by the French, looked to export controls and collective measures as providing the key to stemming the tide of nuclear thefts and/or illegal material sales by the Russian mafia. The Suppliers Regime was created for just this purpose and, together with the Missile Technology Control Regime, arms control measures moved to the forefront of French efforts to address proliferation issues. When the United States decided to abandon the ABM Treaty, which in its view was technologically out of step with emerging threats, and pursue missile defenses as one means of countering the proliferation challenge, the French became convinced that this course would profoundly affect their efforts to dampen incentives for ballistic missile technology transfers, as well as create new incentives for America's adversaries to pursue development of a national nuclear weapons capability (see Gere 2002). In other words, by deviating from the arms control path, the United States was setting an unhealthy precedent for other nations to do the same, and when it came to the nuclear Non-Proliferation Treaty, the French feared that the consequences would be particularly severe, with major defections expected as soon as 2005, the year of the next NPT review conference.

Moreover, coming on the heels of the American rejection of the Comprehensive Test Ban Treaty, to which the French themselves were late converts, U.S. hesitation to enshrine its promised offensive weapons cuts in a formal treaty document was viewed in France as lending support to India's, Pakistan's, and Israel's nuclear programs, none of which are controlled by the NPT, since these countries refused to sign the treaty as avowedly non-nuclear states. However, on this issue in particular, the French really have very little credibility since they themselves followed the path of independent nuclear weapons development, and only signed the CTBT after the PALEN program was in operation.

That said, and although muted in their criticisms now that the ABM Treaty has ceased to exist, the French continue to believe that the Bush approach to arms control is likely to ignite a new round in the arms race, particularly if the Russians and the Chinese decide to pursue significant modernization programs designed to defeat U.S. national missile defense deployments. The logic of this French argument is mired in "old-think" about nuclear weapons and the arms race, and fails to consider adequately the changes that have taken place in U.S. relations with these two nations. On Mr. Bush's first European trip after becoming president, he and Vladimir Putin evidently established some kind of rapport, which subsequently has developed into a rather close personal relationship, despite key differences that exist between American and Russian approaches to various policy issues. As illustrated in their agreement to pursue radical reductions in offensive nuclear weapons, this personal relationship has helped to move the Russian government away from its vehement objections to ending the ABM Treaty restrictions, and it has helped put into place a framework for future U.S.-Russian collaboration on strategic issues, including in the area of missile defense development.

At the same time, the American approach, embodied in the Bush Doctrine, helped to ease Russian military concerns over defense spending and new weapons production, by establishing a ceiling on nuclear weapons holdings and by allowing each nation to define for itself just how it would decide to shape its deterrent posture. French concerns that Russian generals would seek to up the ante by increasing production of offensive nuclear weapons were shown to be baseless once the ABM Treaty was withdrawn, both because of financial limitations on Russian military production and spending and because the Putin government had determined that it had more to gain from working with the United States than against it, certainly in the area of collaborative work on missile defense technologies, which, increasingly, the Russians see as important to Moscow's own counter-proliferation planning.

However, Russian acquiescence to U.S. missile defense plans soon gave rise to another French concern, namely that President Putin had cut some kind of secret deal with the Bush administration, and that the creation of the NATO-Russian Council was the first step in giving Moscow a direct role in Alliance decision-making concerning stability on the Continent. Recalling earlier Cold War-era French allegations of a "superpower condominium," the French are adamant that the EU not be marginalized by Russia's newly established cooperation with an American-dominated NATO. This probably helps to explain why President Chirac is making a special effort to forge a close relationship himself with Vladimir Putin, and why, as well, he appears to be initiating new efforts to get the moribund European Union moving to reform its regulations, its constitution, and its decision-making apparatus.[84]

Apart from the implications with regard to Russia, the French also worry that the American abrogation of the ABM Treaty and its restraints will fuel new arms races elsewhere around the globe, but particularly in Asia, where the Chinese may try to develop systems to penetrate the American defensive shield. Officials in Paris believe that Chinese nuclear modernization efforts would be profoundly destabilizing to China's neighbors in Asia, perhaps stimulating new thought about the nuclear option in Japan, South Korea, and Taiwan, especially now that North Korea has opted to pursue this course. Each of these countries has the capacity to develop nuclear weapons, and several may have already gotten quite close, if they have not actually done so, as appears to be the case with North Korea, which has just revealed the existence of a uranium enrichment-based nuclear program, and, apparently, has begun to remove nuclear fuel rods out of storage for the purpose of reprocessing to produce plutonium-based nuclear weapons. In South Asia, too, Chinese nuclear modernization could influence Indian weapons development; this could have the effect of setting off another round in the arms race between India and Pakistan, which has benefited from North Korea's *No Dong* ballistic missile development program.

All told, the French worry that the American approach to arms control lends greater legitimacy to nuclear weapons possession, and in this context, they can imagine developmental programs in countries such as Egypt, Saudi Arabia, Iran, and

---

84 Former French President Valéry Giscard d'Estaing has been tapped to head a convention designed to assess the options for a "constitutional treaty for Europe." Modeled after the 1787 Philadelphia Convention of America's Founding Fathers, this convention has a mandate to explore deeper integration and the institutions necessary to make the EU a "global force." As for the French, Chirac has clearly stated his position, which is based on a "federation of nation states," having its own constitution, president, and parliament elected from regional districts that cut across national boundaries. In a major speech on March 6, 2002, Chirac also proposed that a "pioneer group" of EU states should "forge" ahead with closer integration, particularly in the defense and foreign policy areas, leaving the "laggards" to catch up later. "As always, the impulse must come from the Franco-German motor" (Chirac 2002a).

Syria, not to mention further efforts in India and Pakistan, whose future stability is a great concern. Indeed, two nightmare scenarios are worrying to the French: one is the prospect of a nuclear war between India and Pakistan over Kashmir, the other is that Pakistan's nuclear weapons will fall into the hands of Al Qaeda or some other extremist group. Thus, for the French, the U.S. pursuit of small-yield nuclear weapons, as described in the Bush administration's Nuclear Posture Review, coupled with America's inclination to set aside formal arms control mechanisms, only reinforces the legitimacy of nuclear weapons at a time when they should be de-legitimized for the sake of global security.

Even as the utility of the Non-Proliferation Treaty has been shown to be wanting in terms of dissuading countries, including Iraq, Iran, and North Korea, that are determined to pursue nuclear weapons development, or in specifying through the International Atomic Energy Agency (IAEA) or United Nations weapons inspections what stocks exist and their locations, the French continue to maintain that without legally binding treaty constraints, the proliferation problem would become unmanageable. This is why, as noted earlier, the French have been ardent proponents of a fissile materials control regime and, more recently, of establishing a framework to create transparency in ballistic missile technology transfers and developments, in the hope of undercutting state and non-state proliferation efforts. To France's relief, the United States has been an active participant in these discussions, and it has done more than the European Union nations to address this fissile material issue through its Nunn-Lugar Cooperative Threat Reduction Program.

The risks of nuclear-related terrorism are growing, a subject of great concern to the French. For the United States, too, this is a concern, more so in the aftermath of September 11 and subsequent speculation about a "dirty" bomb threat against an American city. Arms control frameworks are generally useless in controlling the activities of non-state actors, though they may have some impact on states that sponsor terrorism, or so the French believe. Obviously, the United States is much more skeptical about using arms control to check the behavior of states that are seeking to upset the status quo, and at any rate perceives that the biggest problem in this regard continues to be the potential for Russian stocks to make their way into the hands of rogue actors. Thus, from the U.S. perspective, it is exceedingly important to establish enhanced controls over Russian nuclear weapons and their associated fissile material stocks; for this reason the Bush administration has determined to continue Nunn-Lugar funding, and to work more closely with the Russians to help reduce their vulnerability to theft of nuclear weapons-related materials and technologies.

On this basis, the United States has shown itself willing to compromise on signing a formal document codifying U.S. and Russian strategic nuclear weapons reductions, to remain in force for a period of ten years. This agreement, based on what was euphemistically called the Strategic Offensive Reductions Talks (SORT), provides for deep cuts, down to between seventeen hundred and twenty-two hundred nuclear warheads in the U.S. and Russian nuclear weapons inventories.[85] The French have long supported the idea of deep reductions in the U.S. and Russian nuclear inventories, in part to enhance the status of French deterrent holdings by equating their numbers more closely, and thus they applauded this aspect of the Bush administration's policy, even though they continued to be skeptical of the decision to back away from restrictions on national missile defenses. Why, the French ask, risk damaging security by changing the rules of the game?

The U.S. shift in strategic paradigm that is embodied in the Bush Doctrine also heightens French concerns about U.S. unilateralism and adventurism in Europe's own back yard. Protected by its missile shield, the United States might be more inclined to intervene in crisis regions, where the response might be a threat to Europe, whose vulnerability relative to that of America may make it a more attractive target of opportunity to U.S. adversaries. Ironically, the French have similarly argued the reverse case: that missile defenses will

---

85 According to the agreement that was worked out, both parties would limit their strategic nuclear arsenals to between 1750 and 2200 weapons, defined as either nuclear warheads or strategic nuclear delivery vehicles, depending on the priorities of each country with respect to future force posture and a national decision to base nuclear weapons on land or at sea. In other words, the new agreement provides great flexibility to accommodate the force modernization plans of each side, and it will be in place for ten years, after which time either side can opt to pursue further reductions or leave its current arsenals in place. For a detailed description of the agreement, see Sanger (2002).

release the United States from its ties to European security. Proponents of this line of argument suggest that American invulnerability may occasion a "fortress America" mentality that could produce a new brand of American isolationism. In other words, and in contrast to the Cold War period when French government officials employed the argument that American vulnerability to Soviet ICBMs necessitated French development of the *force de frappe* to compensate for trans-atlantic de-coupling, many now contend that a U.S. missile defense shield will undermine alliance cohesion by creating multiple levels of security protection.

The eventual conclusion to de drawn from this analysis is that French security thought has reached a cul-de-sac. While French analysts struggle to take into account the changing dynamics of the twenty-first century's landscape—dynamics that call for new means of defense—they have yet to come up with a convincing argument as to why missile defenses or preventive defense are unsatisfactory options. At the same time, their troublesome and unwavering emphasis on sustaining arms control frameworks of the past, some of which had already proved to be deficient, falls short of addressing the behaviors of those actors for whom existing arms control regimes have little or no meaning. As viewed in the United States, there may be some benefit to having in place frameworks and mechanisms that provide for greater transparency and confidence-building measures, but, alone, such mechanisms do not suffice when confronted with an uncooperative actor. Missile defenses can provide an important defensive hedge, more so if coupled with the Bush Doctrine's emphasis on dissuasion, coercion, and preemption, particularly in the context of rogue-state and terrorist proliferation efforts.

CHAPTER 6

The War against Terror
and the "Axis of Evil"

French efforts to raise the profile of the European Union and to meet the challenges posed by missile and WMD proliferation have taken on new urgency since the September 11 attacks, for several reasons. First, personal security has become a more prominent concern in Europe, arising in part from the large Muslim minorities that reside in West European countries, but also because of unresolved political issues having to do with Israel and Palestinian statehood, uncertainty in the Balkans, and cross-border criminal activities in Europe. Second, with the attention of the United States focused on the war against terrorism, the Europeans have had to pick up the slack in the Balkans, where ongoing operations are still necessary to ensure regional stability. Finally, because the war on terror has ramifications for European security, manifested most dramatically for the French in the Karachi bomb blast that took the lives of French engineers working with Pakistan's navy, global considerations are lending weight to arguments for a faster development of the ESDP.[86]

In the immediate aftermath of the attacks on the World Trade Center and the Pentagon, President Chirac rushed to New York and Washington, to be the first international leader on the scene to express solidarity with the United States. As the president of the UN Security Council at the time, France was instrumental in "introducing resolution 1368, which, for the first time in UN history, described a terrorist attack as a 'threat to international peace and security'" (Traub 2002), thus giving to the United States international political legitimacy to retaliate against Al

---

86 These points were reiterated by Nicole Gnescotto, director of the EU Studies Institute, in her November 2001 *Le Figaro* article, "Défense: Plus, plus vite, et mieux."

Qaeda and the Taliban regime.[87] Together with other U.S. allies, France supported the employment of NATO airborne early-warning (AWACS) platforms over U.S. territory, and joined with its UN partners in endorsing resolution 1373, which called on states to suppress the funding of terrorist networks and to deny them sanctuary and weapons support.[88] At the same time, they intensified their efforts to get agreement in the EU on common policies relating to anti-terrorism legislation and intelligence exchanges. In retrospect, Paris unquestionably saw the events of September 11 as an opportunity to accelerate momentum in the EU, particularly with respect to the ESDP. Were the ESDP to take off, so reasoned the French, then France's ability to register objections to U.S. actions would be all the more effective.

In several respects, then, the post-September 11 French expression of solidarity with the United States appears to have had a limited shelf-life. Soon after, the French resumed their criticism of the United States on everything from prisoners' rights to the scope of operations in the war against terror. Many in France believe that the United States has been too heavy-handed in dealing with terrorist threats, and the French government has not been as cooperative as Washington would have liked on several fronts, including American efforts to "starve the terrorists of funding," and in the context of building a case against Zacarias Moussaoui, a French citizen who, under U.S. law, could receive the death penalty. French objections to the American pursuit of funding sources for terrorists probably have more to do with intelligence and privacy considerations than with deep-seated differences over this aspect of a comprehensive anti-terrorist campaign. In the case of Moussaoui, however, French hesitations about cooperating with the United States appear to reflect profound cultural and philosophical differences on capital pun-

---

87   UNSC resolution 1368, adopted on September 12, 2001, condemned the terrorist acts of September 11, and "calls on all states to work together urgently to bring to justice the perpetrators, organizers, and sponsors of these terrorist attacks and stresses that those responsible for aiding, supporting, or harboring the perpetrators, organizers, and sponsors of these acts will be held accountable" (paragraph 3). The resolution also goes on to express a readiness "to take all necessary steps to respond to the terrorist attacks of September 11, 2001, and to combat all forms of terrorism, in accordance with its responsibilities under the Charter of the United Nations" (paragraph 5).

88   On September 28, 2001, the UNSC adopted resolution 1373, which addressed the suppression of terrorist funding and financial networks, including the identification and restriction of terrorist use of safe havens for money-laundering purposes. It also provided for measures to prevent the movement of terrorist groups and called for the sharing of intelligence on terrorist operations.

ishment, which, in turn, reveal a deeper disagreement over the rights of the individual versus the well-being of society.

It is certainly true that, to a lesser extent, such disagreements are also apparent within the United States itself, as federal, state, and local government officials contend with the need to balance individual freedoms with homeland security. Between the United States and France, however, the nuances with respect to power politics reflect more fundamental differences over the role of the individual in society, and society's responsibility to the individual. This, together with a divergence of U.S. and French views of how to treat the Al Qaeda prisoners of war, and more broadly how to deal with the challenges posed by radical Islamist fundamentalism, certainly could hamper U.S. efforts to broaden the war on terrorism, or to promote a new U.S.-brokered peace initiative between Israel and the Palestinians. One dominant French view holds that the Arab jihad has its origins in the uneven economic development of Arab societies, while another subscribes to Huntington's clash-of-civilizations thesis,[89] and lays the responsibility for the increase in global terrorism squarely on U.S. shoulders, arising from American support for Israel. For many in France, Palestinian terrorism is a manifestation of the struggle for statehood, and Israeli Prime Minister Ariel Sharon's actions are depicted as terrorist operations, and not the actions of a man desperate to save his country.

So, perhaps it was inevitable that not long after September 11, the French resumed their transatlantic sniping: directing criticisms against U.S. operational planning in Afghanistan, America's widening of the war to include the establishment of a presence and basing infrastructure in Central Asia, and President Bush's inclusion of Iraq and Iran on the "axis of evil" and thus as potential targets of U.S. counter-proliferation operations. Particularly after the president's State of the Union address in January 2002, at which time he coined the phrase "axis of evil," European governments in general, and the French in particular, have decried U.S. policy as heavy-handed and "simplistic" (see, for example, Moore 2002). Editorials and articles in some major French newspapers

---

89 According to Harvard professor Samuel Huntington, future conflicts will not be motivated by ideological or economic interests, but rather from cultural and ethnic differences emanating from the world's great civilizations (1993).

went so far as to speculate whether the attacks on the World Trade Center and the Pentagon might have been justified.[90] To make matters worse, the French public, which often registers greater sympathy for the United States than do their government officials, propelled to the bestseller list a book that questioned whether an attack against the Pentagon even took place (Meyssan 2002). This, coupled with the very public rise in French anti-Semitism and the resurgence of the National Front in the 2002 national elections, raises fundamental questions about the limits of Franco-American cooperation, particularly given the two countries' fundamentally different visions of international relations.

New Threats and Old Nemeses

The convergence of these trends has had a perceptible impact on French foreign and security policy, not the least with regard to attitudes about U.S. policies on several important issues that threaten to exacerbate tensions in the Franco-American relationship further. In this respect, it is extremely revealing that the Sofres poll established that only 34 percent of those polled believe that France is a "loyal ally" of the United States, while 57 percent believe that France is "not always a loyal ally," and 11 percent perceived Americans as their adversaries (Courtois 2002). In three areas in particular, namely the Palestinian-Israeli conflict, Iraq, and Iran, French policies have often conflicted with those of the United States, and in specific instances, the French have used the EU to thwart U.S. initiatives. This has been most pronounced in American efforts to address WMD issues, but it has also been apparent with respect to European efforts to revitalize the flagging Middle East peace process. To the extent that French policies have actively worked against U.S. interests in each of these areas, they have opened up old wounds and created new doubts about France's reliability as an alliance partner.

While the French have historic interests in the Middle East—indeed, their colonial legacy colors their present outlook—there appears to be much more at play than just a desire to effect a positive political outcome for the Palestinians.

---

90 See, for example, Daley (2002) and "How the World Views the War on Terrorism: What the U.S. Media Missed," a Council on Foreign Relations news release that reports that Jean Baudrillard, a leading French philosopher, "expressed his 'jubilation' at the World Trade Center attack on the front page of *Le Monde* [the leading left-of-center French daily newspaper]" (Council on Foreign Relations 2002).

There appears to be an intention to push the United States off center stage and to diminish American influence in the region, although the current French foreign minister protests that this is not so; what France fears most, he says, is "the vertigo of the vacuum of power" rather than the excess of power that is possessed by the United States (Bonnet and Tréan 2002). Still, the French are opposed to American efforts to diminish Yasser Arafat's role, and in their support for Palestinian elections, they already have determined that they will have to certify an Arafat election victory in the face of U.S. protests that until he leaves the scene, no progress is likely in controlling the escalating cycle of violence that has led to Israel's defensive moves. The Arab-Israeli conflict is particularly problematic for U.S.-French relations, given each country's domestic constituencies in support of diametrically opposed solutions. In France, the conflict has the potential to incite the almost six million Muslims, or 10 percent of the French population, who reside in the country but who have never really been integrated into the fabric of French society. It also could spark another Arab oil boycott similar to that of 1973, when Europe's dependence on imported oil from the Middle East influenced French policy positions relating to the Arab-Israeli crisis over the Suez, which escalated into another round of war between Israel and its Arab neighbors.

With the emergence of radical Islam, French concerns over homeland security have grown exponentially and have colored France's responses to post-September 11 security collaboration with the United States. In their souls most French recognize that Islamist militancy is not just a threat to the United States, but to the values of the Enlightenment, which they also hold dear. And yet, in holding to the view that terrorism must be attacked at its supposed roots, that is, poverty and the unequal benefits of globalization, they tend to confuse the problem with the solution. In the case of Iraq, for example, as Kagan points out, "Many officials and politicians in Europe worry more about how the U.S. might mishandle the problems ... than they worry about Iraq itself" (2002a). Moreover, as found in a recent National Bureau of Economic Research study cited in "Limousine Terrorists," published in the *Wall Street Journal*, August 21, 2002, "There is little reason to be optimistic that a reduction in poverty or increase in educational attainment will lead to a meaningful reduction in the amount of international terrorism, without other changes." In fact, the obverse appears to be true in a study of 129 Hezbollah terrorists who died between 1982 and 1994. This compares with a sample of those identified as fighting with Al Qaeda, including American Taliban John Walker Lindh and Mohammed Atta, the middle-class Egyptian who apparently was the operational leader of the September 11 attackers.

The French public sense of personal insecurity first manifested itself in response to the Algerian independence movement. This insecurity has increased as France has become a potential target of Al Qaeda operatives, and as a result government officials tend to try to moderate this trend through domestic political initiatives, including with the decision to allow Muslim representation on the French Council, an official framework to address domestic concerns. Notwithstanding recent initiatives, French concerns over domestic insecurity have not been moderated and indeed have grown in the face of an ever-expanding pool of illegal Muslim immigrants from North Africa. This is a population that suffers from a high rate of unemployment, and its youth have become extremely disaffected with the mores of Western society. More and more, they are finding support from Persian Gulf state-financed *madrasses*, some of which are known to be cultivating radical fundamentalist sentiments.

For the French, who have long tried to keep such extremism at bay, this is proving to be a real challenge, one that requires a scapegoat (the U.S. and/or Israel) and a more prudent course (target the alleged root causes of this disaffection). In this latter regard, many in France perceive U.S. strategy as devoid of a much needed political and cultural dimension to complement its military instruments of power. The French hold that in an ever-contracting "globalized" world, America's reliance on military power is coming at the expense of its capacity to win hearts and minds. From this, the French deduce that U.S. preoccupation with military power is giving short shrift to the concept of soft power, or the ability to shape perceptions using other tools of American diplomacy, including the mass media, the Peace Corps, U.S. Agency for International Development (AID) programs, and the like. This, many in France contend, is a fundamental failing of U.S. policy, and one that can only be remedied by building international consensus on a body of laws and rules for conducting relations between and among sovereign entities. Indeed, the French prescription for dealing with international crises includes being respectful of national traditions and attentive to local concerns, though French interventions in Africa, most recently as demonstrated in Ivory Coast, do not meet France's own criteria in that regard.

Multilateralism, as we have earlier observed, lies at the heart of the French approach to conflict prevention and crisis management, and lately this has been manifested in an emphasis on the institutional role of the United Nations. For France, its membership as one of the UNSC's permanent members—an anomaly given France's present standing in the world community—provides virtually the only means by which the French can attempt to constrain U.S. unilateralist tendencies or to challenge American leadership initiatives. Not surprisingly, in the French world view, the United Nations has emerged as the most important institutional framework, just ahead of the European Union, for dealing with the United States. From this perspective, the international legitimacy that is conferred by the United Nations can only enhance America's strength, not diminish it, as some in the United States have suggested, and on this basis, if it comes to a war against Iraq, the United States will be better positioned to see it through to a successful conclusion if it has obtained a "license" for action from the UN. As the French see it, American disdain for multilateralism is a negation of the very sources of U.S. power. For as viewed from Paris, America's true strength is derived from its permanent alliances, which are based on multilateralism. It is somewhat ironic, in this regard, that most French officials fail to acknowledge, or perhaps even understand, that American actions in building the case for disarming Iraq may in fact restore the legitimacy of the United Nations, and in so doing, confer a new vitality upon post-World War II institutions. Beyond that, the French approach to international relations rests upon American military power and the ultimate knowledge that Western interests, in the end, will be protected by the American penchant to use that power if threatened. This is just as true when it comes to disarming Iraq as it is with respect to prosecuting the war against terrorism.

French efforts to craft a multilateral approach to counter-proliferation planning (that is, reliance on the Security Council, the G-8, or other established frameworks for collective action) have seemed to many Americans to be less than helpful in the broader effort to address terrorism and counter-proliferation worldwide. Nowhere is this more apparent than in the Middle East, where France has created roadblocks for one U.S. policy initiative after another. France's ongoing support of Arafat, even in light of his apparent culpability for terrorist operations directed against Israel, flies in the face of America's support for Israel and, from the U.S. perspective, has been instrumental in continuing the spiral of violence in the Middle East.[91] While pro-Arab sentiments have long shaped the contours of French, and indeed British, Middle Eastern policies, the outright condemnation of Israel by many in France, together with recent anti-Semitic acts committed against synagogues, rabbis, and Jewish property in France, has alienated a significant percentage of the American public. There was a period in the 1980s, when, under François Mitterrand, French policy departed from this line and demonstrated sympathy for the plight of the Israelis, rejecting Arab arguments refuting Israel's right to exist. But this support was tempered by Mitterrand's calls for the creation of a Palestinian state during an address before Israel's Knesset. Not long after he left office, French policy reverted to its familiar pro-Arab tilt, and analysts speculated that the brief departure from the norm stemmed more from a generational concern, probably reflecting a residual sense of guilt about the Holocaust, and less about Arab attacks against Israel.

That said, it is possible to view French policy in another light. France has been practicing balance-of-power politics in the Middle East since its colonial days. Having carved out for itself in the nineteenth century a sphere of influence running, roughly, from Syria through Lebanon and Jordan into Iraq and down to the Persian Gulf states—with the notable exceptions of Saudi Arabia, Bahrain, Oman, and the United Arab Emirates, which tend to lean more heavily on Britain—the French have had a residual interest in the political outcome of the Israeli-Palestinian conflict. Thus, largely at French prodding, the European Union has emerged as the Palestinian Liberation Organization's (PLO)

---

91 The evidence in this regard runs the gamut from payments to the families of Hamas terrorists to culpability in the *Karine A* affair.

largest donor, and in the United Nations soundly endorsed UNSC resolution 1397 calling for the creation of a Palestinian state. The French also are supporting Saudi Crown Prince Abdullah's peace initiative to bring a negotiated settlement to the Arab-Israeli dispute, based on a formula that trades land for peace, pushing Israel to its pre-1967 borders. Alternatively, the French have also agreed to participate in a conference to try to adjudicate territorial boundaries between Israel and a Palestinian entity, if the government in Tel Aviv refuses to accept Abdullah's formula. Without question, throughout the entire period of Ariel Sharon's tenure in office, French policy has been overwhelmingly anti-Israeli, turning a blind eye to Arafat's terrorist connections and arguing that Israel must make the principal concessions in exchange for a lasting peace in the region.

Thus, it is hardly surprising that the French strongly condemned Israel's *Defensive Shield* operation, which was directed against Palestinian Authority compounds on the West Bank that were suspected of harboring terrorist activity. This French policy position was restated in the aftermath of the September 19, 2002, terrorist attacks against Tel Aviv, when the Israelis once again used military force to surround Arafat's Ramallah headquarters, in an effort to pressure the Palestinian Authority into giving up the terrorists who had taken refuge in the compound. From the French perspective, these and further Israeli military operations, undertaken outside of a political framework for a settlement of the larger issue of Palestinian statehood, will only exacerbate tensions in the region and provoke new terrorist attacks. This French position benefits French policy in numerous ways, in addition to securing access to Gulf Arab oil and good relations with Arab countries that are major trading partners of France and the European Union. In these circumstances, it is hardly surprising that the French are worried that any U.S.-led military action in Iraq will upset the status quo and harm French national interests. Indeed, many among the French elite have signed a petition urging the Chirac government to veto any U.S.- or UK-sponsored UN resolution legitimizing the use of force.

Iraq is only slightly less problematic for France than is Palestinian statehood. Without question, the French have come to appreciate U.S. concerns with respect to WMD and missile proliferation, particularly as they have the potential to bolster Saddam Hussein's Ba'athist regime in Iraq. While Frenchmen across the political spectrum proclaim no affinity for Saddam Hussein or his regime, France and Iraq have shared a close economic and political relationship in the past. France even provided Iraq with nuclear reactor technologies for the Osirik reactor that the Israelis destroyed on June 7, 1981—another factor influencing current French views of Israel. As evidence of the special relationship between France and Iraq, as operation *Desert Storm* approached, the highly nationalist defense minister at the time, Jean-Pierre Chevènement, resigned rather than support French participation in the conflict. As a left-wing nationalist republican in the Jacobin tradition, Chevènement rationalized his opposition to the operation on the grounds that it was premature and led by the United States. Like others in the French government and intellectual sector at the time, Chevènement disdained the use of force to resolve what was widely considered to be a political dispute, even though Saddam Hussein had already used force to occupy Kuwait. According to Chevènement, French national interests dictated a "normal" relationship with the regime in Baghdad.

Current French criticisms of U.S. policy vis-à-vis Iraq sound vaguely familiar. Across the political spectrum there is criticism of what is percieved as the rush to use force to impose a regime change and to establish a U.S. protectorate in oil-rich Iraq. Attacking U.S. policy head-on in the United Nations is the first line of the French offensive in support of the status quo in Iraq. It has been accompanied by a renewed French effort to lift or otherwise soften the U.S.-supported sanctions regime, and considerable interest in broadening the "oil for peace" quotas to help stave off what the French contend is a humanitarian crisis in Iraq. Notwithstanding that Saddam is siphoning off funds received for this purpose to rebuild his military machine, and that the Sunni population of the country is thriving (at the expense of the Kurds in the north and the Shi'ites in the south), the French have embarked upon a campaign to remove what they characterize as a restrictive sanctions regime. In this way, they probably hope to gain enormous favor with Saddam, not to mention with the Gulf Arabs, with whom the French lost considerable influence to the United States in the wake of the Gulf war; Paris is, however, beginning to carve out a new role—at least in the Emirates—as opposition to U.S. policies on Iraq and the war on terror, more generally, grows in the region.

Iran, on the other hand, poses no such dilemma because France regards President Khatami as a true reformer. As one French analyst recently said, "With respect to Iran, you can see light at the end of the tunnel" (Moisi 2002b). Thus, from the dominant French perspective, there is much to be gained from engaging Iran rather than making it an enemy in what will only amount to a self-fulfilled prophesy. By seeking to contain Iran, as they perceive the U.S. still attempting to do, French policy elites believe that the United States is creating an adversary where one may not exist. As the French see it, there is much room for shaping Iranian thinking and for enhancing Iran's relationships with the West, based on the yearnings of the younger generation that hungers for Western culture, democracy, and opportunities for economic engagement. The French go to great lengths to point out that the Persians are different from the Arabs and that their world view is much more compatible with that of the West, as exemplified by the offers of cooperation against Al Qaeda and their efforts to carry out political reforms.

On each of these issues, then, there is potential for confrontation with the United States. For the Bush administration, WMD proliferation is the fundamental issue affecting relations with both Iraq and Iran. It must be dealt with firmly and sooner rather than later, lest the United States risk a situation in which American freedom of action is compromised in the strategically important Persian Gulf region. Furthermore, concerns about proliferation in Iraq and Iran extend to the Palestinian issue, in two ways. First, the ability of Israel, a U.S. ally and democratic nation, to survive would be seriously compromised were rogue Arab regimes to gain access to operational weapons of mass destruction. Can anyone seriously believe that American security guarantees to Europe, Japan, and South Korea would be taken seriously by those nations if the United States turned its back on Israel? To be sure, Israel itself possesses a nuclear weapons capability, and over time has shown itself to be ready and willing to take whatever action is necessary to protect the country's security. However, a Ba'athist regime in Iraq that has access to nuclear and other weapons of mass destruction would qualitatively change the balance of power in the Middle East and undoubtedly engender broader nuclear and other weapons of mass destruction proliferation in this already unstable area. As for Iran, if it has not already started down the path to proliferation, it is a prime candidate to do so. Many in the United States believe that Iran has begun to develop nuclear capabilities, with one projection suggesting that Tehran could have an operational nuclear capability as early as 2007.[92] Like a WMD-armed Iraq, a WMD-armed Iran would pose a threat to Israel, particularly if Tehran was emboldened by its engagement with Europe.

Beyond the obvious threat to Israel's existence, the current crisis over Palestinian statehood, the suicide bombings in Israel, and the Sharon government's efforts to contain and destroy the terror have had the effect of diverting European attention from the WMD issue. From the U.S. perspective this could have very serious consequences, particularly now that the United Nations, urged on by the French and the Russians, has been prodded into accepting a new inspections regime for Iraq that gives to the secretary general and the Security Council the power to determine whether Iraq is in "material breach" of previous UNSC resolutions, notably those pertaining to its WMD disarmament. Reflecting some disappointment with the disproportionate attention that was placed on the inspections regime during the course of the UN debate over the wording of the resolution that empowered a new round of weapons inspections, the United States has long maintained, as U.S. Secretary of Defense Donald Rumsfeld observed in recent testimony before Congress, that the inspections are not an end unto themselves, but a device for attaining Iraq's disarmament (Shanker and Sanger 2002a).

The disarmament of Iraq is a goal of paramount importance for the United States, but Washington is also concerned about Iraq's pattern of flagrant violations of the UN-enforced

---

92 Dana Priest (2002) reports a U.S. Central Intelligence Agency estimate that from 2002, Iran is seven years away from having an operational nuclear capability. Israeli intelligence estimates five years. According to the article, both agree that within the next few years, Iran will have acquired enough know-how and technology to produce a long-range missile capability without further foreign assistance.

no-fly zones (NFZ) over the country. As viewed from Washington, recent challenges to U.S. and UK aircraft patrolling the NFZ skies should also be considered in this context, but for the moment they seem to have been dismissed by the majority of the international community, which remains focused on the WMD question. For the United States and its UK partner, Iraq's actions directed against the Allied pilots are more troubling evidence of the regime's defiance of international law; these very actions call into question French assumptions about the feasibility of an international order based on the rule of law in a world community that includes rogue nations and outlaw organizations such as Al Qaeda. In fact, one of the greatest fears of American analysts is that Iraq will supply Al Qaeda with, or facilitate its access to, weapons of mass destruction. This is why, particularly in the aftermath of September 11 and with increasing evidence of Al Qaeda's efforts to obtain WMD capabilities, the United States has redoubled its efforts to discover whether such a link exists. To the discomfort of most of its European allies, a recent report citing credible evidence that Iraq had transferred (nerve agent) VX stocks to Al Qaeda appears to support U.S. fears in this regard. The evidence subsequently laid out by Secretary Powell in his address before the Security Council on February 5, 2003, builds on that contention, although French officials continue to find it "unpersausive." For their part, the French continue to oppose any military intervention against Iraq, particularly an intervention that results from a unilateral U.S. decision and is divorced from an empowering UNSC mandate.

The French position on the use of force against Iraq did evolve over the fall and winter of 2002-03, maintaining that military intervention may be justified were Iraq to be found in "material breach" of UN Security Council resolutions, but only if the UNSC passed an empowering mandate crafted specifically for that purpose. "War," in the words of Jacques Chirac, "would be an admission of failure," and everything must be done to avoid it. Only after the weapons inspectors have completed their mission—an event that now is alleged to take many more months—and the Security Council has assessed their findings should a decision be taken on the use of force. That has been and continues to be the French position on Iraq.

For its part, the United States accepted the principle of going to the United Nations to get a mandate for new inspections, but it had tried to insist that the same resolution should contain a clause authorizing the use of force to compel Iraq's compliance and to ensure that the weapons inspections were unimpeded. France, of all the permanent members of the Security Council, was the most vociferous in its opposition to what it regarded as an "automatic trigger" for the American resort to force. On this basis, and mired in their own "special interests" as described above, the French engaged in a protracted effort to block U.S. action in the Security Council, with the help of Russia and China both. The resulting resolution was a mixed bag for both France and the United States, with diplomats in Paris getting Security Council agreement on the need for a two-step process before UN consideration of the use of force, but not agreement on the French position that the UNSC had to pass a second resolution calling for the use of force before the U.S. could take action, if Saddam is found to be in "material breach." Even as President Bush warned that the United States would invoke its right to use force against Iraq if there is no Security Council consensus on the way ahead after Hans Blix's January 27, 2003, report, the Bush administration nevertheless sought to placate its critics by once again taking its case to the United Nations, this time revealing previously classified intelligence pointing to Iraq's efforts to mislead and subvert the weapons inspection process mandated by UNSC 1441. Because of the centrality of these developments to the future of the French-American relationship, a closer look is warranted.

Iraq and the Use of Force to Compel Compliance

For some time now, the United States and France have pursued different approaches to Iraq. Ever since the Gulf war, the French have been highly critical of the U.S. over-reliance on military means to coerce the Iraqi leadership to cease and desist on issues ranging from their use of chemical weapons against the Kurds in the north of the country to enforcement of the no-fly zones by U.S. and UK aircraft. The French, in contrast, have been willing to enter into negotiations with the regime on issues of mutual concern, and more recently have expressed a willingness to spearhead a campaign to get the post-*Desert Storm* sanctions lifted, because, as the French

Chronology of UN Resolutions on Iraq

1991

March 3	Safwan Accord ending hostilities signed.
April 3	UNSCOM established.
April 23	UNSC passed resolution 687 requring Iraq to end its WMD programs, recognize Kuwait, return POWs and property, and end support for international terrorism.
August 15	UNSC passed resolution 707, calling on Iraq to comply with weapons inspections and to make full discolsures of its WMD capabilities.
October 11	UNSC passed resolution 715 establishing a long-term weapons monitoring program.

1996

June 12	UNSC passed resolution 1060, demanding Iraq's full compliance with UNSCOM.

1997

June 21	UNSC passed resolution 1115, which threatened to impose travel restrictions on Iraq's government officials.
October 23	UNSC passed resolution 1134, banning consideration of lifting of sanctions against Iraq until compliance is verified.
October 29	Iraq barred American UNSCOM inspectors from conducting weapons inspections.
November 12	UNSC imposed travel restrictions on Iraqi government officials.

1998

February 23	UN secretary general brokered a compromise that allowed UNSCOM to resume work, but exempted inspections of "presidential sites."
August 3	Iraq barred UNSCOM from inspecting any new sites.
August 14	U.S. Congress passed a resolution declaring Iraq to be in "material breach" of the cease-fire terms.
September 9	UNSC adopted resolution 1194, suspending any review of the sanctions.
October 30	UNSC offered Baghdad another chance to comply, but Iraq refused and suspended "all cooperation" with UNSCOM.
November 15	UNSC passed resolution 1205 condemning Iraq's actions and called them a violation of the February 1998 compromise.
December 15	Iraq refused to comply with UNSCOM, and the inspection team withdrew from the country.
December 16	U.S. and UK initiated operation *Desert Fox* to compel Iraq's compliance with all UNSC resolutions.

1999

December 17	UNSC passed resolution 1284, creating UNMOVIC and offering Iraq sanctions relief if it allowed inspections to resume.

2002

November 8	UNSC passed resolution 1441, mandating the return of the weapons inspectors to Baghdad on November 18.
December 7	Iraq presented to Hans Blix an accounting of its WMD stocks, capabilities, and facilties.
December 19	UNSC members received UNMOVIC's initial assessment of Iraq's weapons declarations.

2003

January 27	Hans Blix delivered his report to the UNSC.
February 24	U.S./UK draft resolution concerning Iraq's compliance with UNSC 1441.

explain, they are having a negative impact on public opinion "on the Arab street." When Iraq blocked the activities of the UN weapons inspectors in 1998, the United States worried that this was in aid of their resumption of covert WMD programs. In response, the United States and the United Kingdom launched an air campaign over Iraq to try to force compliance on WMD disarmament. France, too, expressed concerns in this regard, but it refused to participate in *Desert Fox* and instead sought to reinvigorate established arms control mechanisms (in particular, the MTCR and the Nuclear Suppliers Group) to constrain Iraq's ability to obtain weapons components and other WMD materials.

Unfortunately, the pattern of technology transfers between Iraq, on the one hand, and Russia and China, on the other, continued, and there appears to be substantial evidence that Saddam Hussein's regime has resorted to deception and covert initiatives to resume development of its WMD programs. A number of articles have been written in the popular and professional media supporting this contention. One article in the popular press that has received considerable attention is David Rose's "Iraq's Arsenal of Terror," in the May 2002 issue of *Vanity Fair*. The author, using interviews from Iraqi defectors, lays out a chilling picture of the breadth of Iraq's WMD and missile programs, all of which have benefited from Saddam's 1998 expulsion of the UN weapons inspectors from the United Nations Special Commission (UNSCOM), the UN program designed to prevent Iraq's development of these types of capabilities. The article weaves a telling story of Iraq's deception efforts in this regard, and of its use of front companies to evade Western sanctions and intelligence-gathering. Specific sites are identified where, Rose's sources contend, Iraq is developing and testing WMD technologies. These allegations are corroborated in the professional and academic literature, where, for example, Richard Butler, the former head of UNSCOM, illuminates Iraq's deception programs to conceal its covert WMD activities in his 2000 work, *The Greatest Threat: Iraq, Weapons of Mass Destruction, and the Crisis of Global Security* (262). In *The Greatest Threat*, Butler contends that Saddam is "building—building weapons, as are other rogue states" (2000, 242).

Similarly, Kenneth Pollack, a former CIA analyst and member of the National Security Council during the Clinton administration, writing in his book, *The Threatening Storm* (2002), lays out a case for attacking Iraq now, before Saddam can operationalize a nuclear weapons capability, which would, according to Pollack, have devastating consequences for regional stability.[93] In Pollack's words, "It is clear that Saddam sees nuclear weapons as being in a category by themselves and that if he has a nuclear weapon the world will have to treat him differently" (2002, 178). Pollack then goes on to describe the extent of Saddam's WMD programs and the measures that he has taken to keep them concealed, so as not to alienate Iraq's traditional "friends," the French included. None of this, however, justifies a military intervention, particularly since the level of juridical proof is questionable and subject to interpretation, or so contend the French.

So, too, the French contend, Secretary Powell's case linking Iraq to Al Qaeda is circumstantial. French analysts, more generally, speculate that it would be very unlikely for Iraq to share its nuclear technologies with Al Qaeda, since the secular government in Baghdad and the fundamentalist organization hold different operating philosophies and fundamental objectives. Those holding to this view clearly reject the U.S. contention that Iraq is trying to benefit from Al Qaeda's hatred of the West by giving to the terrorists sanctuary as well as access to WMD assets, especially chemical or biological weapons, that could be used against the United States or U.S. operational forces. In so doing, Saddam may hope, as Pollack contends, to enhance his ability to forestall defeat, or at the very least, to ensure that any American victory could come with a high price tag. Pollack also observes the operational importance of Israel's preemptive attack on the Osirik nuclear reactor in 1981, assessing that in light of what we have learned since, "the operation looks like eminent good sense and may have saved the lives of millions of people" (2002, 369). With this in mind, the United States decided to make public the evidence of Iraq's complicity with the

---

93 Pollack goes on to write, "Once he (Saddam) has acquired a nuclear weapon, he believes that he will be able to deter the United States and Israel under all circumstances except if he were to launch his own nuclear strike against them. He also believes that with nuclear weapons he could largely disregard the United Nations' demands and bully most of the regional states to ignore the sanctions altogether" (2002, 179).

terrorists in order to give substance to its belief that Al Qaeda may be able to mount an even more devastating attack using WMD provided by Saddam's regime.[94] For most of Europe, and the French in particular, it is essential not only that such a link be established, but also that the evidence be incontrovertible before they will consider mandating the use of force against Iraq. Without such proof, the French hold that U.S. action against Iraq is unjustified and outside the scope of action for the war against terrorism. While the French do concede concern over Iraq's prospective development of chemical and, more worrisome, biological weapons, they are generally complacent about nuclear weapons, undoubtedly because officials believe that Baghdad's nuclear program was effectively dismantled by the UN inspections and subsequently abandoned. According to French officials, Saddam's B/CW capabilities are being developed "in small laboratories in other parts of the Middle East, and pose a management problem rather than a cataclysmic challenge" (Evans-Pritchard 2002).

From this, French officials, as reflected in Villepin's response to Secretary Powell's UN presentation, remain to be convinced that a show of force over Iraq is justified. In his remarks, Villepin sought to dilute the U.S. case by asserting that "the absense of long-range delivery systems reduces the potential threat" of Iraq's chemical and biological weapons. He also went on to dismiss U.S. concerns about Iraq's nuclear weapons programs, though he did suggest a need "to clarify" Iraq's attemps to acquire those aluminum tubes that Secretary Powell singled out as a "material breach" of previous UNSC disarmament resolutions.[95] The preferred French strategy for doing so was to expand the process by introducing more UN weapons inspectors into Iraq. If this approach fails, France signalled that then it would consider the use of force, but only under a UN mandate to do so.

The French position on Iraq is telling, and reveals the extent to which the French government is prepared to go to protect French national interests, even to the point of compromising their "principles" relating to the legitimacy of the United Na-

---

94 See, for example, Jeffrey Goldberg (2002) and Stephen Hayes (2002).
95 According to Foreign Minister Villepin, "In the nuclear area, we need to fully clarify any attempt by Iraq to acquire aluminum tubes. This is a *démarche* which is difficult, but it is anchored in resolution 1441, which we should conduct together" (2003).

tions. As Pollack points out, in 2000, "when Iraq began demanding that countries fly commercial aircraft into Baghdad in violation of the U.N. flight ban in return for further oil-for-food contracts, Paris suddenly discovered a new 'interpretation' of the U.N. resolutions that indicated that there was no such flight ban—even though it had voted for the original resolution and had respected the ban for the preceding ten years" (Pollack 2002, 204). As one of Iraq's largest trading partners, France was still owed upwards of $4.5 billion from pre-*Desert Storm* arms sales. Further, since the implementation of the UN-directed oil-for-food program, designed to alleviate the suffering of the Iraqi people but being manipulated by Saddam for his own purposes (including to promote Iraq's military modernization and its WMD activities, in defiance of UN intentions), French commercial interests have received the lion's share of Iraq's oil-for-food contracts. Pollack characterizes French policy in this regard as "shameless pandering" (2002, 204). Others, including Henry Kissinger, see it as a "test case for another French effort to define a European defense identity distinct from and in opposition to the United States" (Kissinger 2001, 194).

By focusing attention on the "plight of the Iraqi people," and taking the spotlight off of U.S. disarmament concerns, the French have rather successfully, with the aid and support of Russia and China, moved the focus of the UN debate on Iraq, and in doing so, have sought to discredit the American position on Saddam's WMD activities. They have also, in that context, worked to ensure that it is incumbent upon the UN to prove a negative, namely that Iraq has not complied with previous UN resolutions, instead of demanding evidence of Iraq's compliance with UN dictates. This, together with a weaker mandate for the weapons inspections (than that originally contained in UNSC 687 empowering UNSCOM), and with no senior-level American inspectors in the delegation (to challenge either Hans Blix or the Iraqis), virtually guarantees a less aggressive inspections regime, and hence a significantly lower probability of success in rooting out Saddam's most dangerous WMD programs.

Most likely it was just this type of pre-determined outcome that was uppermost in the mind of President Chirac, when, in late January 2003, he and his German counterpart, Chancellor Gehard Schroeder, ruled out participation by their respective armed forces in a military action against Iraq. Since then, and as Chancellor Schroeder's domestic position has eroded, the French appear to be waffling on this issue, with Villepin at the UN proclaiming the use of force to be "a final recourse," and Chirac dispatching the aircraft carrier *Charles de Gaulle* to the Mediterranean to cover a prospective operational contingency, though he still refused to say whether France will commit forces to a military action, even if it is specifically endorsed by a new UN Security Council resolution. That said, most observers of the French scene assume that France would grudgingly join a U.S.-led operation rather than be left on the sidelines, particularly if it meant a say in the disposition of post-Saddam Iraq's power structure. However, by leaving their options open, the French obviously have to prevail no matter what ultimately happens. If they can forestall American action by extending the inspections or by blocking a second UNSC resolution on the use of force, then their immediate interests will be served. Alternatively, if the United States acts outside of a UNSC mandate, or if it manages to convince the Security Council to pass a use-of-force resolution, the French can jump on board at the last moment and therein secure their position in a post-conflict peace settlement. Either way, the French may reason that they cannot lose, except perhaps in their relationship with the United States, which is fast losing patience with its recalcitrant ally.

To all appearances, France's position on military action against Iraq is based on a narrow interpretation of international law and the broadest possible support for a United Nations mandate for further action. The United States, on the other hand, has argued that ample legal authority already exists, based first on UNSC resolution 678, adopted in 1990, which gave member states the right, under Chapter 7, to use "all necessary means" to restore peace and stability in the region.[96] In a powerful address before

---

96 Apart from UNSC resolution 678, UNSC resolution 687, adopted on April 3, 1991, established, among other provisions, the creation of the United Nations Special Commission (UNSCOM) designed to enforce Iraqi compliance with international treaties dealing with ballistic missiles and weapons of mass destruction development. In 1998, the government of Iraq refused compliance with UNSCOM inspections, and in November of that year finally ejected the inspectors from the country. In December, the United Nations adopted UNSC resolution 1284, creating the United Nations Monitoring, Verification, and Inspection Commission (UNMOVIC) to replace UNSCOM. At the same time, largely at French insistence, it also provided for a partial lifting of the sanctions on Iraq, expressly for humanitarian purposes, although it has subsequently been demonstrated that some of this aid and the proceeds from the oil exports authorized under this provision have been siphoned off for use in military projects.

the UN General Assembly on September 12, 2002, President Bush carefully catalogued the case against Iraq, referring to the sixteen UNSC resolutions that had been passed and violated by Saddam's regime. As President Bush stated:

> The conduct of the Iraqi regime is a threat to the authority of the United Nations, and a threat to peace. Iraq has answered a decade of UN demands with a decade of defiance. All the world now faces a test, and the United Nations a difficult and defining moment. Are Security Council resolutions to be honored and enforced, or cast aside without consequence? Will the United Nations serve the purpose of its founding, or will it be irrelevant?

Since the Gulf war, Iraq's repeated violations of UN resolutions, in particular its expulsion of the weapons inspectors in 1998, are enough to justify the use of force, including for the purpose of regime change, or so argue two Washington lawyers, Lee A. Casey and David B. Rivkin, in a very persuasive article published in the *Wall Street Journal* on September 25, 2002. The French, on the other hand, contend that the use of force now, some eleven years after the cease-fire, is not automatically authorized by UNSC resolution 678, much less for the purpose of regime change, which has been the outcome that the Bush administration desires.

While French government officials are not opposed per se to ending Saddam's reign of terror, indeed, according to President Chirac, they would welcome it, they nevertheless are insistent that regime change through outside intervention should not be the objective of UN actions.[97] For the French, the issue should not be framed around the objective of regime change, but rather whether the United States acts without UN authorization to enforce Iraq's WMD disarmament.

For its part, the United States claims that it does not need UN approval before it can act, based on Iraq's past actions, its violations of international law (e.g., creation of a smuggling regime to augment oil exports, challenges to NFZ operations, and the use of chemical weapons against its own minorities),

---

97 In his *New York Times* interview, Chirac also said that he personally would like to see a new Iraq government, and he called Saddam Hussein "a man who is especially dangerous to his own people." At the same time, he said, "I am totally against unilateralism in the modern world," and implied that American military action against Iraq threatened to destroy the "international coalition formed to fight terrorism in Afghanistan and accentuate what he called rising anti-Americanism and anti-Western sentiment in developing countries" (Chirac 2002b).

and its prospective threat to regional stability. As pointed out in a *New York Times* opinion piece by Fletcher School professor Michael Glennon, the United States is not the first nation to contest the role of the United Nations in assessing the need to use force in accordance with the UN Charter. According to Glennon, "Since 1945, dozens of [UN] member states have engaged in well over 100 inter-state conflicts that have killed millions of people" (2002).[98] For example, NATO used force to compel Milosevic over Kosovo without recourse to a use-of-force mandate from the United Nations. Even as France, at the time, had warned against such use without a UN mandate, France, itself, on numerous occasions and especially in Africa, did the same when its national interests were at risk. Thus, while it may be politically useful to obtain UN endorsement, the French are less than honest when they try to portray the United States as the "rogue hyper-power," because it chooses to reserve for itself the right "to decide whether or not action is required."

Perhaps recognizing their own complicity in the erosion of international consensus on the "rule of law," the French have also been careful to couch many of their arguments against the use of force in Iraq on the premise that as a sovereign state, Iraq is entitled to define its own governmental structures and leadership. Presumably, this also extends to Saddam's regime, whose legitimacy can only be challenged by the Iraqi people themselves. This helps to explain why, after *Desert Storm*, the French were opposed to regime change in Baghdad, and now their position with respect to the intervention of the United Nations to try to enforce Iraq's compliance with Resolution 1441's disarmament objectives. The French are very uncomfortable with the proposition of violating Iraq's sovereignty, even though to do so would inevitably alleviate the suffering of the Iraqi people, especially its Shi'ite and Kurdish minorities. Quite clearly the concept of national sovereignty is a value that many in France must uphold at all costs, especially when it corresponds to

---

98 According to Glennon, "This record of violation is legally significant. The international legal system is voluntary and states are bound only by rules to which they consent. A treaty can lose its binding effect if a sufficient number of parties engage in conduct that is at odds with the constraints of the treaty. The consent of United Nations member states to the general prohibition against the use of force, as expressed in the Charter, has in this way been supplanted by a changed intent as expressed in deeds ... It seems the Charter has, tragically, gone the way of the 1928 Kellogg-Briand Pact which purported to outlaw war and was signed by every major belligerent in World War II" (2002).

French interests, which also depend very heavily on the status quo. In other words, as viewed in Paris, regime change in Iraq, more than a decade after the end of the Gulf war, requires an international consensus that Saddam has forfeited his protections of sovereignty under the law. Regime change, brought about by an American use of force, inevitably would cause France to lose its preferred position in Iraq, and place into doubt the repayment of the country's pre-*Desert Storm* debt and its post-*Desert Storm* contracts.

As discussed earlier, the issue of a mandate for crisis interventions outside of Europe and in Europe beyond the confines of the NATO treaty area has long been a matter of great contention between the United States and France. Emerging initially in the context of intervention in the Balkan crises throughout the 1990s, the issue has taken on new significance amid talk of military intervention in Iraq. As with NATO action in non-Article 5 crises, the French believe that an empowering political mandate is required before the United States intervenes in Iraq, otherwise it risks setting a precedent that would be "extraordinarily dangerous ... As soon as one nation claims the right to take preventive action, other countries will naturally do the same" (Chirac 2002c). Were the United States to act without an explicit UN mandate specific to this particular situation, the French allege that the U.S. action would give other nations free license to do the same. In particular, the French believe that without a separate, second UN mandate, following one providing for the return of the weapons inspectors, the United States in effect has legitimized Russian intervention in Chechnya and may be setting up a basis for the leadership in Moscow to justify military action against Georgia.

Until quite recently, the official French position on Chechnya conveniently ignored the fact that, whatever one's view of Russia's brutality, Chechnya is a constituent part of the Russian Federation. Over the summer of 2002, however, this French position subtly changed, in a rather transparent effort to engage Putin's Russia in a security dialogue that marginalizes the United States. Thus, during his July 2002 visit to Sotchi to meet with Vladimir Putin, President Chirac proclaimed that "France unreservedly condemns any terrorist act, of any kind, and believes that no cause can justify terrorist acts" (Chirac 2002d). In retreating from France's former sharp criticisms of Russia's policy toward Chechnya and by offering to explore alternatives to the EU's desire that Lithuania and Poland put in place a system of formal controls to monitor the movement of Russian nationals into and out of Kaliningrad, Chirac undoubtedly has hopes of forging a special relationship with Russia and using it to curb American efforts to engage with Russia, without EU participation, on issues ranging from Iraq to European security.

At the Sotchi meeting, Chirac also endeavored to attract Putin's support for the French position on Iraq, and in a subsequent meeting between the two countries' foreign ministers, the French sought a Russian pledge to veto the American and British Security Council resolution identifying Iraq as being in "material breach" of previous UNSC resolutions and authorizing the use of force if a new round of UN weapons inspections proved that case or were the subject of Iraqi interference or non-compliance. What the French may have feared most was an American effort to stage an end run on the UNSC by co-opting Russian acquiescence on Iraq. Superpower condominium, as it was termed in the decade of the 1980s, provided a rallying point for the French in the European Union, and now with respect to Iraq.

However, over the past several months, Russian intransigence on a number of strategic issues in Moscow's relationship with the United States creates doubts about the validity of such a condominium being established. First, there was Russia's agreement to supply Iran with additional reactor technologies, beyond those already being delivered to Bushehr. Then, there was the negotiation of an economic agreement between Russia and Iraq, worth about $40 billion. Finally, in 2001, Russia welcomed Kim Jong-il in Vladivostok, to the consternation of the United States. These initiatives, targeted at the "axis of evil" states, certainly have an economic origin, but they also may be intended to demonstrate that Russia is an independent actor, with strategic interests that are different from those of the United States. For the French, Russian disappointment with the tangible, and pragmatic, results of Putin's rapprochement with the United States opens the door for the French to walk through and press upon Moscow their insistence on support for Chirac's Iraq initiatives. In this sense, as in other areas, French policy is intended to outflank the United States in its attempt to circumvent the machinery of the United Nations, illustrating very clearly the zero-sum nature of U.S. and French policy approaches to Iraq.

That said, it is evident that Washington undoubtedly would prefer to obtain the blessing of the Security Council before commencing action against Saddam and his regime. However, in the current international climate this may not be feasible, even if the French were to abstain from voting. Practically, with the membership of the UN Security Council composed of five permanent members (the United States, the Peoples' Republic of China, France, the United Kingdom, and Russia), and ten rotating members,[99] the United States could attempt to get a use-of-force resolution, although it will have to persuade skeptical members and counter French efforts to promote the Franco-German initiative to deploy additional weapons inspectors to Iraq. This is certain to protract UN debate and, in the process, raise a fundamental question about the organization's future relevance if it refuses to back up with force previous UNSC resolutions mandating Iraq's compliance and disarmament. That said, the gaps and inconsistencies in Iraq's initial weapons declarations are just as troubling to the French as they are to the United States, but they are not enough to justify a *casus belli*, according to French officials. All of the members of the Security Council have a responsibility to avoid war and, on this basis, further attempts to defuse the crisis must be considered before mandating any use of force.

For its part, the United States holds that the French position establishes a dangerous precedent for flouting international law—precisely the obverse of what the French maintain that they hope to achieve by arguing for time to extend the weapons inspection process. In the words of John Chipman, director of the International Institute for Strategic Studies in London, the practical effect of arguments in support of this

---

99   The ten rotating members of the UNSC currently are Bulgaria, Cameroon, Guinea, Mexico, and Syria, whose terms end in 2003; Angola, Chile, Germany, Pakistan, and Spain, whose terms end in 2004. Conceivably, from this group, the United States could find the necessary eight nations to support its position, but a veto from any one of the permanent members would forestall a vote, and the mandate issue would not get off the ground.

position "suggests that an outlaw state has only to engage in a diplomatic war of attrition to be released from its legal obligations and be freed from the threat of military action to enforce compliance with UN legislation passed in an effort to end hostilities" (Chipman 2002).[100]

Without question, Iraq has pursued such a strategy, all the while flaunting its non-compliance with successive UN resolutions aimed at monitoring, verifying, and destroying its ongoing WMD programs. For years after the terms of the cease-fire were spelled out, the leadership of Iraq systematically resisted and undermined UN weapons inspections, and in 1998, it finally ejected the UNSCOM inspectors from the country over a contrived incident involving the inspection of so-called presidential sites.[101] In response, the United States and the United Kingdom, relying on UNSC resolution 678 authorizing the use of force to compel Iraq's compliance with the UN weapons inspections, initiated military operations, designated *Desert Fox*. The military operation, which involved the use of U.S. cruise missiles, lasted for four days. The Americans and the British justified their action on the basis of UNSC resolution 687, which was passed under Chapter 7 of the United Nations Charter and dealt with Iraq's non-compliance with the UN-mandated operations of the weapons inspectors, constituted under UNSCOM, which was chartered specifically to deal with this issue. France, which condemned Iraq's actions, both with respect to the weapons inspectors and to the military's increasingly aggressive stance in challenging Allied pilots enforcing the no-fly zones over Iraq, nevertheless refused to participate in the operation and justified its position on the grounds that there had been no

---

100 Chipman goes on to note, "It would penalize states that had exercised restraint and chosen the path of negotiation by denying them recourse to the use of force to buttress international law, and strengthen diplomacy and meet an emerging threat, once diplomacy had failed" (2002).

101 Richard Butler makes this point clearly in *The Greatest Threat* (2000). In the foreword, which documents UNSCOM's efforts and struggles in relation to Iraq, Butler writes, "The failure of the world community to deal effectively with Saddam Hussein—a man determined at all costs to obtain, stockpile, and if possible, make use of weapons of mass destruction in pursuit of his personal and political goals—is a profound one, constituting a crisis in the management of global security" (xxii). Elsewhere, in commenting on the effectiveness of the UN Security Council to deal with this threat, Butler observes, "Three permanent members of the Security Council ... have decided to end any serious effort to disarm Saddam, to oblige him to conform with the law. Russia, France, and China have done this because they prefer to pursue their own national interests rather than to carry out their international responsibility" (xvi).

new UNSC mandate for action after the expulsion of the UNSCOM inspectors.

At the heart of French and American differences over the weapons inspections are divergent U.S. and French views of the utility of either the United Nations or multilateral arms control frameworks in controlling state behaviors, especially with respect to states that flout UN disarmament directives. As the Bosnia experience clearly showed, UN peacekeepers were ineffective in carrying out successive UNSC mandates, not to mention their inabiltiy to deter agression against the UN-designated safe havens. For their part, Americans are reluctant to waste any more time by trying to gain Iraq's acceptance for an inspection regime that is dependent upon Baghdad's total compliance, which is doubtful at best. Viewing arms control as essential for stability in the broader Middle Eastern region, the French contend that a less than perfect inspection regime is better than having none at all. This quite clearly accords with their position that France's only objective is to obtain Iraqi compliance with Security Council resolutions, in particular with resolution 687; regime change has never been on their agenda, in part because of apprehension over its impact on broader regional stability.

Furthermore, the French remain extremely critical of what they perceive as a lack of vision on the part of the United States with respect to the endgame in Iraq and in the Persian Gulf region more broadly. Like their criticisms of the U.S. involvement in Bosnia and Kosovo, the French complain that the American propensity to rely on military power as the premier crisis management tool fails to address the fundamental issues underlying Iraqi behavior, and while it might provide a quick fix, the longer-term concerns will remain unresolved. Paradoxically, there is a nagging suspicion on the part of some French analysts that contrary to what is generally believed, the United States does have a long-term strategy for Iraq, and that includes gaining access to the country's oil reserves. Notable French experts on the Middle East contend that "the installation of a pro-American regime in Baghdad would enable [the United States] to kill two birds with one stone" (Barochez 2002a). Not only will the United States gain unprecedented access to Iraq's oil reserves, which would offset Saudi Arabia's unpredictability as a U.S. ally, but by installing a pro-American regime in Baghdad, it has the potential to "disarm the opposition to a settlement of the Palestine question in accordance with Israel's interests" (Barochez 2002a).

Others in France are less certain of America's long-term commitment to the region, although they, too, tend to believe that a major motivating factor behind the U.S. penchant for military action is, indeed, access to Iraq's oil wealth. Still, they question the staying power of the United States and contend that post-Saddam Hussein, a major effort at nation building will be required to hold the country together and to ensure that a dangerous power vacuum does not emerge in this volatile region. In this respect, many in French policy circles believe that absent a ten- to twenty-year commitment—similar to that taken on by the United States after World War II in Japan and Germany—Iraq could very well implode into three entities, with the Kurds in the north declaring independence, the Shi'ites in the south reuniting with Iran, and the Sunni middle of the country forming a rump state. The French fear that in the aftermath of American action, when U.S. forces are withdrawn from Iraq, they and their EU partners will have no option but to intervene to fill the resulting power vacuum and provide support for rebuilding the country.

Lessons Learned from *Enduring Freedom* for French Military Interventions

To make matters worse, EU capabilities are not yet established to take on a major post-conflict role in Iraq, with the Helsinki Headline Goal of creating a European Rapid Reaction Force of sixty thousand not scheduled to be met before 2003 at the earliest. Without the cover of the ERRF, the French, by themselves, are far less prepared than the British to implement peacekeeping operations—at least on the scale that is likely to be required in Iraq. Peacekeeping aside, French forces have demonstrated difficulties in operating in a coalition framework as well, raising frustrations for all parties when it comes to operational deployments. In part this is the result of France's prolonged absence from NATO's integrated command structure, and the operational consequence of de Gaulle's political decision to emphasize French autonomy in defense decision-making. But it also relates to France's failure to keep up with defense investments, especially in the area of equipment modernization. Even as the Chirac-Raffarin government has decided to raise defense spending, as noted earlier, there is no guarantee that spending increases in the defense sector can be sustained, given structural weaknesses in the French economy that include an ambitious social welfare program, a strong labor union movement, and high unemployment rates, particularly in the French youth population. So, in one sense, France is no better off than many of the other NATO allies, although psychologically the French consider themselves to be "special" in this regard, probably because of their nuclear deterrent power.

It is true that France, like many other U.S. allies, offered to contribute to the U.S.-led operations in Afghanistan. The offer was declined, very likely because French participation would have caused more problems than it was worth, if the U.S. experiences in Bosnia and Kosovo serve as an example. Moreover, the nature of the war against Al Qaeda and the Taliban was assessed to demand the ultimate in flexibility and, in truth, very few Allied forces or contingents are capable of improvising when it comes to operational adjustments. Still, the United States did move back from its original impulse to conduct the operations alone, or at most with its UK and Australian allies, and invited those nations that had volunteered to send representatives to the headquarters of U.S. Central Command at Tampa to help plan and participate in the International Security and Assistance Force (ISAF), the humanitarian assistance mission. For a proud nation like France, this was hardly satisfying, but without the requisite capabilities, there was little else for French forces to do, except in the areas of intelligence collection and combat strikes during operation *Anaconda*. In these areas in particular, French forces were employed with their U.S. counterparts, and for the most part they have done very well together, but on a larger scale, French forces still are unable to mount operations on a scale with the British.

In this respect, it is instructive that during the opening stages of operations against the Taliban and Al Qaeda in Afghanistan, the French had difficulty in deploying forces to the region. French officials note in this context that it took the *Charles de Gaulle*, France's one nuclear-powered aircraft

The French Contribution to Enduring Freedom

Operation *Hercules*

Task Force 473

1 aircraft carrier (with 16 *Super-Étendards,*
   2 *Hawkeyes,* and 5 or 7 *Rafales*)
1 air defense frigate
2 anti-submarine frigates
1 nuclear-attack submarine
1 tanker/supply ship

Mine Warfare Group

1 mobile support ship
2 minesweepers
2 maritime patrol aircraft, based at Djibouti
2 *Mirage-IVs* (reconnaissance and observation)
1 *Transall Gabriel* (electromagnetic intelligence)
1 research and experimentation ship (intelligence)

Special Forces and Intelligence Personnel

2 companies of the 21st RIMA (230 personnel)
   at Mazar-i-Sharif
1 GTO (60 personnel and 2 C-160s) at Dushanbe
6 *Mirage* 2000-Ds at Manas
2 C-135s (tanker aircraft) at Manas
460 personnel at Manas

Operation *Pamir*

1 battalion consisting of elements of the 21st RIMA,
the 17th RGP, and the COS (some 513 personnel)
at Kabul (French participation in the International
Security Assistance Force)

carrier, more than a month to mobilize for an operational deployment in the Arabian Sea area. During that time, repairs had to be made to the vessel, so that it did not reach Persian Gulf waters before December 19, more than a month after the start of operations. Moreover, negotiations between France and Northern Alliance commanders over the roles and missions of French forces in Afghanistan stalled the deployment of 240 French soldiers. Part of the reason for this delay was the Jospin government's ambivalent stand on the Northern Alliance. In addition, French forces were late in deploying to operational sites near Mazar-i-Sharif to prepare for the arrival of humanitarian aid. The reason for this was a disagreement with Uzbekistan, the staging area for these French forces, over the precise French role. That said, during operation *Anaconda* in March 2002, six French *Mirage* jets based in Kyrgyzstan, together with sixteen *Super-Etendard* aircraft based on the *Charles de Gaulle,* struck thirty-one targets, the only non-U.S. aircraft to have conducted strike operations in Afghanistan. In addition, French special forces provided important support to U.S.-led counter-terrorist operations in the mountains of Afghanistan. Beyond these deployments, the French have approximately 500 soldiers participating in the International Security and Assistance Force in Kabul, and additional soldiers to support airbase operations at Manas, Kyrgyzstan, and Dushanbe, Tajikistan. French deployments to Mazar-i-Sharif ended in February 2002; French forces stationed in Kyrgyzstan departed the region in October 2002 and were replaced by troops from Denmark, the Netherlands, and Norway.

During the Gulf war, the French also had difficulty in mobilizing forces for deployment to the Gulf region, but that was largely due to the constraints imposed by their conscription-based force structure and an inability to find suitable numbers of volunteers to mobilize complete units. When they eventually were able to find sufficient forces (i.e., elements of the 6th Armored Division) for deployment to the theater, they had to be deployed with the U.S. 18th Airborne Corps to provide the political cover for the fact that this coalition partner could not keep up with the American advance. While the technology gap between French and American forces was an issue, of greater concern to American military planners were the political constraints surrounding the employment of French forces. There was also a profound difference between American and French operational philosophies, with the French appearing to be "alarmingly laissez-faire" about detailed planning, and the need for blitzkrieg-paced operations. During the campaign to take Al Salman, for example, French forces, led by Brigadier Bernard Janvier—who was later to become the UNPROFOR commander in Bosnia—ordered French forces to laager for the night, before the objective was taken, even though it was in sight and at least two hours of daylight remained. Frustrated at Draquet's (the Young Deer Division) slow pace throughout the campaign, the American commander of the 82nd Airborne, Major General Jim Johnson had, in mid-February, offered to take the town on his own. His offer was rejected by then-Lieutenant General Gary Luck, commander of the 18th Airborne Corps, because the French would have been left without a role, and this was politically infeasible. Thus, on February 24, 1991, French forces initiated the attack, but not without crucial supporting fire from the Americans. As Janvier later lamented, "Everything worked against our movement: the spreading out of units, a dense night, violent sandstorms, and rain. . . The difficult terrain resulted in multiple flat tires" (Atkinson 1993, 383, 433-37).

Since the Gulf war, the French government has abandoned conscription and has created a professional army, precisely to get around the problems that plagued French deployments during *Desert Storm*. However, defense modernization was viewed as a secondary priority for Lionel Jospin's government, leading President Chirac to observe, in his Bastille Day 2002 press conference in Paris shortly after his successful bid for a second term, "For some time we have failed to keep up with the United Kingdom in defense efforts, and this has consequences as regards our political power among European countries." President Chirac's identification of the United Kingdom's armed forces as a model for French defense planning is instructive, for it clearly draws a connecting line between military power and the political currency that is derived from that power. In this context, then, it is plausible to suggest that French criticisms of American unilateralism stem more from envy of U.S. military capabilities and the capacity of the United States to back up its policy initiatives with the use of force, if need be, than from a fundamental disagreement over the use of force to backstop political directives. This is why, as pointed out earlier, the French are determined to join the "cruise missile club," and why, as well, they retain nuclear weapons, are blocking reforms of the UN Security Council (either to support Germany's application as a permanent member or to give up its seat to allow for one rotating EU seat), and have decided to procure a second nuclear-powered aircraft carrier to enhance the operational flexibility of French forces.

That said, the fact remains that the French and the Americans have a fundamental disagreement on how the use of force should be applied in specific conflict scenarios. This was an issue during *Desert Storm*, and it practically paralyzed operations over Kosovo at one point. More recently, during operation *Enduring Freedom*, after France had asked to be part of the coalition, French forces failed to carry out some of their assigned missions, "due to differences of evaluation with the Americans on their potential impact" (Isnard 2002a). According to French sources, French aircraft, operating with those of the United States near Gardez, had to have each target validated by French authorities in the president's and the prime minister's offices. Most of the targets that were rejected were so-called targets of opportunity for which there had been no advance planning. The reasons given for refusing to strike these targets varied from their posing a significant risk to civilian populations to imprecise intelligence about the target in question.

In their increasing criticism of U.S. actions since September 11, the French contend that the United States is acting as though it had a blank check to intervene anywhere in its war against terror. In a very telling statement, former French Foreign Minister Hubert Vedrine commented, "What characterizes American power currently is that it manifests itself from aircraft carriers to CNN, in Hollywood, the universities, the dollar, the economy, technology, the armed forces, and so on" (Vedrine 2002a). French influence in all these areas has faded to a vestige of France's past glory. This fact notwithstanding, France still perceives the world according to a paradigm that accentuates French *exceptionalisme* but fails to take into account that this paradigm is a legacy of a past that can no longer be recreated. Predictably, the result is a country that is badly out of step with its transatlantic partner, and one that consistently tries to save face by criticizing the strategies and policies of the United States.

That said, there have been suggestions that French policy is open to change, now that the experience of the last cohabitation government is in the past. President Chirac is said to be much more interested in working with the United States than was his former prime minister, Lionel Jospin, who was widely regarded as anti-American. However, as events of the winter of 2003 have demonstrated, the French remain difficult partners and reluctant U.S. allies. To win their support will not be easy, and a growing body of American decision-makers are not convinced that the time required is worth the trouble. Patient diplomacy on the part of the United States and a willingness to listen to French concerns and suggestions are required, as is a French willingness to bend when necessary, to sustain something far more important than its presumption of world power—that is, to know who its friends are and how they deserve to be treated, in the face of a pernicious, and shared, threat. There is no question that most French officials would welcome the downfall of Saddam Hussein, though again, timing and context are important to France. Working through the United Nations and obtaining the support of Russia are two key French conditions for participation in an intervention. Officials in Paris would also require thoughtful planning of the endgame, together with U.S. backing for a Middle East peace plan to forestall the prospect of a further escalation between Israel and the Palestinians.

Time will tell whether or not this is an accurate reflection of the new reality of French politics, and thus far, the evidence of change is unconvincing. Even if this is true, it is too much to hope that the sour notes of the last decades will disappear completely. Like the United States, France pursues an interest-based foreign policy, which is informed by that country's unique historical experiences, its culture, values, and geographic location. Tellingly, when the United States initiated operations in Afghanistan and immediately sent special operations forces to the theater to prepare the battlefield for the subsequent military campaign, the French dispatched a noted philosopher, Bernard-Henri Levy, to assess the role that France might take in the country's reconstruction (Mallet 2002). To a certain extent this reflected France's inability to deploy a significant military force far from home in a timely fashion.[102] More fundamentally, however, it reflects the French capacity to make a virtue out of necessity. In present circumstances, France has little alternative but to employ its own soft tools of power, seeking to spread French values and cultural icons with a missionary zeal. This helps to explain Vedrine's statement about CNN, and it lies at the heart of President Chirac's announced intention to establish France's own 24/7 international news service.[103]

In any event, there is every likelihood that France, and, for that matter, other U.S. allies, will jump on the bandwagon to support the United States if action against Iraq is swift and decisive, and if the United States makes clear its long-term vision

---

102 The 1994 French *Defense White Paper* was intended to modernize and redress the shortcomings of French conventional forces, as made painfully clear by their inability to keep pace with American forces during *Desert Storm*, and by their inability to transport forces in a timely fashion to Africa for crisis interventions. Chirac's election in 1995 signaled a new opportunity to modernize French non-nuclear forces, but budget constraints and the election of a Socialist majority in the National Assembly elections of 1997 placed major constraints on initiatives in the defense area. Consequently, in the aftermath of the September 11 attacks against the United States, the French were unable to contribute in a meaningful way to operations in Afghanistan. As characterized by one French officer, "The modest French participation in the operations in Afghanistan was an eye-opener. We have come across as damned fools." According to another account, "[t]he special forces were not engaged and the aircraft carrier arrived at the end of the bombing. As for providing the combat airplane 'reinforcements' that Jacques Chirac formally announced on November 16, 2001, they may arrive in central Asia at the end of February [2002] at best." Six *Mirage* 2000 fighters, two KC-135 tankers, one C-130 aircraft, and one C-160 aircraft did arrive in Kyrgyzstan in March 2002 (Merchet 2002).

103 See, for example, Philip H. Gordon (2002). In his comment, Gordon observes that "French efforts to protect their culture are often less successful than they think. Regulations on the use of the French language are hard to enforce, fast-food outlets are proliferating despite state support for French gastronomy, and while subsidies for French cinema ensure that more French films are made, they do not make them widely watched or exported." Likewise, we can infer, it will be very difficult for the French to compete with CNN globally.

for regional stability. Although in terms of its actual military contribution to the operation, practical constraints suggest that in addition to some air and naval support for interdiction missions over Iraq and in the waters surrounding the country, the French contribution to an Iraqi contingency operation would be relatively small, and centered around these and special forces units. French government officials have already made clear their intention to ensure a French role in Iraq's post-conflict reconstruction. On this issue in particular, the French have expressed their own view that the endgame in Iraq must go well beyond regime change and encompass nation-building and creation of a network of economic and cultural ties to the West. Because of Iraq's geostrategic position in the wider Middle East, and given its vast oil reserves, the French are adamant that the country not be allowed to sink into civil war as a result of any U.S. operation, and they have expressed real concerns about relying on the Iraqi National Congress (INC) for leadership in the country after Saddam is deposed. It is perhaps too cynical to suggest that the French are worried about losing their privileged position as one of the current regime's largest trading partners, but the fact remains that the INC has already raised the issue of future oil contracts with the French, and any change in the status quo is unsettling in French decision circles for what that might mean for energy prices and the French economy.[104]

Iran: Engagement or Rollback?

The French are also concerned about the potential implications of an American intervention in Iraq for Iran, with whom Paris also shares a close relationship. A power vacuum in Iraq could work to the interests of Iran, which could attempt to occupy the southern Shi'ite-dominated portions of the country. Absent that, Iran has the potential to emerge as the region's strongest power—one that is armed with nuclear, chemical, and biological weapons, though the French tend to downplay U.S. fears in this regard, too. More so than with respect to Iraq, the French were incensed that President Bush included Iran in his "axis of evil" speech, charging that U.S. policy is counterproductive to the "reformist" impulses of Iran's "moderate" president, Mohammed Khatami.

The United States, in contrast, views with growing alarm Iran's efforts to develop WMD and advanced missile capabili-

---

104 See Alançon (2002).

ties. Regardless of what one thinks of Khatami, Iran's pursuit of WMD is viewed as an outgrowth of Tehran's aspirations to attain major-power status, and on this point the country's clerics are united. U.S. analysts are thus wary about making false distinctions between Ayatollah Ali Khamenei and President Khatami, suggesting that both have similar goals for the country, with each presenting a different face to the outside world in order to normalize relations with the West and thereby benefit from its trade and economic ties.

To that end, the leadership in Tehran made a tactical decision to cooperate with the United States during the Clinton years, seeking engagement rather than isolation from the United States. Since the 1979 Islamic revolution, Iran had characterized America as "the Great Satan." But sometime in the mid-to-late 1990s, with the coming to power of Khatami, elements within the Iranian government were persuaded that there were areas in which the two countries did share a common interest, namely in containing the activities of the Taliban in Afghanistan, stemming the flow of drugs out of that country, and continuing to ensure that Saddam Hussein remained compliant with the post-*Desert Storm* sanctions and restrictions on weapons developments and deployments. On this basis, debate over lifting Washington's dual-containment policy was engaged in by the Clinton administration, only to be rejected when Iran's support for Hezbollah and Hamas, and its efforts in the WMD arena, continued unabated. Once in office, the Bush administration undertook a sweeping review of proliferation issues, and very quickly came to the same conclusion about Iran as did its predecessor, although not without protracted debate over engagement as a means of moderating Iran's policies in these two areas.

In the immediate aftermath of September 11, and sharing a common perception of the Taliban and Al Qaeda enemies, the Iranians demonstrated visible support for the United States, and even offered limited intelligence cooperation about the situation on the ground in western Afghanistan. At the same time, however, Iran failed to prosecute those same terrorists as they fled Afghanistan in the opening salvos of the war. And, despite much hype, the professed intelligence cooperation with the United States has been less than meets the eye, while the regime continued to support Hezbollah and Hamas against Israel and continued its work on its WMD arsenal. With this as the backdrop, President Bush opted to include Iran in his January 2002 State of the Union address, in part to signal the seriousness with which his administration views Iran's support to terrorists and its WMD buildup. He also used this speech to alert all nations to looming WMD threats, and signaled as well that the war on terror extends well beyond Al Qaeda.

Consequently, the United States has kept Iran on its list of state sponsors of terrorism, a move that had little chance of changing after the January 2002 discovery of weapons contraband aboard the freighter *Karine A* bound from Iran and intended for the Palestinian Authority, presumably to be used against Israel. It also served notice that it intended to ask Congress to extend the Iran-Libya Sanctions Act (ILSA), which it did, to the utter consternation of the French, who have led the charge for normalization of relations with Iran. For their part, the French, together with other European countries and the EU collectively, have lifted the sanctions that were imposed during the Iran-Iraq war, and since 1995 and Chirac's first presidency, they have been focused on deepening relations with Iran. In part, this is undoubtedly intended as a challenge to America's predominant role in the Persian Gulf arena. Iran's ratification of the Chemical Weapons Convention in 1997 demonstrated to the French the wisdom of their approach, and they perceive that they can influence Iran's nuclear aspirations in the same way, with a little help from the Russians, who are providing nuclear reactor technologies to Iran, allegedly for civilian purposes.

American concerns about Iranian nuclear proliferation are heightened by Russia's agreement to provide Tehran with two nuclear reactors and reprocessing capabilities, as well as advanced missile technologies.[105] Despite repeated efforts of the

---

105 In the summer of 2002, Russia announced plans to build as many as five more nuclear-power reactors in Iran, in addition to the highly contentious Bushehr plant that is currently under construction and scheduled for completion by early 2003. Subsequently, and apparently to appease U.S. concerns in this regard, "Russia appears to have watered down plans to build five nuclear reactors in Iran, after the issue threatened to sour improving ties between Moscow and Washington" (Myers 2002). According to the minister of atomic energy, Alexander Rumyantsev, political factors would be taken into account in any Russian decision to construct more than the Bushehr reactor. See Chazan (2002). However, in December 2002, American intelligence revealed that Russia had supplied Iran with equipment and expertise to build two new facilities that appear to be part of a nuclear weapons program. According to one report, at one site there appears to be a heavy-water plant, while satellite photography has shown another facility that looks like a site for producing highly enriched uranium. See Sanger (2002b).

Bush administration to get Russian agreement to stop dangerous technology transfers to proliferating countries, the United States stands virtually alone on this issue, with the French convinced that their approach is the one that will yield results. France's decision to convene an international conference on ballistic missile proliferation and to issue an invitation to Iran served just that end. In February 2002, the French Foreign Ministry convened a conference in Paris to address the ballistic missile proliferation issue "in a comprehensive manner from the perspective of newly emerging missile powers" (Farooq 2002). As described by Quai d'Orsay officials, this meeting was designed to get consensus on a "code of conduct" among proliferators with respect to crisis stability. Iran, as a participant, endorsed the final communiqué, which was hailed by EU participants as an important starting point from which to resolve the issue of the Bushehr nuclear-power plant (*Tehran Jam-e Jam* 2002).

The Paris communiqué is not, however, politically binding, and the Iranians are free to pursue their ballistic missile and nuclear programs in the interim, the latter program a reflection of Iran's refusal to sign the Non-Proliferation Treaty and its apparent contempt for the French approach. In this context, preemptive military action to take out the reactors before they are operational might emerge as an option for debate, as it did when, in 1981, the Israelis destroyed the Osirik reactor in Iraq. Just as they opposed Israel's preemptive strike against Iraq in 1981, the French would undoubtedly voice strenuous objections to any consideration of a strike to cripple Iran's emerging WMD capability. On the issue of how best to deal with Iran's WMD programs, France and the United States may well part company, since there is neither agreement now on the emergence of Iran as a nuclear threat nor Allied consensus on the role that Tehran should play in Persian Gulf security decision-making. Without question there is even less French support for the use of force against Iran than there may be for action against Iraq. This is not just because the French perceive the Persians to be more culturally and historically attuned to Europeans, but because of the implications of U.S. action against Iran for the balance of power in Central Asia. The French have already made some tentative moves to offset America's new influence in the region, basically by establishing a military presence in Kyrgyzstan and by engaging both India and Pakistan, in addition of course to bolstering relations with Putin's Russia, which regards Central Asia as its "near abroad." Moreover, in August 2002, French officials traveled to Uzbekistan to explore the prospects for basing French forces in that country, and there continues to be discussion with the oil-producing Caspian Basin nations to get a foothold into oil production and pipeline development in the region.

Beyond their national initiatives, the French have also actively pushed the European Union to seek cooperative ventures with Iran, stemming from their assessment that "Iran is on the eve of major changes" (Guetta 2002). With half its population born after the Iranian revolution, Western values and culture are no longer scorned, according to French analysts. Rather, they are embraced, and, as the older generation passes on, popular pressures for reform and increased secularization are only likely to build. Thus far, French officials contend, such aspirations have been stifled because of the nature of the *sharia* government which gives a political veto and control over the security apparatus to the mullahs. Reformers have been imprisoned and media outlets closed, but still the pressures for reform have continued to grow, placing the country in an "invisible civil war," which members of the EU believe can end in a peaceful evolution if they offer the country the cooperation that it needs. From the French perspective, such cooperation would be dependent upon certain political conditions, including an end to the repression of the free press and greater freedoms for the country's female population. Thus, whereas the Europeans believe that they can effect political change through engagement, the United States has chosen to pursue a different strategy, one that promotes the liberal, democratic aspirations of the Iranian people, but that also undercuts the regime's dangerous behavior, the same objectives that the United States seeks in Iraq, and for that matter, in North Korea.

North Korea

The third point on President Bush's "axis of evil" is North Korea. For most Europeans, Korea is a long way off and attracts relatively little interest, except now that it has withdrawn from the NPT and appears to be pursuing its own national nuclear weapons program. That said, the Democratic People's Republic of Korea's (DPRK) ballistic missile capabilities and its WMD programs are not regarded as very serious threats to European security, at least in the interim, although there is recognition, at least in French defense policy circles, of the adverse effect of DPRK programs on other states' efforts in this area, particularly those of Iran and Pakistan. Consistent with their general preference for engagement over containment, the French have offered, through the EU and on their own, to mediate between North and South Korea to facilitate reconciliation and the Republic of Korea's (ROK) sunshine policy, its policy of engagement rather than confrontation with the North. In January 2003, Foreign Minister Villepin visited Seoul in an effort to help defuse the nuclear crisis and offered to mediate between the DPRK and the United States to establish a dialogue on North Korea's economic plight.

From the beginning of the Bush administration, the French have been critical of American disparagement of South Korean President Kim Dae-Jung's policy of engagement, and they have downplayed U.S. concerns about North Korean nuclear development, to the extent of providing whole-hearted support for the Clinton administration's 1994 Agreed Framework with North Korea; their support continues even now in the wake of North Korea's flagrant violation of that accord. Under this agreement, a U.S.-led coalition was to have built two light-water nuclear power reactors for civilian energy use, in exchange for a pledge by North Korea to end its nuclear weapons program and allow for inspections by the International Atomic Energy Agency (IAEA) to certify that it is no longer in violation of its pledges under the Non-Proliferation Treaty.[106] The assumption at the time was that North Korea only had one nuclear weapons development program, and it had been based on plutonium reprocessing. North Korea's subsequent revelation that it was pursuing a covert uranium-based nuclear weapons program shocked the French, but since has been rationalized as a "tool" to get the Americans to take Pyongyang more seriously. In other

---

106 The Korean Energy Development Organization (KEDO), which was set up under the Agreed Framework, had just started to pour the concrete for the first reactor when North Korea revealed the existence of a parallel-path nuclear development program, one that is uranium-based, as opposed to plutonium-based. This development has put the nail into the coffin of the Agreed Framework, although officials in South Korea and Japan are trying to resuscitate the accord. From the American perspective, unless and until the North Koreans renounce their nuclear program and open the country up for a new round of IAEA inspections, all bets are off and there can be no engagement with the regime in Pyongyang.

words, from a French perspective, North Korea's nuclear program is currency to be used in great-power bargaining, and the decision to reveal its existence, while perhaps reflecting a lack of understanding of the American reaction, nevertheless was meant to underscore the urgency for Western and, in particular, U.S. engagement with the regime in the DPRK.

As with Iraq, the French are concerned that the United States might resort to force to contain North Korea's nuclear program. However, the close proximity of Seoul to North Korean artillery fire and, indeed, the situation on the peninsula more generally, including a South Korean electorate that supports dialogue over the use of military power, makes preemption a highly risky option for the United States—and one that may not yield the intended results because of the difficulty in locating and targeting buried and hidden North Korean nuclear weapons and their associated infrastructure. For the French, the clear preference of the Bush administration to avoid the use of military force to solve the North Korean nuclear crisis is both a relief and a contradiction. As viewed in Paris, the North Korean case points out the bankruptcy of the Bush doctrine, namely because of American unwillingness to consider the use of force when U.S. nationals are endangered. In his 2003 State of the Union address, President Bush observed that "different threats require different strategies," and in the case of North Korea, the United States would work with its regional partners to find a solution. By choosing to take its time and coordinate its policy with key regional partners, the United States is pursuing a path that should be applauded by the French. Instead it has become another source of friction and a bone of contention in the Franco-American relationship.

Although French policy positions regarding North Korea are consistent with the general French penchant for engagement as a means of bringing about indigenous political reform, it is also likely that the French adopted their positions on North Korea to better situate themselves in the South Korean marketplace, including with respect to the possibility of large defense exports. Indeed, the United States and France came head-to-head in the recent ROK fighter aircraft competition, and they are likely to find themselves facing off against each other in other potentially lucrative defense competitions, including for missile defenses, as the South Koreans move forward with their defense modernization plans.

However, while arms sales to the ROK are an important economic concern for the French, the role of peace broker on the Korean peninsula is a major political aspiration for the EU and is one that could solidify Europe's relationships with a uniting Korea as well as with China, on whom both South Korea and France are now concentrating much effort. For France, China has the potential to stymie U.S. actions in Asia, and with its seat on the UNSC is an important French ally on Iraq. Whereas, since the 2002 Crawford summit, Sino-American relations have warmed considerably, the French contend that U.S. and Chinese interests will ultimately clash over differences on Taiwan, the North Korean nuclear crisis, and the war on terror. As viewed from Paris, Bush administration policies, including the Nuclear Posture Review, which singles out the PRC as a potential adversary, will force a new confrontation with China and make it all that much harder to loosen the heavy-handed control of the Communist Party over everyday life and commerce. Here, as with Iran, France regards engagement as more productive than containment, leading many French elites to assert that current U.S. policies are more dangerous to regional stability than are Chinese regional power aspirations. Were China to perceive itself to be encircled by the United States and its allies, including a Russia more compliant with Western interests, the government in Beijing could also decide to step up its support of anti-American forces, by increasing trade and technology transfers, for example, to North Korea or Iraq.

China is an important regional actor and a global power with permanent representation in the UNSC. Many in France perceive in China a formidable ally against U.S. hegemonic aspirations. Others, with more narrow motives, see China as an important market for French goods. China is a major economic center of power and as such is a pole in the multipolar system configuration that the French identify as crucial to the conduct of international relations in the twenty-first century. For this reason, the French have conferred singular focus on China in the Asia-Pacific region, identifying it as a major spoke in France's global economic and political strategy.

CHAPTER 7

A Final Word and a Roadmap for the Future

At the conclusion of their book, *The French Challenge: Adapting to Globalization*, Philip Gordon and Sophie Meunier describe the French perception of the need for alternatives to a world dominated by the United States alone. Paraphrasing President Chirac, they argue for alternatives in the face of alleged U.S. tendencies toward unilateralism, "messiahism," and isolationism. For a majority of French elites, a unipolar world dominated politically, culturally, and economically by the United States is unacceptable and strategically unsound. This is why, Gordon and Meunier claim, there is a groundswell of support in France for a world that is "multipolar, diversified, and multilateral" (2001, 112). From this perspective, it is logical to support a strong, integrated Europe, which in the future could speak with one voice in international organizations and act on the basis of its interests and preferences.[107]

Most French elites are quick to point out that the Europe that they are building will be predisposed to be on the U.S. side in international discourses, but it also will reserve the right to challenge U.S. unilateralist decisions and to act independently on the basis of its own assessment of emerging global realities. In this, the French suggest that they are doing precisely what the Americans are doing; namely, developing policies that accord with their interests, based on a *realpolitik* assessment of emerging power trends, global challenges, threats, and alignments in the international system. From this French perspective, as described

---

[107] In 2002, a number of French books were published, supporting this view. However, there was one notable exception: Emmanuel Todd's, *Après l'Empire: Essai Sur la Décomposition du Système Américain*. In this book, Todd argues that the American system is in decline and that U.S. military initiatives, including a war against Saddam, are merely a pretext to cover the loss of American power. To offset the dangerous tendencies in the American decline, Todd argues for greater European unity and espouses the creation of a European-Russian alliance to challenge U.S. policy initiatives.

throughout this study, France's interests are better served in a multipolar international system, in which the European Union is a major pole in the new order, and from which basis France has a better opportunity to influence the shape of world events and decision outcomes.

If the EU offers a forum where the French voice will be heard and heeded, it also raises the prospect for both acting in and creating multilateral frameworks with an even greater possibility to influence strategic decisions. To be an even more powerful determinant of behavior, however, multilateralism, from the French perspective, must rely on an empowering mandate, preferably given by the EU or the United Nations, depending on the circumstances of a particular contingency. And finally, the French always prefer an element of predictability, giving rise to an emphasis on "rules of the road" that can either be provided in an operational mandate (given by the EU or the UN), or negotiated under the rule of law and established in a binding international agreement. With this exacting and legalistic approach, the French tend to be very literal in their interpretation of EU and UN mandates, international arms control frameworks, and institutional collaboration in Europe and beyond, reflecting one means by which France hopes to be able to influence U.S. decisions and actions on the global stage.

In stark contrast, the United States as the lone superpower has less need for elaborate gamesmanship to effect change on the international scene. Accordingly, Washington cares less about elaborate theories about world order and more about influencing trends and dealing with concrete problems. In this context, the United States is increasingly skeptical about the roles and relevance of traditional alliance frameworks. Equally questionable in the eyes of U.S. policy-makers is the value of formalized arms control frameworks in an age when technology is changing so fast that it is hard to keep up with its innovations, particularly in the security setting where transformation takes time and money and requires new and creative strategic thought. At a political level, the United States has always valued cooperation with like-minded states and for major international crises has depended on its allies for support and military aid. The traditional notion of alliances is, however, changing, particularly in the aftermath of September 11 and with the new recognition of the vulnerability of the American homeland.

In the absence of a shared assessment of future threats and operational challenges, it is difficult to support arguments for the type of tight collective decision-making and action that was necessary during the Cold War. As seen in the Kosovo conflict, the Alliance's decision-making process was convoluted, cumbersome, and contentious. It worked against timely action, and the rules of engagement were such that they were a drag on operational planning. Successive U.S. commanders have said that they never again want to fight a war under these conditions, and their frustration only grew with the realization that the forces they were commanding were highly disparate and uneven, because of technology gaps and differences in tactics and procedures.

Military problems arise with alliances, with respect to interoperability, rules of engagement, and even military doctrine, as this monograph also points out, all of which have contributed to the perception of a "go it alone" U.S. mentality. Sometimes out of necessity that perception has indeed been accurate, as was the case with respect to the military strikes against Sudan and Afghanistan after the bin Laden-sponsored bombings of U.S. embassies in Africa. It is legitimate to debate how best to respond to global terrorist threats, but all the while recognizing that the United States is not the only country to have used military force in retaliation for terrorist acts. States acting in self-defense are under no legal obligation to consult with other states before taking military action. The principal case for such consultations would be a need to secure Allied support or participation, assuming that such assistance would be useful or necessary. Unhappily, however, recent experiences have proved to be wanting in several respects, most notably because of the comparative paucity of military forces to deal with contemporary threats, and based on fundamentally different U.S. and Allied perceptions of the use of force in dealing with such threats. Against Al Qaeda, U.S. allies have provided important support, including in the military field, but as noted throughout this study, a widening technology gap between the United States and its partners is affecting operational planning in NATO and in the wider war on terror. In the case of Iraq, the UN has authorized the enforcement of the no-fly zones in separate resolutions, as well as mandated Iraq's compliance with non-proliferation regimes, but the United Kingdom, alone among America's European partners, participates in the NFZ enforcement missions. The United Nations has been particularly ineffective in dealing with Iraq, and as an institution has been unwilling to face down Saddam Hussein over his illegal proliferation activities, from oil sales outside of the UN embargo to WMD development.

More often than not, what passes for U.S. unilateralism is nothing more than the United States acting alone because its allies are constrained by their lack of appropriate military capabilities, or because of other restrictions, as in the case of Japan, which has legal constraints on the employment of its Self-Defense Forces. With respect to the specific case of Iraq, moreover, the United States diverges seriously from many of its allies, including France, on how to deal with Saddam Hussein, as noted elsewhere in this study. This divergence extends as well to fundamental political differences over engagement of Iran and the Middle East peace process more generally. Because Europe (and for that matter, Japan and China) are more dependent on Gulf oil than is the United States, it is inevitable that the transatlantic partners will have different views on how to deal with these intractable issues.

In reality, the unfortunate truth is that in many cases when the United States does act unilaterally, it does so because there is no effective alternative. If the U.S. does not do it, who, you might ask, will? In a world where threat perceptions, risks, and challenges have been transformed by, among other things, the European revolutions of 1989, security planning has become more complex and global in nature. Economic competition has emerged as a more prominent aspect of security planning, with many Americans wondering if the European Commission's decisions—including the one to block the merger of General Electric and Honeywell, two American companies operating in the EU—portend new trade frictions that could further erode support for NATO in the United States. For their part, the Europeans ask how the Bush administration's decision to impose tariffs on steel imports and to give new subsidies to U.S. farmers accords with a commitment to free trade.

On both sides of the Atlantic, the post-World War II generation is being supplemented, if not assiduously replaced, by another generation largely unfamiliar with the history of American intervention on the Continent. In Europe, this generation seems increasingly preoccupied with issues directly related to the deepening and widening of the EU, and has little time for NATO, whose relevance is increasingly questioned now that Russia has become a half-way member of the club. In one sense, the new generation has a more parochial outlook, and appears to be much more interested in establishing a new European identity and institutional structures than in promoting a Europe-based world view. The French, in particular, have become much more inward-looking; as characterized by one French analyst, as the French become more narcissistic, they also have become more insular, whereas the United States has become more outward-looking in its perspectives (Moisi 2002b). It is certainly true that on the U.S. side there is interest in promoting a more global approach to foreign policy and national security—an approach that would relegate Europe to a less prominent role than it commanded in the bipolar Cold War era. To be blunt about it, many Americans simply no longer care what the French—or, for that matter, the other Europeans—think about the United States; for them the future lies in a new relationship with the "new Europe," and with Putin's Russia, based on more traditional balance-of-power considerations. Still others point to Asia and recommend a revitalization of the Sino-American relationship, identifying China and the Pacific region as the real priority for American foreign and national security policies. Those holding to this perspective argue that the Taiwan "problem" is likely to be resolved peacefully over time, as more and more Taiwanese engage in business enterprises with mainland China. Whether or not this is true, the future, for them, lies in Asia, with China's emergence as the preeminent regional power the key factor influencing the way in which U.S. interests are to be sustained.

Furthermore, those who believe that the United States must focus on China and the Pacific region see the United States as a Pacific power, and three of the five, or four of the five, depending on how Russia is characterized, emerging poles of the French multipolar concept are Asian nations. Added to this is India, whose rising economic power, democratic structures, and heritage make it a natural partner for the United

States, regardless of how Sino-American relations evolve. In the war against terrorism the United States has a major interest in strengthening relations with numerous countries, especially India, despite the very real, immediate imperative to ensure that Pakistan does not become a failed state. In other words, the United States, in coming years, may be less inclined to rely on Europe than it did during the Cold War.

This would be unfortunate and, more to the point, detrimental to the interests of both Europe and the United States, as global stability and European security could benefit from a reaffirmation of the transatlantic tie. Since its birth, the United States has had allies in Europe, and France was its first. The Marquis de Lafayette was a French aristocrat who fought with George Washington at Valley Forge, and 226 years after he first arrived on American shores, he was made an honorary U.S. citizen, only the sixth foreign national to have achieved that distinction. The French provided important political support for the American war for independence, and throughout the history of the Franco-American relationship, and particularly in the twentieth century each has demonstrated a need for the other. Yet, in the first years of the twenty-first century, the two nations appear to be talking past each other, and in some instances, attempting to score points at the other's expense. If America's global power and influence are a source of envy and concern for many in France, French efforts to constrain American actions on the global stage, either through the United Nations or the European Union, risk fueling a rivalry in which the two partners consciously find ways to marginalize each other, whether in the area of military planning or diplomatic initiatives. French behavior surrounding UN resolution 1441 may have been heralded as a great political achievement in Paris, but in the United States it served to reinforce anti-French sentiments.

Contrary to what many in France believe, America does not aspire to hegemony; in point of fact, Americans are reluctant to exercise their power, and for the most part would prefer not to intervene in a crisis. America will act when challenged by threats to its values, as it did in Bosnia and Kosovo, and when its vital national interests are at risk, as after September 11. The United States has come to rely more on the use of force as an instrument of policy than its allies, in large part because it has the ability to summon military strength that is not available to France or other NATO-European allies. For France, multilateralism, as Kagan points out, may very well be the refuge of the weak (2002a, 1-21). French policy elites, on the other hand, vehemently disagree with this characterization, and argue that through multilateralism constructive dialogue is possible, and only on that basis can peace and stability be attained. Against U.S. arguments that America does rely on multilateral policy approaches when possible and where appropriate, French analysts reply that the U.S. brand of multilateral diplomacy is not real multilateralism, but rather U.S. unilateralism with selective, international support. To be truly multilateral, the United States would have to involve its allies directly in consultations and planning from the start and be willing to incorporate their suggestions and criticisms when there was disagreement on strategies, operations, and even the endgame (see, for example, Achcar 2001). In response, U.S. policy practitioners contend that recent U.S. experiences in this regard have not made the multilateral approach an attractive option to the United States.

By the sheer expanse of their territory and vastness of their resources, Americans view the world from a unique geostrategic perspective. In a sense the French seek to redress the resulting power imbalance by strengthening the EU as the basis for their global initiatives and for projecting their views onto the global stage. Seen through the U.S. lens, collective defense is an important construct for U.S. planning, although multilateralism is not the preferred U.S. operational approach. However, to the extent that the United States needs allies, and surely it does in many contingencies for political or even material support, American perspectives of alliance arrangements, or of multilateralism more generally, are conditioned by what its partners can bring to the equation in support of common interests. To paraphrase Secretary of Defense Donald Rumsfeld's thesis, the mission must shape the coalition, and not the other way around. In this respect there is no question but that U.S. perspectives have been conditioned by recent experiences in which multilateral decision-making proved to be more of a liability than had been anticipated, although in the case of Afghanistan, such concerns were muted given the nature of the coalition operations and the

Security Planning After September 11

Changed Political Context	New Operational Priorities	Military Transformation	Geostrategic Factors

• Bush Doctrine
o Prevention
o Preemption
o Dissuasion
o Coercion
 	
• Partner paradigms
o Alliance Futures
  - NATO
  - ESDP/ERRF
 	
• Coalitions of the willing
o OEF
o Iraq
o Maritime intercept
 	
• National-bilateral
o UK
o Australia
	• Homeland Defense
	o Counter BW
	o Weapons of mass effect
	o BM/CM defenses
	o Counter-terror
	o Cyber security
	
	• Asymmetric Warfare
	o Urban operations
	o Force protection
	o Non-military campaigns
	
	• Allied vulnerabilities
	o West a target
	o Divergences exploited
	o Assumes U.S. protection
		• U.S. emphasis on:
		o Crisis response
		o Force projection
		o Missile defenses
		o SOF
		o Expeditionary and urban warfare
		o Technology offsets
		
		• NATO reform
		o Transformation and command HQs
		o Capabilities gaps/niches
		o EU competition
		o Enlargement
		
		• Allied constraints
		o Budget shortfalls
		o Capabilities shortfalls
		o Access restrictions
			• Base access and overflight
			o New opportunities (e.g., NATO enlargement)
			o Shrinking U.S. presence "footprint"
			
			• Forward deterrence
			o Port & sea-lane security
			o Base and expeditionary force protection
			
			• Cross-border crime
			o Al Qaeda's global reach
			o CNA/CND
			o MNCs, NGOs, mafias

operational imperative arising from the direct attack against the United States.

Largely on this basis alone, U.S. alliance frameworks are destined to change, reflecting perhaps a new understanding of the diversity of Allied interests. From this, the larger notion of the West as a formative force in U.S. alliance dynamics may be giving way to more practical considerations, although, indeed, bin Laden seems not to have noticed the erosion of this concept. Accordingly, alliance considerations likely will assume greater weight in U.S. policy only if allies bring useful capabilities or if they enhance political support at home and abroad for specific American initiatives. Consequently, in the context of twenty-first century security planning, we may have to come to grips with the reality that U.S. alliance frameworks will be less rigid and, depending on the situation, function more pragmatically, relying, for example, on so-called coalitions of the willing to implement specific taskings and combined joint task forces (CJTFs) to operationalize mission planning. For the United States this will entail the need to tailor its thinking about U.S.-Allied command relationships and, even more difficult, to consider new formulas to attain forces "complementarity," if interoperability is really beyond its grasp. For U.S. allies it very clearly means taking the necessary steps to meet defense spending goals, and in certain instances, a serious reexamination of policy constraints on the employment of military forces and their rules of engagement.

To return to one of the central themes of much of the French critique of U.S. policy, trends in world politics are driving the United States toward unilateral policies, and this, in turn, has profound implications for transatlantic relations. If this is so, it is true not because alliances have outlived their usefulness, but rather because alliance cohesion is more or less held hostage to the lowest common denominator, which in most cases is an inadequate basis upon which to formulate coherent policy responses. As many in the United States increasingly believe, the only alternative to unilateral action is inaction—a policy choice that also carries with it potentially profound risks and threats to vital U.S. interests. Thus, it is neither the reorientation of American foreign policy nor the transformation of the international system from unipolarity to multipolarity per se that is driving U.S. security decision-making, but rather an inability to attain alliance consensus on the way ahead. In part, this is a reflection of cultural differences, manifested in disputes over the death penalty in the United States, contending perspectives on international organizations, mandates, and human rights. It also arises from philosophical differences on the use of force in international relations and from the unique role and position of the United States in the post-Cold War era. For whatever one's view of the United States, there can be no doubt that it presently occupies a unique position in the international system. Just how nations react to that reality depends in no small measure on each nation's interests and political, strategic, and economic objectives.

In this context, the United States and its European allies, collectively or selectively, could part ways. The conventional wisdom that, in the end, the United States and the EU will always be on the same side may be proven wrong on issues such as Iran, or, for that matter, the future of Israeli-Palestinian relations. These are hard problems for which there is no easy solution, and differences between American and European security perspectives suggest that the two may, indeed, be following different paths. This does not mean that there is justification for tossing NATO aside, as some in the

United States and France have suggested. It does imply the need to re-think very carefully just how the Alliance goes about reforming itself to make it more relevant to the threats and challenges of the post-September 11 world. To that end, the United States may determine a need to recalibrate U.S. force deployments in Europe. So, too, the creation of an EU defense entity that is synergistic with NATO's strategic concept, its role and missions, and its decision structures would enhance transatlantic security, not diminish it. If, as some in France suggest, it is necessary to define the ESDP in opposition to the United States in order to lend it credibility, doing so will surely wound the Alliance, perhaps critically. To be sure, NATO is much more than a military alliance; it is first and foremost a political organization, created to safeguard and promote a concept of values, freedoms, and choices that is sorely lacking in other parts of the world. It represents a notion of the West that should not be allowed to erode, no matter how different its members' perspectives of difficult and challenging issues.

Just as it would be short-sighted of the United States to resist the development of a European defense entity, it would be foolhardy of the Europeans to take U.S. solidarity for granted. There is a limit to American patience, and pragmatism is an essential element of the American character, as has been generally observed, including by Tocqueville who so many years ago wrote, "I think there is no country in the civilized world where they are less occupied with philosophy than in the United States" (2000, 403).[108] There is a real danger that events will conspire on both sides of the Atlantic to push the United States further and further away from its oldest ally. Thus, both sides need to work to sustain the Franco-American relationship, making allowances when necessary for tactical differences, in order to sustain a strategic connection.

There is some reason to hope in this regard, although there is still a danger of miscalculation on both sides. There continues, as well, to be a profound misunderstanding of each

---

108 Tocqueville goes on to observe that Americans "manage to resolve unaided all the little difficulties that practical life presents" (2000, 404). He continues, "In America, the purely practical part of the sciences is cultivated admirably, and people attend carefully to the theoretical portion immediately necessary to application; in this way, Americans display a mind that is always clear, free, original, and fertile; but there is almost no one in the United States who gives himself over to the essentially theoretical and abstract portion of human knowledge" (2000, 434).

other's motives. The "conservatives" are in power in France and in the United States, but Chirac's Union for a Populist Movement has more in common, politically, with the American Democratic Party than it does with the Republicans, but even this connection is tenuous. In general, European "conservatives" are libertarians who have more in common with British Prime Minister Tony Blair's "third way" philosophy, which has moderated and evolved to hold free market views on the economy, for example, than they have in common with Americans of either political stripe. In this context, it cannot be over-emphasized that we are products of our own, unique environments, and our world views are shaped and conditioned by factors that have no real analogue on the other side of the Atlantic.

There is a presumption in French policy circles that much of U.S. policy, regardless of political persuasion, rests on the nation's religious moorings, which were present at the creation and still are perceived as exerting significant influence over all aspects of American life, including the way in which the United States relates to the outside world. Viewing the United States in this way, French analysts contend that the Bush administration's approaches to the war on terrorism and counter-proliferation planning reflect a fanaticism that is at once illogical and not easily refuted. Terminology such as the "axis of evil" and a "crusade against terrorism" reinforce this view and lead the French to the conclusion that on certain issues they will be compelled to adopt the leadership role in forcing the United States to moderate its policy pronouncements, if not its positions on issues viewed as important to global politics, European security, or French economic interests.

That said, on the fundamental issue of weapons of mass destruction there is a greater convergence of U.S. and French perspectives than the differences of approach would lead one to believe. Like the United States, France would like to ensure that Iraq has been divested of its capacity to produce weapons of mass destruction, in particular nuclear weapons, the possession of which would profoundly affect regional stability. For the French, the preferred path to gain that assurance lies through the United Nations, using the weapons inspections mandated under UNSC resolution 1441 and other multilateral arms control mechanisms, notably the Non-Proliferation Treaty and a global conference on disarmament. At no time have the French suggested the forcible removal of the Ba'athist regime, although they, too, would like to see Saddam and his sons removed from power. As viewed from Paris, the only legitimate rationale for contemplating the use of force against Iraq would be if there is irrefutable evidence, gleaned after completion of the weapons inspections process, of WMD activity, in violation of the UNSC resolutions 687 and 1284, or if there existed a "smoking gun" linking the Iraqi leadership to Al Qaeda and the events of September 11, 2001.

In this context, Iraq's willingness to allow UN weapons inspectors to reenter the country in November 2002 was a moment of considerable hope for the French. After years of duplicity on the issue of Iraq's disarmament, Baghdad's announced intention to comply with the UN demand for an accounting of Iraq's WMD assets by December 8, 2002, was a welcome development for the French, who, with the Russians and sometimes the Chinese, have been Iraq's champion in the United Nations, first over the sanctions and lately with respect to the consideration of the use of force. While French elites were disappointed at the inadequacy of Iraq's subsequent weapons declarations, and have signaled an awareness of the gamesmanship being employed by the leadership in Baghdad in this regard, particularly in the expectation of creating deeper fissures between the United States and its European allies, they nevertheless disagree with U.S. arguments that Iraq is in "material breach" of UNSC 1441, therein opening the way for military intervention to achieve Iraq's disarmament. For their part, the French have adopted a strategy that aims at dragging out indefinitely the weapons inspection process, making it all the more difficult for the United States to obain a UNSC consensus on the advisability of a military intervention before that process reaches a more definitive conclusion.

This approach is widely supported among the French electorate, as made plain in recent public opinion polling, much of which reveals the depth of French opposition to the use of force to disarm Iraq. This very strong expression of French public opposition to military intervention in Iraq is reflected in the French government's frenetic attempts in the United

Nations to forestall what is perceived now as more or less the inevitable, and to buy time by calling for a broader dialogue on peace and stability in the region. A large segment of the French elite believes that the road to stability in Baghdad lies through Jerusalem; that is, the more pressing issue influencing politics throughout the Middle East region is the conflict between Israel and the Palestinians. Finding a resolution to the question of Palestinian statehood, it is argued in Paris, will open the door to other options for addressing Saddam Hussein. For it is also a very specific French view that Israel's own nuclear weapons provide a major incentive for Saddam and possibly other Arab states and Iran to pursue the acquisition of national nuclear capabilities. Reflecting a dominant view on the "Arab street," some in French analytical circles cling to the belief that if Israel can be held accountable for its nuclear weapons by being, for example, sanctioned (by the UN) for its nuclear capability, then there is a chance that other regional powers will be dissuaded from pursuing their own nuclear programs, particularly if the consequences for doing so are exacting. Others, while acknowledging that Israel's nuclear deterrent is a problem when considering new approaches to nuclear proliferation, are also aware of the perceived hypocracy of such an approach given France's own decision to deploy a national nuclear capability.

Perhaps, to turn attention away from France's own proliferation behavior, the French attempt to deflect criticism from their own case by pointing out that "in its war on terrorism, Washington is being very selective in its definition of nuclear proliferation, depending on whether or not the countries in question are its allies" (Consea and Lepick 2002). Thus, Iraq and Iran, together with North Korea, are unfairly singled out for international censure, when Pakistan, India, and Israel are not, prompting French criticisms of a double standard and, worse still, of a duality of approach in security decision-making that makes no allowances for differences of opinion. As President Bush has expressed it, "either you are with us or [you are] with the terrorists." The stark choices explicit in this approach are very difficult for the French polity to accept, having preferred to adhere to Kagan's Kantian paradigm that allows for nuanced options. If the ABM Treaty was long regarded in France as the touchstone of strategic stability, the Non-Proliferation Treaty is the sine qua non of arms control. Yet, its inability to control the proliferation-related activities of Iraq and Iran, which were NPT signatories, to constrain North Korea from withdrawing from the treaty, or to compel Israel to sign it, raises, from the American perspective, fundamental questions about the utility of relying on arms control to shape the behaviors of states, as well as with respect to expecting that offensive nuclear weapons by themselves will deter transnational, non-state terrorists. Outlaw states and non-state actors are not deterred by established arms control mechanisms, and the chaos of the global international order requires new concepts for dialogue with disaffected and rogue actors.

Without question, the nature of the emerging international system, and the challenges and threats to which it is giving rise, demands collective action, particularly when allies share the same values and concerns. However, the question is whether in this new, emerging international order, this is enough, particularly when allies perceive their interests to be asymmetrical with those supported by the United States. Walter Russell Mead, writing in *Special Providence*, notes that:

> As the dominant global power for most of the twentieth century, the United States entered the twenty-first as a global hegemonic power on a novel scale ... The American hegemony today is militarily supreme, culturally pervasive, technologically dominant, and economically dynamic. Its allies and enemies alike fear being swallowed up in it; it is the basic fact of international life (2001, 323).

Just how France and other U.S. allies and coalition partners relate to that power delineates the major challenge of alliance relations today. For the Chirac government in France, there appears to be a greater willingness, in comparison to its predecessor, to leverage U.S. power where it can to support French interests. Indeed, this was the message delivered by French Foreign Minister Dominique de Villepin, during his visit to Washington just after the June 2002 National Assembly elections, when he stated, "France must have a relationship of trust and frankness with the United States, even if it sometimes means being abrupt" (Villepin 2002b). But whether in fact this will prove to be the case over time remains in question, particularly in light of the anti-American obsession, to use Revel's characterization, that pervades many levels of French thought. In this regard, it is instructive that the late French President François Mitterrand was alleged to have said, "France does not know it, but we are at war with America. Yes, a permanent war, a vital war, a war without death. Yes, they are very hard, the Americans, they are voracious, they want undivided power over the world" (Benamou 1996).

What the French want is to influence that power, and bend it to suit their purposes. Toward that end, they have sought to use the EU as a surrogate for French power, and in so doing, to constrain American actions or initiatives when they are perceived to be in conflict with French interests. In the opening years of the twenty-first century, the predominant French impulse has been to attempt to block American initiatives, because they are generally perceived as threatening to an emerging French agenda that not only seeks to create a stronger European entity, but to regain French influence in the Middle East, where once it played a defining role. But the record of the recent past is less encouraging to French aspirations in this regard. In 1984, when François Mitterrand stood together and clasped hands with German Chancellor Helmut Kohl at the commemoration of the Battle of Verdun, French expectations were great that the Franco-German "motor" would once again be fired up for Europe. Two decades later, in the wake of significant Franco-German differences over EU reform, enlargement, and institutional changes, most notably with regard to the Common Agricultural Policy (CAP), the euro is a noteworthy success, but the ESDP is only sputtering along, notwithstanding their common initiative on Iraq. In fact, this Franco-German initiative has served to polarize the EU, and as the ensuing declarations of support for the U.S. position from other European leaders make clear, France and Germany do not speak for Europe on security matters.

Hubert Vedrine, writing about François Mitterrand's tenure as president, observed, "No secular world trend on any level—diplomatic, commercial, military, cultural, linguistic—is intrinsically favorable to France" (1996, 760). This is why, Vedrine goes on to explain, a unified Europe, arising from the intensification of Franco-German collaboration, is necessary, and the key to regaining French *exceptionalisme*, which has been lost by globalization and the unsurpassed rise of American power. Unfortunately for the French, however, the Germans appear to be less interested in using the EU to provide a basis for European foreign policy and interventions than in applying the power of the EU to advance Germany's global economic interests. Thus, in terms of building a separate and independent European defense identity, the Germans are proving to be problematic for the French.[109]

Even more problematic for the French is the United Kingdom, which is seen in French policy circles as being particularly unhelpful at this point. There is no question but that French policy elites are very concerned over the perceived solidarity with the Bush administration that the Blair government is demonstrating on Iraq. Prime Minister Tony Blair's February 2003 meeting with President Chirac at Touquet was brief and to the point but found little common ground on Iraq. Jean-Pierre Raffarin's emphasis on the establishment of what he calls "creative humanism" is proving to be the essence of his approach, as prime minister, to international relations (Raffarin 2002). A disciple of former President Valéry Giscard d'Estaing, Raffarin argues that France must not be seduced by the illusion of power, but rather, it must endeavor to establish policies on the basis of laws and the principle of humanism, the latter being a reference to France's multicultural society and in particular to its sizable Muslim minority.[110] Inevitably, this conception, which also harkens back to the principles of international law as a point of departure for international action, will come into conflict with America's efforts to respond to a new enemy who rejects Western juridi-

---

109 See, for example, Jacques Isnard (2002c). He writes, "Two major arms projects are blocked in Europe at present: the Airbus A400M military transport aircraft and the Meteor long-range air-to-air missile. [This] could cause European defense to break down," particularly at a time in which the United States is launching a political and commercial offensive to discredit both European projects. "In reality, what is at issue in this trial of strength is the possibility—or otherwise—of promoting a dialogue over security between the two sides of the Atlantic Ocean, which is balanced and respects each country's national sovereignty."

110 See, for example, Hazim al-Amin (2002.). According to this author, the third-generation immigrants from the Maghreb to France are the target of "jihad-oriented Islamists." This generation is "the fruit of the disappointment of the two generations that had come before them. They are Arabs and Muslims but they do not command Arabic and their knowledge of Islam is barely sufficient for them to perform a single rite of the religion. But neither are they French, doors having been slammed in their faces thanks to their dark complexions. They have long suffered the feeling that they are not wholly French, which has made it somewhat easy to cobble together a violent form of Islam in their incoherent and split mentality."

cal frameworks and who has turned on their head civilized tenets of war.

The fundamental truth of recent times is that America is at war, although the French refuse to characterize the terrorist acts against the United States in that way. Terrorism is but one manifestation of this war, one that targets the soft underbelly of democratic and open societies. To fight terrorism and the jihad that is being waged against the West, all facets of national and international power must be used. This is a reality that cannot be changed by the utopian aspirations of international law. Neither will it be altered by French efforts to force the United States to moderate its behavior and to address the Palestinian issue before responding to the threat of weapons of mass destruction. Just as France has less and less understanding of Americans today, Americans have less and less patience for French efforts to constrain Washington's ability to react to the threats that America faces.

Terrorism is a challenge that is not going to go away even if Al Qaeda is eliminated. Terrorism has revealed America's vulnerability. It also has exposed the tenuousness of America's alliance relationships, most dramatically with respect to France. Iraq and the conflict between Israel and the Palestinians are likely to widen the fault lines between America and France even further. Until France gives up its attachment to status quo policies, its relations with the United States are doomed to remain difficult and at times hostile. Contemporary Franco-American relations are complex and paradoxical: at one moment there is a special closeness derived from the beginnings of the American nation, manifested in the inclusion of New York firefighters and West Point cadets in the 2002 Bastille Day parade; at the next moment, France is contesting U.S. efforts to exempt American soldiers and diplomats from the jurisdiction of the International Criminal Court—notwithstanding the fact that France itself negotiated a seven years' exemption for its forces.

In the post-September 11 environment, the French argue that the submission by nation-states to international authority and universal principles is much preferable to the nation-state system, which was the legacy of the 1648 Treaty of Westphalia. More than this, the French suggest that September 11, 2001, is likely to prove to be a "transitional moment" in which the fundamentals of the international system of order were challenged and demonstrated to be wanting in the face of new transnational terrorist threats, globalization, and the growing incidence of failed states. In Europe, with the slow but steady evolution of the European Union, state sovereignty already is being eroded, with the establishment of the euro and efforts to create an EU defense identity being the most noticeable manifestations of this trend. As a charter member of the European club, France has exhibited alternating tendencies either to embrace the EU and fashion it in France's own image or to hold it at arm's length when EU policies conflict with those of the French government. In many respects, the French are ambivalent about the EU, largely because of what it may mean for the notion of French *exceptionalisme*. France is no longer the largest EU country; that honor goes to Germany, which increasingly appears to be drawing Europe's locus of power eastward. To compensate for that, France alternates between trying (as it has done historically) to seduce the Germans with talk of their centrality to Europe's emergence as a great power, and trying to outflank the Germans by establishing a special relationship with Russia, creating, in effect, a new Entente Cordiale.[111] However, France may be disappointed in this endeavor, since the Russians appear to be more interested in dealing with the United States, over the heads of the Europeans, when it suits their purposes to do so.

As the notion of French *exceptionalisme* fades away, France is changing, and with a diverse population base and a young generation that is steeped in European culture, the nation is struggling with its identity and role in the international system. Thus, while French power attributes have great potential to be magnified and exploited for the EU cause, ordinary Frenchmen are anxious about what the loss of their "Frenchness" may mean for their futures. As they have done in the past, the French are turning more and more to shoring up their relations across the

---

111 Originally signed in 1891 between France and Russia after Germany refused to renew the Reinsurance Treaty of 1887, which had been created to put in place a system of "overlapping alliances" among the great European powers, this agreement was designed to provide French support to Russia in any colonial dispute with Great Britain, and to end French isolationism on the Continent. See Kissinger (1994, 179-81).

Mediterranean littoral and into Africa, where the French colonial legacy still commands some influence. But it really is on the global stage, principally as a permanent member of the United Nations Security Council, that France has concentrated its efforts to reassert its weight in global affairs. To do so, however, it has more than once had to take on the United States, its oldest ally and its nemesis, too. For France's loss of its own sense of identity comes at a time of unparalleled rise of American power on the world stage.

As we have seen, the Franco-American relationship has never been easy, although in the face of commonly perceived threats it has stood both parties well. The end of the Cold War era, brought to a close by German unification and Russia's shedding of its empire, has given way to a time of great uncertainty that, after the terrorist attacks against New York and Washington, has opened new possibilities for U.S.-Russian relations. America's historic withdrawal from the ABM Treaty, an arms control icon for almost thirty years, followed by the establishment of the NATO-Russian Council, enlargement of the Alliance to include the former Soviet Baltic republics, and the war on terror, has provoked a fundamental reassessment of de Gaulle's "certain idea of France." For diehard Gaullists, including, in many respects, the current French president, the French destiny is to assume the leadership mantle in the EU. From this pedestal, France will be better able to cope with future challenges, and just as important, credibly challenge American power and policy positions, when that is deemed necessary to French and EU interests. For if Russian-American "condominium" is of concern to the French polity, the potential for the United States to act on its own, without consulting with its Alliance partners, is the ultimate Parisian nightmare. This is why George Bush frightens the French, and why, despite honest differences over policy positions, their government officials continue to criticize, belittle, and assign dubious motives to virtually anything that emanates from Washington these days.

In Washington, there is an inclination to tell the French to get over themselves; after all, France today is a small shadow of its former self. But, that would be too easy, and in the final analysis, not necessarily in the best of U.S. interests. When all is said and done, the United States and France continue to share common interests, although increasingly it is also true that the countries' interests are diverging, and for that reason, they will have to work all that much harder to emphasize the positive elements of their relationship. In the war against terrorism they have a common enemy, though the French desire to ensure security at home often appears to undermine its efforts abroad. France's considerable Muslim population is always a worry and a potential constraint on the country's relationships with the Arab world and with Israel, over whom the U.S. and France will have to agree to disagree. That said, it has become apparent that France is a status quo power whose world view is tied up with its efforts to warn the United States off from invading Iraq and to take the path of engagement to influence and shape elite behaviors in Iran. The perturbations from September 11 resonate uncomfortably in France, while the United States, having no other choice, is energetically moving ahead to meet these new challenges and to transform its way of doing business in much of the world.

With the enunciation of the Bush Doctrine, the United States has developed a new national security strategy, one that puts potential enemies of America on notice. Preventive action, encompassing the military concept of preemption, is an important element of the Bush administration's more forward-leaning security stance. Although the Bush Doctrine integrates all the levers of national power in support of its fundamental tenets, including diplomatic engagement as an important aspect of prevention, the French and other Europeans have been highly critical of what they regard as its direct challenge to international law. More than this, the French believe that with the Bush Doctrine, the United States is making enemies where none need to exist.

With the Bush Doctrine's three-pronged emphasis on preventive action, democracy building, and homeland security, the French, who hold to their no-nuclear war philosophy, fear that with the Bush Doctrine the United States is lowering the nuclear threshold, and that American consideration of a new generation of small-yield nuclear weapons only increases that likelihood. Deterrence remains the essence of French strategic thought, and the missile defense concept has the potential to undercut French deterrent capabilities. On this issue, though, the greater French fear is that the United States, with a national missile defense capability in place, could well become "fortress America" and uncouple its security from that of the Europeans, as they have long suspected would occur. In 1962, it was alright for the French to develop their own national deterrent capability and subsequently pull their forces out of NATO's integrated command structure when it suited their interests to do so. But in 2002, the United States was criticized for pursuing a missile defense deployment that Washington believes offers a better basis for its security than did the "balance of terror."

Of course, much of the Franco-American debate is semantics and posturing. On missile defenses, the French have expressed industrial interest in collaborating with the United States, and there is considerable interest in French policy circles in joining with the Americans in key space-oriented programs. The Raytheon-Thales industrial cooperation and EADS project collaboration with Lockheed offer a framework for industrial collaboration in the security arena, while the Group of Eight forum, for example, provides the transatlantic partners with another framework for dealing with new and emerging global challenges in which they have shared interests. Identifying ways to maximize those interests and minimize their differences is the challenge of alliance relations today. However, unless France moves closer to the new NATO, its ability to influence the EU's security evolution will be limited by the fact that its partners are more comfortable using NATO standards, command structures, and capabilities. Interoperability with the United States remains a priority concern for a majority of the NATO partners, although transformation of the alliance, which undoubtedly will happen, can only realistically occur if the EU's defense development proceeds in tandem with NATO's evolution.

Before September 11, 2001, there were serious doubts about the ability of NATO to survive. After September 11, those doubts persist, notwithstanding the NAC's September 12, 2001, proclamation of solidarity with the United States and the Alliance decision to deploy forces, for the first time in its history, to help defend a member country against an attack. France, with one foot in and one foot outside of Alliance decision circles, has consistently plotted to reduce the power and influence of the United States within the Alliance. Having failed in recent years to attain that objective, French policy elites have promoted the concept of a separate and equal European defense capability. To date, the ESDP is more of an illusion than a reality, although there can be no question but that the EU will one day have at its disposal a credible military capability for use in any number of contingencies, some of them featuring U.S. cooperation, others not. For this reason, it would be ill-advised of the French to continue to press for development of that capability as a means of pushing away or marginalizing its U.S. ally. The old adage warns, "Be careful of what you wish for, you might get it;" it is entirely possible that a future generation of American policy elites will decide to opt out.

For now, there appears to be little likelihood of that occurring, although if the French and others keep pushing the United States in that direction, who knows what the future will bring? Villepin's harsh criticisms in January 2003 of the U.S. stance on Iraq's need to comply fully with the provisions of UNSC 1441 tend to empower anti-European sentiments in the United States. If it is true, as Robert Kagan (2002a) asserts, that Europeans and Americans no longer share a common view of the world, then they should embrace their differences and work to minimize the tensions to which they give rise. However, France and Germany's joint declaration that they opposed a U.S.-led invasion of Iraq, certainly not before U.N. weapons inspectors are given more time does not bode well in this regard, particularly when their former champion, U.S. Secretary of State Colin Powell, declared at the 2003 World Economic Forum held in Davos, Switzerland, that the U.S. was prepared to act even if its allies were not.

Reflecting Secretary Rumsfeld's characterization of the disconnect between "old Europe and the new Europe," former Czech Presdient Vaclav Havel has opined that "reason often needs force." With this in mind, it is more than a little disingenuous for the French to speak about universal values and multilateral frameworks as a substitute for raw military power in international affairs, when one of the principal reasons that they are pursuing the development of an EU constitution is to create a basis for that power and its uses. In 1991, at the start of the crisis in Yugoslavia, Jacques Poos, then president of the European Council, proclaimed, "This is the hour of Europe" (Simms 2001, 54). Only, it wasn't, and American intervention was necessary to arrive at a solution. It has been almost two years since the Helsinki Summit established its Headline Goals, and the Europeans have yet to increase their defense spending or begin to close the capabilities gap with the United States. The new French government has vowed to do that, but it remains to be seen just how firm that commitment is in the face of other, contending spending priorities. Even as the Chirac-Raffarin government has presented a new defense plan that increases defense spending, the real question is where that money will go and how long the programmed spending increases can be sustained. Thus, whatever happens in this regard, the French still will need to leverage the EU in the security planning area, and the issue here becomes one of how much sovereignty the French are prepared to surrender in order to participate in a quasi-federal structure that allows the EU to speak with one voice on foreign and defense policy matters. Until that occurs, however, the new French government, for all its bluster, is wary about breaking relations completely with the United States and, at the very least, hopes to maintain the appearance of amicable relations.

What does this mean for the future of the Franco-American relationship? From crisis management to cultural influence, the French recognize that the United States occupies a position of dominance that, even at the height of empire, the French had no hope of achieving. With such a large and perceptible imbalance of U.S. power relative to France, and for that matter to the EU as well, there is a growing resignation among the French that the United States, inevitably, will act unilaterally when its interests so dictate. What bothers the French is that, from their vantage point, the United States is not using its power as effectively as it might, and, they argue, it would benefit greatly from closer consultation and dialogue with its allies, who just might have something to offer.

From a U.S. perspective, this may be a reasonable approach in some circumstances; in others not. Above all, it comes across as a rather transparent effort to retain for France and Europe some relevance in policy areas where they have been demonstrated to be marginal to a political or military resolution. Despite French efforts to push the EU into a more proactive foreign and security policy stance, its members have become much more inward-looking, and even on issues where European interests are readily apparent, as with the crisis between Morocco and Spain, it was the United States, not the Europeans, that brokered the solution. Recent experiences in Bosnia and Kosovo underscore this point, while further suggesting the need for transformation in U.S-Allied relationships. Henry Kissinger argues that the "central issue is just how much unity the Atlantic democracies need to manage their future and how much diversity they can stand. It is in America's interest that Europe becomes a more active participant in world affairs. But it is not in America's interest that this identity be defined in opposition to the United States" (Kissinger 2001, 81).

In coming years the French will have much to say about Europe's evolution. They also have it within their grasp to nurture a more cooperative relationship with the United States, as Foreign Minister Dominique de Villepin claims he wishes to do. In this endeavor however, deeds will matter more than words. This does not imply the need for unconditional support for U.S. policies at every turn. Nations, like honest people, may have disagreements and still remain friends. What it does mean, though, is a commitment of support when the United States puts itself on the line for those interests or principles that are shared by the Atlantic democracies. Editorial writers on both sides of the Atlantic are talking about a "values gap," and "a growing divergence of interests and capabilities" between the United States and France, to which a "perceptions gap" has given rise. WMD and ballistic missile proliferation are considered on both sides of the Atlantic to constitute a profound challenge, but there is no sense of an urgent need in France to address these threats now. For the United States these are fundamentally important challenges.

Neither is there an understanding of just how much America has changed since September 11, 2001. Whereas many in France would argue that they have been fighting terrorism for decades, it is hard for them to understand that America is at war against a pernicious and global enemy whose sole purpose is to destroy the fabric of Western society. Perhaps the presence of a large Muslim population increases the French sense of personal vulnerability, and hence, France's inability to connect with the Americans on the war on terror and their sense that Western civilization itself is threatened. It is ironic, though, because on this issue, the two nations have much more in common than divides them, and it provides a useful starting point for recalibrating their relationship. Only time will tell, although the United States may be running out of patience with France, its reluctant ally. Or, has France become a competitor and an unreliable partner?

Sources Cited

Achcar, Gilbert. 2001. Wish lists of Washington, Moscow, and Beijing: A trio of soloists. *Le Monde Diplomatique*, December. Internet version/English edition (http://MondeDiplo.com/2001/12/05trio).

Ailleret, Charles, chief of French General Staff. 1967a. Défense dirigée ou défense 'tous azimuts.' *Revue de Défense Nationale*, December: 1923-32.

———. 1967b. As quoted in Lacouture 1991, 428-9.

al-Amin, Hazim. 2002. Conditions of North African immigrants in France. *Al-Hayah* (London), August 1. Translated and reprinted in FBIS, document GMP20020801000115, Internet version, August 1.

Alançon, François. 2002. Interview with Ahmed Chalabi. *La Croix*, February 27.

Atkinson, Rick. 1993. *Crusade: The untold story of the Persian Gulf war*. Boston: Houghton Mifflin Company.

Bailey, Thomas A. 1946. *A diplomatic history of the American people*. New York: Appleton-Century-Crofts, Inc.

Barber, Tony, and David Usborne. 1995. France accuses the U.S. of arming the Muslims. *The Independent*, July 1.

Barochez, Luc. 2002a. Europeans and Arabs opposed to strike: U.S. allies not convinced by Washington's arguments against Saddam Hussein's regime. *Le Figaro*, August 9. Internet version, translated and reprinted in FBIS document EUP20020809000059, August 9.

———. 2002b. Une guerre préventive en Irak?. *Le Figaro*, September 11. Internet version (http://www.lefigaro.fr).

———. 2002c. The new situation: America's anti-terrorist obsession deals new hand. *Le Figaro*, September 11. Translated and reprinted in FBIS document EUP20020912000165, September 11.

Baudrillard, Jean. 2001. L'esprit du terrorisme. *Le Monde*, November 3.

Beaumont, Peter, and Ed Villiamy. 1994. U.S. spells out ban on intelligence sharing in NATO. *The Observer*, November 13.

Benamou, Georges-Marc. 1996. *Le dernier Mitterrand*. Paris: Plon. Referenced in Conrad Black, Britain's American option-and America's stake, *National Interest*, spring 1999, Internet version (http://www.lexis-nexis.com):8.

Blair, Tony, et al. 2003. Europe and America must stand united. *Wall Street Journal*, January 30.

Bobbitt, Philip. 2002. *The shield of Achilles: War, peace, and the course of history*. New York: Knopf Random House. See especially the epilogue, where the author presents his view of Al Qaeda.

Boniface, Pascal. 2002. Introduction. *L'Année stratégique*, 2003. Paris: Institute for International and Strategic Relations (IRIS).

Bonnet, François, and Claire Tréan. 2002. Interview with Foreign Minister Dominique de Villepin: France wants a "frank" relationship with the United States. *Le Monde*, July 29. Internet version, translated and reprinted in FBIS document EUP20020731000030.

Brenner, Michael, and Guillaume Parmentier. 2002. *Reconcilable differences: U.S.-French relations in the new era*. Washington, D.C.: Brookings Institution Press.

Brichambaut, Marc Perrin. 2002. Interview with author, Washington, D.C., February 14.

Brittan, Samuel. 2002. The U.S. is more nearly right. *Financial Times*, August 1.

Bush, President George W. 2002. Remarks before the UN General Assembly, New York, September 12.

Butler, Richard. 2000. *The greatest threat: Iraq, weapons of mass destruction, and the crisis of global security*. New York: Public Affairs, a member of the Perseus Books Group.

Casey, Lee A., and David B. Rivkin, Jr. 2002. The U.S. Constitution trumps the U.N. Security Council. *Wall Street Journal*, September 25.

Champion, Marc. 2003. Eight European leaders voice their support for U.S. on Iraq. *Wall Street Journal*, January 30.

Chazan, Guy. 2002. Russia waters down plans for nuclear plants in Iran. *Wall Street Journal*, August 5.

Chipman, John. 2002. America's right to fight Iraq. *Financial Times*, August 13.

Chirac, Jacques. 2001a. Quoted in Halberstam 2001, 316.

———. 2001b. Remarks made before the Institute of Higher National Defense Studies (IHEDN) in Paris, June 8. (http://un.int/france/documents_anglais/010608_mae_chirac_desarmement.htn).

————. 2002a. Quoted in Evans-Pritchard and Helm 2002.

————. 2002b. Threats and responses: Perspectives. Interview by Elaine Sciolino. *New York Times*, September 8.

————. 2002c. Chirac offers Iraq plan. Interview with Elaine Sciolino. *International Herald Tribune*, September 10.

————. 2002d. Quoted in Marie-Pierre Subtil, Chirac abandons any criticism of the war in Chechnya. *Le Monde*, July 21-22. Internet version, translated and reprinted in FBIS document EUP20020722000043, July 21.

Clark, General Wesley K. 2001. *Waging modern war*. New York: Public Affairs.

Consea, Pierre, and Olivier Lepick. 2002. Threats to disarmament and international security: The new world disorder. *Le Monde Diplomatique*, July. Internet version/English edition (http://www.MondeDiplo.com/2002/07/04disarmament): 2.

Conze, Henri, former French armaments director. 2002. Interview with the author, Paris, June 16.

Council on Foreign Relations. 2002. How the world views the war on terrorism: What the U.S. media missed. *Council on Foreign Relations News Release*, no. 9 (spring).

Courtois, Gerard. 2002. U.S. image strongly deteriorated in France over the past year. *Le Monde*, September 11. Internet version, translated and reprinted in FBIS document EUP2002091100275, September 11.

Daley, Suzanne. 2002. French minister calls U.S. policy 'simplistic.' *New York Times*, February 7.

Davis, Jacquelyn K., Charles M. Perry, and Robert L. Pfaltzgraff, Jr. 1989. *The INF controversy: Lessons for NATO modernization and transatlantic relations*. An Institute for Foreign Policy Analysis Special Report. Washington, D.C.: Pergamon-Brassey's International Defense Publishers.

Davis, Jacquelyn K., and Micheal J. Sweeney. 1999. *Strategic paradigms 2025: U.S. security planning for a new era*. An Institute for Foreign Policy Analysis Book. Dulles, Virginia: Brassey's, 1999), 353pp.

De Gaulle, Charles. 1956. *L'Appel*, 1940-1942. Vol. 1 of *Memoires de guerre*. Paris: Plon.

————. 1962. Quoted in Lacouture 1993, 340.

————. 1970. *Le renouveau* (1958-1962). Vol. 1 of *Memoires d'espoir*. Paris: Plon. Quoted in Lacouture 1992, 367.

Delpech, Thérèse. 2002. *Politique du chaos*. Paris: Seuil, 2002. Referenced in Quentin Peel, An empire opts out, *Financial Times*, August 19.

Dempsey, Jack. 2002. EU military operation in Macedonia at risk. *Financial Times*, May 16.

Douin, Jean-Philippe. 1996. Vers un nouvel équilibre entre les fonctions opérationnelles. *Revue de Défense Nationale*, July 14:57-65.

Evans-Pritchard, Ambrose. 2002. America's plans for military action threaten to divide EU. *Daily Telegraph*, March 13. Internet version (http://www.telegraph.co.uk/news/2002/03/13).

Evans-Pritchard, Ambrose, and Toby Helm. 2002. Chirac lays out plan for federation of Europe. *Daily Telegraph*, March 7. Internet version (http://www.telegraph.co.uk/news/2002/03/07).

Executive Office of the President of the United States. 2002. The national security strategy of the United States of America. September 12. Washington, D.C.: The White House.

Farooq, Umer. 2002. France reportedly invited India, Pakistan to anti-ballistic missiles talks. *The News* (Islamabad), January 26. Translated and reprinted in FBIS document SAP20020126000006. Internet version, January 26.

Foreign Broadcast Information Service (FBIS). 2002. Poll shows growing French opposition to U.S. policy. Translated and reprinted in FBIS document EUP20020831000038, August 31.

France, Ministère de la Défense. 1972. *Livre blanc sur la défense, 1972*. Paris: Ministère de la Défense.

France, Ministère de la Défense. 1994. *Livre blanc sur la défense, 1994*. Paris: Ministère de la Défense.

France-2 television. 2002. Results of an IFOP-*Journal du Dimanche* poll, reported in Paris on France-2 television. Also reported in *Large majority of French reject military intervention against Iraq*, FBIS document EUP20020811000070. Internet version, August 1.

Frears, J.R. 1981. *France in the Giscard presidency*. London: George Allen and Unwin Ltd.

Gallois, Pierre. 1961. *The balance of terror*. Boston: Houghton Mifflin Company.

Gere, François. 2002. Le nucléaire déchaîné. *Libération*, May 31.

Gildea, Robert. 1996. *France since 1945*. Oxford: Oxford University Press.

Glennon, Michael J. 2002. How war left the law behind. *New York Times*, November 21.

Gnescotto, Nicole. 2001. Défense: Plus, plus vite, et mieux. *Le Figaro*, November 20.

Goldberg, Jeffery. 2002. The great terror. *The New Yorker*, March 25, 25.

Goldschmidt, Bertrand. 1980. France, Europe et Alliance Atlantique. In *Le complèxe atomique: Une histoire politique de l'énergie nucléaire.* Paris: Fayard.

Gordon, Philip H. 2002. Liberté! Fraternité! Anxiety! *Financial Times,* Weekend Section, January 19-20.

Gordon, Philip, and Sophie Meunier. 2001. *The French challenge: Adapting to globalization.* Washington, D.C.: Brookings Institution.

Gormley, Dennis. 1998. French sale cripples MTCR. *Defense News,* May 11-17:19.

Guetta, Bernard. 2002. Comments on Radio FranceInter, 0518 GMT, June 19. Translated and transcribed in FBIS document EUP20020619000202. Internet version, June 19.

Halberstam, David. 2001. *War in a time of peace: Bush, Clinton, and the generals.* New York: Scribner.

Hayes, Stephen. 2002. Why the CIA can't keep up with the New Yorker. *Weekly Standard,* September 13 (Lexis-Nexis version).

Heisbourg, François, director of the Foundation for Strategic Research (Paris). 2001a. *Hyperterrorisme: La nouvelle guerre.* A Foundation for Strategy publication. Paris: Odile Jacob Publications.

———. 2001b. NATO can manage current strains on missile shield. *International Herald Tribune,* Saturday-Sunday, January 13-14, Editorials/Opinion.

———. 2002. Interview with the author, June 19, Paris.

Hobbes, Thomas. 1914. *Leviathan.* With introduction by A.D. Lindsey. London: J.M. Dent and Sons.

Huntington, Samuel P. 1993. The clash of civilizations. *Foreign Affairs* 72, no. 3 (summer): 22-49.

Imbert, Claude. 2002. Anti-American obsession. *Le Point,* September 6. Translated and reprinted in FBIS document EUP20020906000376, September 6.

Institute for Foreign Policy Analysis (IFPA). 2000. *European security institutions: Ready for the twenty-first century?* An Institute for Foreign Policy Analysis Special Report. Dulles, Virginia: Brassey's/Quicksilver Press.

Isnard, Jacques. 1997. Le grand déballage nucléaire. *Le Monde,* February 14. Internet edition (http://www.lemonde.fr). Quoting Charles de Gaulle, May 15, 1962.

———. 2002a. Les Français ont été amenés à refuser des missions fixées par les Americains. *Le Monde,* March 10.

———. 2002b. Defense of Europe via cruise missiles. *Le Monde,* July 13. Translated and reprinted in FBIS Internet version, document EUP20020715000035, July 13.

———. 2002c. Arms Europe has broken down. *Le Monde*, August 13. Translated and reprinted in FBIS, French commentator: Germany blocking European arms projects. Internet version, document EUP20020813000041, August 13.

———. 2002d. Les crédits d'équipement militaire en forte hausse. *Le Monde*, September 6. Internet version (http://www.lemonde.fr).

Joffe, Josef. 2002. The axis of envy. *Foreign Policy*, September/October: 68-69.

Kagan, Robert. 2002a. Power and weakness. *Policy Review*, no. 113 (June/July). Internet version (http://www.policyreview.org/JUN02/kagan_print.html): 1, 2.

———. 2002b. Multilateralism, American style. *Washington Post*, September 13.

———. 2002c. France's dream world. *Washington Post*, November 3.

Kant, Immanuel. 1939. *Perpetual peace*. With introduction by Nicholas Murray. New York: Columbia University Press.

Kettle, Michael. 1993. *De Gaulle and Algeria 1940-1960*. London: Quartet Books.

Kissinger, Henry A. 1994. *Diplomacy*. New York: Simon and Schuster.

———. 2001. Does America need a foreign policy? In *Toward a diplomacy for the twenty-first century*. New York: Simon and Schuster.

Kohl, Wilfred. 1971. The nuclear program of the Fourth Republic. In *French Nuclear Diplomacy*. Princeton: Princeton University Press.

Lacouture, Jean. 1992. *De Gaulle: The ruler, 1945-1970*. Translated from the French by Alan Sheridan. New York: W.W. Norton and Company.

———. 1993. *De Gaulle: The rebel, 1890-1944*. Translated from the French by Patrick O'Brian. New York: W.W. Norton and Co.

Lellouche, Pierre, Guy-Michel Chaveau, and Aloyse Warhouver. 2000. France and the challenge of WMD proliferation: A report of the Defense Commission of the French National Assembly [in French], December 7. Paris: Assemblée nationale.

Mallet, Victor. 2002. The French disconnection. *Financial Times*, February 26.

May, Clifford D. 2002. The West-West divide: Just how close will America and Europe remain? *Washington Times*, September 12.

Mead, Walter Russell. 2001. *Special providence: American foreign policy and how it changed the world. A Century Foundation book*. New York: Alfred A. Knopf.

Merchet, Jean-Dominique. 2002. First ills in the professional armed forces. *Libération*, February 4. Internet version translated and reprinted in FBIS document EUP20020204000356, February 5.

Messmer, Pierre. 1993. Quoted in Williams 1993, 411.

Meyssan, Thierry. 2002. *Le Pentagate*. Chatou, France: Carnot.

Miller, Paul-David. 1994. *Retaining Alliance relevancy: NATO and the Combined Joint Task Force concept*. Cambridge, Mass.: Institute for Foreign Policy Analysis.

Mitterrand, François. 1987. Quoted in Pierre Favier and Michel Martin-Roland, *La décennie Mitterrand*, vol. 2, Les épreuves (1984-88) (Paris: Editions de Seuil, 1991), 645.

Moisi, Dominique, vice-director of the French Institute for International Relations. 2002a. Yesterday's man versus yesterday's policies: French voters face an uninspiring choice that has turned the presidential election into an exercise in damage limitation. *Financial Times*, March 11.

———. 2002b. Interview with author, Paris, July 15.

———. 2002c. Europe must not retreat from America's army. *Financial Times*, August 26, Opinion/Editorial.

Moore, Charles. 2002. Our friends in Europe. *Wall Street Journal*, March 8.

Myers, Steven Lee. 2002. Russia says it may reconsider its nuclear plant deal with Iran. *New York Times*, August 3.

National Bureau of Economic Research. 2002. Study referenced in Limousine terrorists. *Wall Street Journal*, August 21, 2002 (Internet edition).

Nye, Joseph S., Jr. 2002. *The paradox of American power: Why the world's only superpower can't go it alone*. New York: Oxford University Press.

Odom, William. 1995. Send in the troops. *Pittsburgh Post-Gazette*, June 4.

Papandreou, George. 2002. Quoted in Jack Dempsey, EU military operation in Macedonia at risk, *Financial Times*, May 16.

Pollack, Kenneth M. 2002. *The threatening storm: The case for invading Iraq*. A Council on Foreign Relations book. New York: Random House.

Priest, Dana. 2002. Iran's emerging nuclear plant poses test for U.S. *Washington Post*, July 29.

Raffarin, Jean-Pierre. 2002. *Pour une nouvelle gouverance*. Paris: l'Archipel.

Reuters. 2002. U.N. closer to Iraq vote, Bush sees inspectors. *New York Times*, October 30.

Revel, Jean-François. 2002. *L'obsession anti-américaine: Son fonctionnement, ses causes, ses inconséquences*. Paris: Plon.

Rose, David. 2002. Iraq's arsenal of terror. *Vanity Fair*, May, 120-31.

Rosett, Claudia. 2002. America's true friends. *Wall Street Journal*, September 12.

Rumsfeld, Donald H. 2002. Transforming the military. *Foreign Affairs* 81, no. 3 (May-June): 31.

Rutten, Maartje. 2002. From *Saint Malo to Nice: European defense: Core documents*. Chaillot Paper #47. Paris: Institute for Security Studies.

Sanger, David E. 2002a. Bush and Putin to sign treaty to cut nuclear warheads. *New York Times*, May 14.

———. 2002b. U.S. says Russia helped Iran in nuclear arms effort, adding to concerns about allies. *New York Times*, December 16.

Schultz, George P. 2001. Quoted in *Mead* 2001, 31.

Shanker, Tom, and David E. Sanger. 2002. Rumsfeld says other nations promise to aid attack on Iraq. *New York Times*, September 19.

Simms, Brendan. 2001. *Unfinest hour: Britain and the destruction of Bosnia*. London: Allen Lane/ Penguin Press.

Smith, Michael. 2002. Crack NATO unit disbanded as Britain pulls out. *Daily Telegraph* (London), August 14.

Stimson, Henry. 1971. *On active service in peace and war*, 456. New York: Hippocrene Books. Quoted in Williams 1993, 264.

Sullivan, Andrew. 2002. America knows who its friends are. *Sunday Times* (London), May 5.

Tehran Jam-e Jam. 2002. EU states' relations with Iran will continue. February 7.

Tertrais, Bruno. 2001. *U.S. missile defense: Strategically sound, politically questionable*. A working paper of the Center for European Reform. London: Center for European Reform.

———. 2002. Interview with the author. Paris, June 16.

Tiersky, Ronald. 2000. *François Mitterrand: The last French president*. New York: St. Martin's Press.

Tocqueville, Alexis de. 2000. *Democracy in America.* Translated, edited, and with an introduction by Harvey C. Mansfield and Delba Winthrop. Chicago and London: University of Chicago Press.

Todd, Emannuel. 2002. *Après l'empire: Essai sur la decomposition du systèm américain.* Paris: Gallimard.

Tournoux, Jean R. 1967. *La tragédie du général.* Paris: Plon.

Traub, James. 2002. Who needs the U.N. Security Council? *New York Times Magazine,* November 17: 47-48.

Ullman, Richard. 1989. The covert French connection. *Foreign Policy* 75 (summer):3-33.

United Nations. Security Council. 2001. *Resolution 1368 (2001).* S/RES/1368 (2001).

Vedrine, Hubert. 1996. *Les mondes de François Mitterrand: A l'Elysée 1981-1995.* Paris: Fayard.

———. 2001. *France in an age of globalization.* With Dominique Moisi and translated by Philip H. Gordon. Washington, D.C.: Brookings Institution Press.

———. 2002a. Interview by Jean-Philippe Samarcq. Question de génération. *La Croix,* March 11.

———. 2002b. Quoted in Wolfgang Proissl and Daniela Schwarzer, France demands proof and UN mandate before military strike against Iraq. *Financial Times Deutschland,* March 25.

Villepin, Dominique de. 2002a. *Le cri de la gargouille.* Paris: Albin Michel.

———. 2002b. Quoted in Patrice de Beer, Europe - Etas-Unis: L'incompréhension. *Le Monde,* August 4. Internet version (http://www.lemonde.fr).

———. 2003. Quoted in In their words: The Security Council, *New York Times,* February 6, A17.

Wijk, Rob de. 1997. *NATO on the brink of the new millennium: The battle for consensus.* English edition. London/Dulles, Virginia: Brassey's.

Williams, Charles. 1993. *The last great Frenchman: A life of General de Gaulle.* London: Little, Brown and Company.